# Kittever Memorial Book
# (Kuty, Ukraine)

## Translation of
## *Kittever yisker-bukh*

By: Eisig Husen

Originally published in New York 1958

**A Publication of JewishGen, INC**
Edmond J. Safra Plaza, 36 Battery Place, New York, NY 10280
646.494.5972 | info@JewishGen.org | www.jewishgen.org

JewishGen, Inc. 2023.
An affiliate of New York's Museum of Jewish Heritage – A Living Memorial to the Holocaust

MUSEUM OF
JEWISH HERITAGE
A LIVING MEMORIAL
TO THE HOLOCAUST

**Kittever Memorial Book (Kuty, Ukraine)**
Translation of *Kittever yisker-bukh*

Copyright © 2023 by Rhoda Kuflik. All rights reserved.
First Printing: January 2023, Tevet 5783

By: Eisig Husen
Translated from Yiddish by Stanley Scheindlin, D. Sc.
Project Coordinator: Melina Kuflik McCauley
Cover Design: Rachel Kolokoff Hopper
Layout: Jonathan Wind
Name Indexing: Stefanie Holzman

JewishGen Inc. is not responsible for inaccuracies or omissions in the original work and makes no representations regarding the accuracy of this translation. Digital images of the original book's contents can be seen online at the New York Public Library website or the Yiddish Book Center website.

Printed in the United States of America by Lightning Source, Inc.

Library of Congress Control Number (LCCN): 2022934820

ISBN: 978-1-954176-47-8 (hard cover: 208 pages, alk. paper)

# About JewishGen.org

JewishGen, an affiliate of the Museum of Jewish Heritage - A Living Memorial to the Holocaust, serves as the global home for Jewish genealogy.

Featuring unparalleled access to 30+ million records, it offers unique search tools, along with opportunities for researchers to connect with others who share similar interests. Award winning resources such as the Family Finder, Discussion Groups, and ViewMate, are relied upon by thousands each day.

In addition, JewishGen's extensive informational, educational and historical offerings, such as the Jewish Communities Database, Yizkor Book translations, InfoFiles, Family Tree of the Jewish People, and KehilaLinks, provide critical insights, first-hand accounts, and context about Jewish communal and familial life throughout the world.

Offered as a free resource, JewishGen.org has facilitated thousands of family connections and success stories, and is currently engaged in an intensive expansion effort that will bring many more records, tools, and resources to its collections.

Please visit https://www.jewishgen.org/ to learn more.

**Executive Director:** Avraham Groll

# About the JewishGen Yizkor Book Project

Yizkor Books (Memorial Books) were traditionally written to memorialize the names of departed family and martyrs during holiday services in the synagogue (a practice that still exists in many synagogues today).

Over the centuries, as a result of countless persecutions and horrific atrocities committed against the Jews, Yizkor Books (Sefer Zikaron in Hebrew) were expanded to include more historical information, such as biographical sketches of famous personalities and descriptions of daily town life.

Following the Holocaust, the idea of remembrance and learning took on an urgent and crucial importance. Survivors of the Holocaust sought out other surviving residents of their former towns to memorialize and document the names and way of life of those who were ruthlessly murdered by the Nazis. These remembrances were documented in Yizkor Books, hundreds of which were published in the first decades after the Holocaust.

Most of these books were published privately, or through landsmanshaftn (social organizations comprised of members originating from the same European town or region) that still existed, and were often distributed free of charge. Sadly, the languages used to document these crucial histories and links to our past, Yiddish and Hebrew, are no longer commonly understood by a significant percentage of Jews today. As a result, JewishGen has undertaken the sacred responsibility of translating these books into English so that the culture and way of life of these communities will be preserved and transmitted to future generations.

In 1986, a group of farsighted JewishGenners started a project to pool their efforts together in groups based upon their ancestors from each town and donate money to get the Yizkor books of their ancestral towns translated into English.  As the translated material became available, it was made accessible for free at www.JewishGen.org/Yizkor. Hardcover copies can be purchased by visiting https://www.jewishgen.org/Yizkor/ybip.html  (see below).

It is our hope that the translation of these books into English (and other languages) will assist the countless Jewish family researchers who are so desperately seeking to forge a connection with their heritage.

**Director of JewishGen Yizkor Book Project**: Lance Ackerfeld

## About JewishGen Press

JewishGen Press (formerly the Yizkor Books-in-Print Project) is the publishing division of JewishGen.org, and provides a venue for the publication of non-fiction books pertaining to Jewish genealogy, history, culture, and heritage.

In addition to the Yizkor Book category, publications in the Other Non-Fiction category include Shoah memoirs and research, genealogical research, collections of genealogical and historical materials, biographies, diaries and letters, studies of Jewish experience and cultural life in the past, academic theses, and other books of interest to the Jewish community.

Please visit https://www.jewishgen.org/Yizkor/ybip.html  to learn more.

**Director of JewishGen Press:**  Joel Alpert
**Managing Editor** - Jessica Feinstein
**Publications Manager** - Susan Rosin

The author Eisig Husen
Born on October 18th, 1904 in Kittev (Kuty), Poland
Passed away January 2nd, 1979 in New Jersey, United States

Photo not in original book. Courtesy of the author's daughter Rhoda Kuflik.

## Notes to the Reader

The images in the original book were reproduced from photographs from the time of the first edition.

A reader can view the original scans of the book on the websites listed below.

The original book can be seen online at the Yiddish Book Center website:

https://www.yiddishbookcenter.org/collections/yizkor-books/yzk-nybc313844/husen-eisig-kitever-yizker-bukh

OR

at the New York Public Library Digital Collections website:

https://digitalcollections.nypl.org/items/a1060250-79c5-0133-c5b1-00505686d14e

To obtain a list of Shoah victims from Kitev (Kuty, Ukraine), the reader should access the Yad Vashem web site listed below; one can also search for specific family names using family name option. These lists are continually updated by Yad Vashem, so it is worthwhile to periodically search these lists.

There is more valuable information (including the Pages of Testimony, etc.) available on this website: https://yvng.yadvashem.org/

A list of all books available from JewishGen Press along with prices is available at: https://www.jewishgen.org/Yizkor/ybip.html

## Cover Caption and Credits

**Front Cover Photograph:**

*Author of this book, Eisig Husen and his family (from the year 1937).*
*From left to right: Eisig Husen and wife Rivka (Rebecca), his mother Sheindel, his nephew Chaim Druckman, sister Malka Druckman, his brother-in-law, Abraham Druckman.*
*[Page 236].*

**Cover Design:** Rachel Kolokoff Hopper

# Foreword

## By Eisig Husen's daughter, Rhoda Kuflik

I was born in Kuty, Poland in October of 1937 just before the start of World War II.  When I was about four years-old, my parents and I miraculously escaped Kuty during the Holocaust.  The night that we decided to make our escape from Kuty was after a major pogrom that had taken place in our town, during the Passover holiday on April 10, 1942.  Most of that day, my parents, some relatives and I hid inside an underground hole in our home while the Nazis ransacked our home in search of us.  Incredibly, we survived. Once we came out of hiding, I realized that we were leaving home. I looked for something that I wanted to have.  There were photographs thrown about in a closet, and I took as many as I could and put them in a jacket that was nearby.  My parents did not take anything with them when we left our home except for the clothing they were wearing.  My father put a jacket on, took me on his shoulders, and we started on our journey.  The jacket that he chose to wear had my photographs in the pockets. Those are the photographs from Kuty that are in this book.

After leaving home, we crossed the border and were able to get on a train to Chernovich, Romania. Once there, my father managed to procure working papers, which enabled us to live there safely until the war ended.  As soon as we arrived in Chernovich, my father began the process of trying to help other Jews from Kuty to escape to Chernovich.  One of the first was my grandmother, Shaindle, my father's mother, whose picture is on the cover of this book.  On April 24, 1942, the Gestapo rounded up many of the remaining Jews and started them on the March of the Living Dead, taking them to certain death.  My grandmother was part of this march.  However, my father had sent two men, who formerly worked for him at a lumberyard which he owned in Kuty, to help her escape.  They somehow managed to pluck her right out of the line of prisoners and take her across the border to Chernovich.  My father was also able to help save his sister, Milka, and her husband, Avram Drukman, and their son, Chaim, whose pictures are also on the cover of this book.  Chaim Druckman went on to become a highly respected Orthodox rabbi and politician in Israel.  My father also helped save the life of my young cousin, Sally, and my Aunt Chuma, who came to live with us in Chernovich.  My father tried to help save as many people as he could.

My father began writing this book the day that the Nazis invaded Poland, and he kept writing whenever he could throughout the war.  He said that it kept him alive, the idea of being able to tell the story. It was difficult to get information during the war because the first thing that the Nazis would do when they invaded a town would be to disrupt communications.  But, my father, who was a very successful and well-respected businessman, managed to find people who helped him get information.  It was his mission. Former workers from his lumberyard brought him information on what was going on in Kuty and in surrounding villages. He kept a record of the people who were killed, those he was told about and those he saw with his own eyes.  He knew how they were killed and the precise date of their death. He knew exactly what was happening, and he kept all this information in his book.  My father believed that he had to expose the atrocities to a world that did not know about these things.  For five years, during every free minute, day and night, he wrote about what was happening in Kuty and other Polish towns. When he came to America, he got a Yiddish typewriter and sat and typed this book.

After my parents passed away, my husband and I decided to have my father's book translated from Yiddish to English so that it could be read by our family.  We wanted our children, grandchildren, extended family and future generations to know their family's history and to never forget what happened to six million Jews. We also wanted the world to remember what happened, so that it should never happen again.

Many years later, when one of my grandsons, Evan, was eight years-old, he asked to interview me for a school project. He wanted to know about the night that my parents and I left Kuty. He called his report, "The Escape." At that time, I felt compelled to write my own memories and experiences down. I knew that it was my turn to write a book. I wrote a book, "I Remember", which was published in 2016. It is the story of my family's escape from Kuty and journey, afterwards, to America, as I recall the events. Like my father, it became my mission to tell my family and the world what I had seen and experienced, first-hand, so that it would be known and never be forgotten.

On the following pages are several more photos which I feel belong here too.

Rhoda Kuflik
January 27, 2023

## Photos

All photos courtesy of Rhoda Kuflik, the author's daughter

*Wedding photographs of my mother Yetta and my father Eisig*

*My mother's youngest brother Yosel with his beautiful bride in Kuty*

*My mother (front row, right) with her sisters in Kuty*

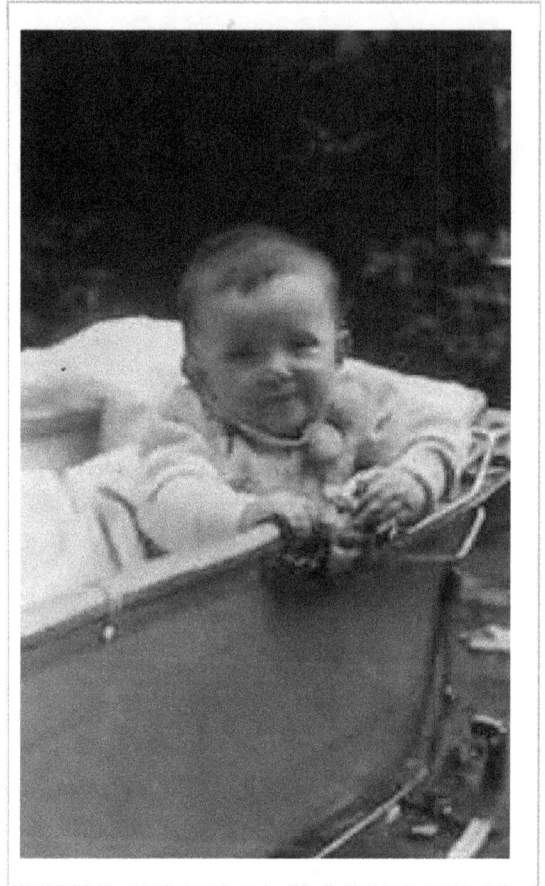

*Baby photos of me in Kuty*

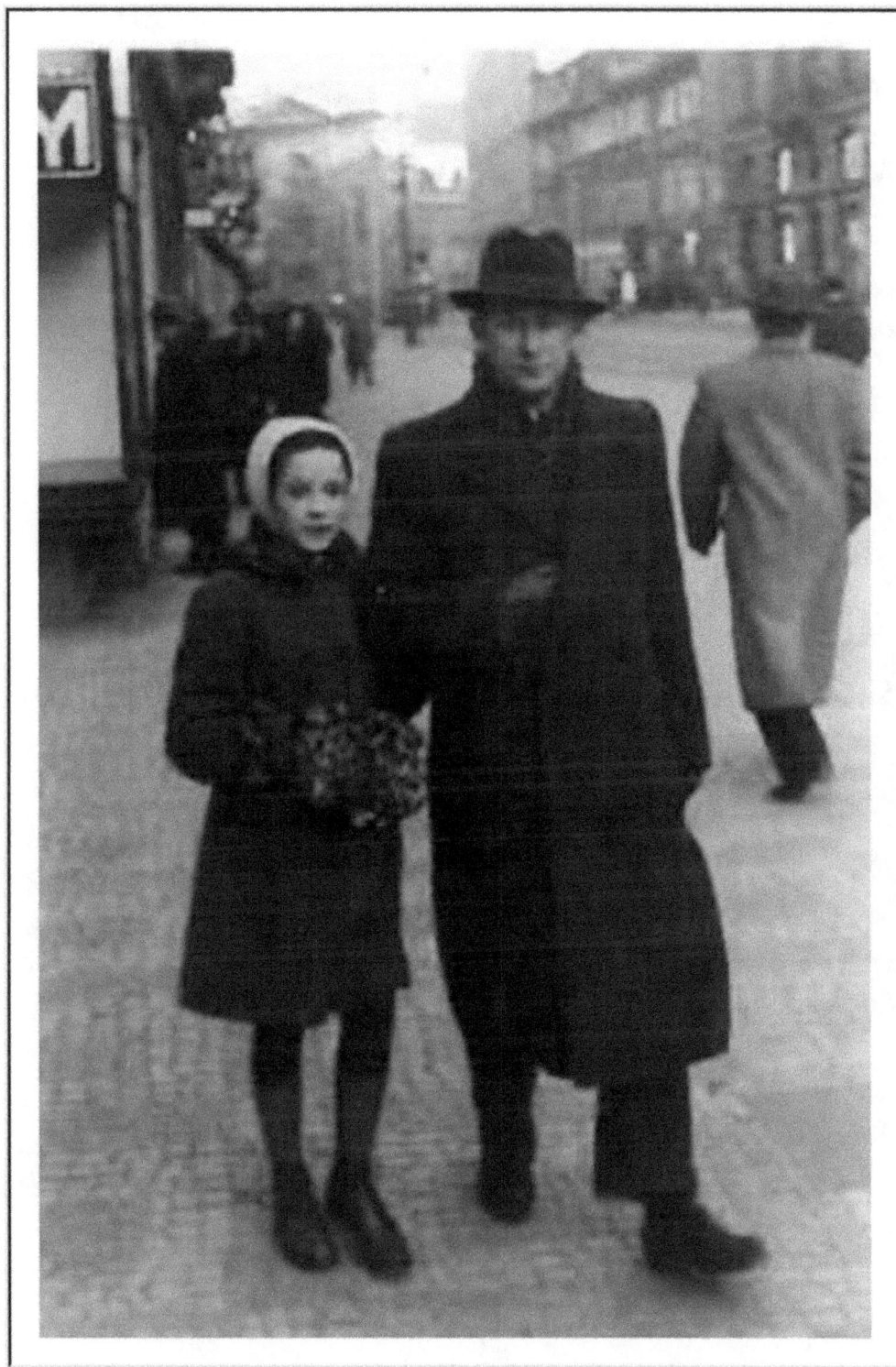

*Father and me in Prague after the war*

*My mother, my father and myself at a window of our home in Kuty*

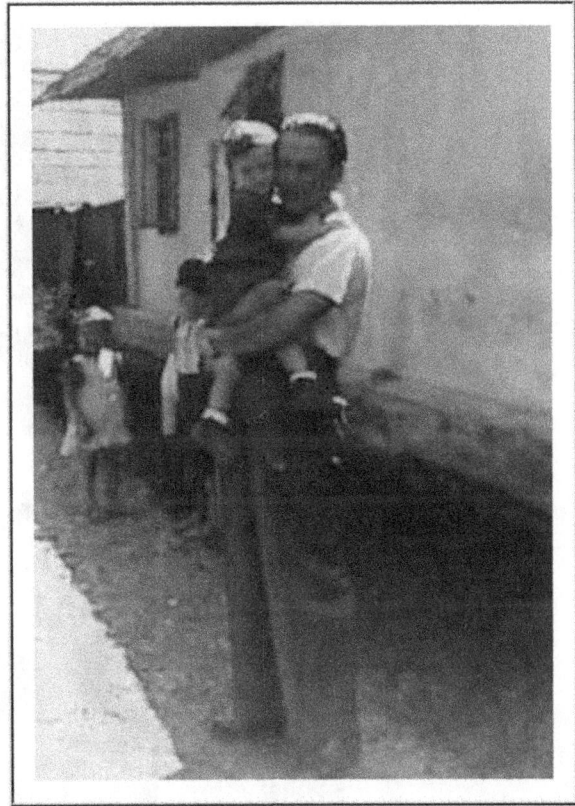

*My father and myself in the backyard of our house in Kuty*

*My mother and myself in Kuty*

# Geopolitical Information

**Kuty,** Ukraine is located at 48°15' N, 25°11' E and 283 miles WSW of Kyyiv

|  | Town | District | Province | Country |
|---|---|---|---|---|
| Before WWI (c. 1900): | Kuty | Kosów | Galicia | Austrian Empire |
| Between the wars (c. 1930): | Kuty | Kosów | Stanisławów | Poland |
| After WWII (c. 1950): | Kuty |  |  | Soviet Union |
| Today (c. 2000): | Kuty |  |  | Ukraine |

## Alternate Names for the Town:

Kuty [Ukr, Pol, Rus], Kitev [Yid], Kutten [Ger], Cuturi [Rom], Kitov, Kutev, Kutow, Kutty, Kuty nad Czeremoszem

## Nearby Jewish Communities:

Vyzhnytsya 0 miles N
Vyzhenka 2 miles SSW
Moskalivka 5 miles NW
Kosiv 6 miles NW
Roztoky 7 miles SW
Miliyeve 7 miles NE
Berehomet 8 miles ESE
Rozhniv 8 miles NNE
Pistyn 11 miles NW
Korytne 11 miles ENE
Myhove 11 miles SE
Ust'-Putyla 11 miles SSW
Banyliv 12 miles NE *
Dzhuriv 12 miles NNE
Yabluniv 15 miles NW
Dikhtinets 15 miles SSW
Zabolotiv 16 miles NNE
Pechenizhyn 23 miles NW

Zhadova 16 miles ESE
Demiche 16 miles NNE
Knyazhe 16 miles NE
Vashkivtsi 18 miles ENE
Putyla 18 miles SSW
Banyliv-Pidhirnyi 18 miles SE
Nyzhni Stanivitzi 18 miles ENE
Serhiyi 19 miles S
Verkhovyna 19 miles WSW
Kostintsy 19 miles E
Yablunytsya 19 miles SW
Kolomyya 21 miles NNW
Kabeshti 21 miles E
Cheresh 22 miles ESE
Panka 22 miles ESE
Snyatyn 22 miles NE
Nepolokivtsi 23 miles ENE
Banya Bereziv 23 miles WNW

Pechenizhyn 23 miles NW
Hvizdets 23 miles N
Drachyntsi 24 miles E
Chudey 24 miles SE
Hlynytsia 24 miles ENE
Krasnoyilsk 24 miles SE
Storozhynets 25 miles ESE
Stetseva 25 miles NE
Dzhurkiv 26 miles N
Selyatin 27 miles S
Bili Oslavy 28 miles NW
Straja, Romania 29 miles SE
Davydivtsi 29 miles NE
Lanchyn 29 miles NW
Mykulychyn 29 miles WNW
Tatariv 29 miles WNW
Kitsman 30 miles ENE

**Jewish Population:** 3,137 (in 1900), 2,900 (in 1931)

Map of Ukraine showing the location of **Kuty**

# Table of Contents

# Kittever Memorial Book
# (Kuty, Ukraine)

# 48°15' / 25°11'

Translation of
*Kittever yisker-bukh*

**Author: Eisig Husen**

Published in New York 1958

---

**Acknowledgments:**

**Our sincere appreciation to Rhoda Kuflik
for donating the translation of her father's book
and permission to place it in the JewishGen Yizkor Book site.**

**We wish to thank Ala Gamulka for editing the translation
and to Genia Hollander for typing
up the English text to facilitate its addition to this project
and to Sondra Ettlinger for extracting the pictures
from the original book, enabling their addition to the project.**

This is a translation of: *Kittever yisker-bukh* (Kittever memorial book),
Author: Eisig Husen, Kittever Sick and Benevolent Society in New York, Published: New York 1958 (Y 240 pages)

**Note:** The original book can be seen online at the NY Public Library site: <u>Kuty (1958)</u>

---

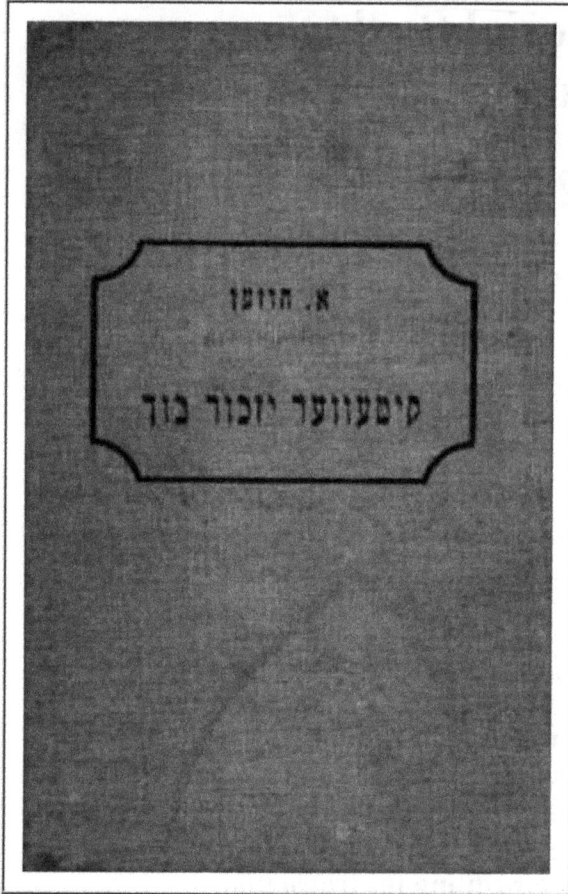

# Kittever Yizkor Book

In Three Parts:

First Part:         The Life and Work of the Kittever Jews

Second Part:     The History of the Destruction

Third Part:        The Names of the Martyrs

**By Eisig Husen**

New York, 1958

Published by the Kittever Sick and Benevolent Society in New York
All Rights Reserved

**Translated from the Yiddish by Stanley Scheindlin. D.Sc.**

# Preface

[Page 7]

In the dreadful summer months of the year 1942, when the German mass-murderers were each day shooting, burning and gassing thousands of Polish Jews; in the fateful days – after the Yuden action in Kittev – when I myself wasn't sure about the next day, I resolved that as long as I still lived, to record the appalling events. I began to write the record, the daily events and experiences of Kittev and the surrounding cities and towns, according to the authentic reports we received from those places.

One of the main reasons that moved me to record all these bloody events was my then naïve belief that the great democratic world had no idea of what was happening, because if they did know what the Germans were doing, they would surely employ all means to stop the horrible destruction-work of the Nazis, their murderous actions against the innocent Jews. All Polish Jews shared this belief, as did the Jews of our city, Kittev.

Since nobody believed that any Jew could be saved from the bloody talons of the Nazi evil beast and the Ukrainian murderers, that he might be able, after the war, to appear as a living witness and accuse the mass-murderers before the world tribunal, I resolved to make my modest contribution to the history of the German murder-actions that they should not be forgotten. I employed every free minute and wrote down every day what we experienced until the complete destruction of Kittev and her Jews.

[Page 8]

I wished to ensure that what was written should not be lost. In those months, weeks and days when I and my family were hiding in the cold, damp and dark cellars, under red-hot tin roofs on the attics, days when our lives hung by a hair, I turned over this book with its glowing Yiddish letters to a Polish acquaintance and asked him, in case we will perish, to send the notebooks to my sister and brother-in-law in America.

This year will be sixteen years since the great people -destruction of our city. The Jews of Kittev were destroyed. I and my family were saved from the murderous hands through a miracle. We had the privilege of coming to the great and free America and here to start a new and free life. However, the atmosphere here of commotion and tumult could not cause me to forget the tragic past. I felt that I would not be able to go on peacefully with a normal life in the new home for me and my family as long as I would not have fulfilled my debt towards the martyrs of Kittev. I resolved to erect a written gravestone, a monument of the word to the beautiful and creative life of the Jewish city – Kittev; to tell how the Kittever Jews lived and how they perished.

Five full years I collected the needed materials for this Yizkor book. Every free minute virtually day and night, my thoughts were occupied with the sacred work. I strove to give an all-round picture of the creative life of the Kittever Jews.

The second section of the Yizkor Book – "The Destruction" is devoted to the experiences of the Kittever Jews and the life of the Jews in the neighbouring towns and villages under Nazi occupation. Everything is based on my exact observations as I experienced it as an eye-witness of the great destruction.

[Page 9]

The book is written in a simple Yiddish language by a person who describes the history of his home-town, from its founding to its destruction. I wanted to get across the joys and sufferings of Jewish Kittev, its way of life and its folklore.

The third part, the written monument of Kittev, is dedicated to the luminous memory of the martyrs. Let this book be found in the home of every Kittever landsman and landswoman. Let our children acquaint themselves with the martyrology of our city and its martyrs, and remember them forever.

**Eisig Husen,  April 10, 1958**

*[Page 10]*

*Blank*

*[Page 11]*

**First Part: The History of Kittev**

# <u>The life and work of the Kittever  Jews</u>[1]

*[Page 12] Blank [Page 13]*

## Chapter I

# Kittev and Its Landscape

Geographically, the city Kittev lies in the left-hand corner of Eastern-Galicia, near the Carpathian Mountains, not far from the former Polish-Romanian border. Nature bestowed on the city an abundance of beauty. Its landscape captures the human eye. Were an artist to undertake to paint a fantastic colorful landscape, he would, it seems, be unable to paint a more beautiful landscape than Kittev was in reality.

The city and its market-place, the shops and the Jewish streets lay on a hill. When one looked down from the hill into the valley, one saw the Dolina like a beautiful panorama in a thousand hues spreading its scattered bright houses around a green sea of aromatic flowers, gardens and orchards, with blooming and ripe fruit trees. At the foot of the Dolina there snaked the stormy mountain-stream – the Chermesh – which formed the natural boundary between Poland and Romania. The Chermesh was half covered by a belt of yellow-grey sands and green willows. From the green willows, the Kittever Moshe'lech and Shlome'lech used to cut Hoshanos, or willow branches, for Hoshanah Rabba. In the stillness of the night, you could hear in the city the rushing of the Chermesh waves and the stormy racing of its waters.

From the north and west sides of Kittev, a long chain of green forests surrounded Kittev and fell in places into the valley and then rose again so high that it looked as if the tops of the trees were touching the heavens.

*[Page 14]*

Above the road leading from Kittev to Toodiav, there rose majestically the "Oidiush" which, with its grey sandy mountain, looked like an unscalable wall. Its surrounding bare rocks looked like a fortress of walls defending the Garden of Eden Forest which loomed green over them. When one stood above, on the "Oidiush" mountain, one saw all of Kittev.

Every street, lane, houses, the big synagogue (shul) and the houses of study and also every blooming corner of the Dolina, the swift foaming Chermesh which stretched like a green snake and separated Kittev from Vizshnets. Far and wide, as far as a human eye could reach, one saw spacious blooming fields, gardens and orchards of Kittev and the nearby villages.

Above, over the "Oidiush", there spread for miles the Garden of Eden Forest which blended together with the Kossover woods and the woods of the surrounding hill-villages.

In these forests, folk legend tells, the Holy Baal Shem would come to be in seclusion – to pray with the magical Nature, with the birds in the woods, with the grasses and herbs of the fields, and to pour together his soul with divine Nature.

At the foot of the "Oidiush" there was spread like a magic carpet, the mysterious "Levadeh". This was a network of hidden paths and footpaths. Under a green "succah covering" of odorous flowers, there were hidden nooks, blooming orchards and hilly young woods. There did the longing youth of Kittev meet to spin their most beautiful youthful dreams. Couples in love would meet there and romanticize. Would the thick trees along the narrow footpaths be able to speak or sing, they could relate much or sing out magnificent heartfelt melodies of longing and youthful love, better and stronger than a human story-teller or composer.

*[Page 15]*

On the other side of the city, on the Sniatiner road, the "Zsharibiz" was located. This was a delightful resting place among odorous fruit orchards and green gardens. There, the Kittever Jews, especially the youth of the city, amused themselves in their free time.

A magical panorama surrounded the city. No wonder that the famous Yiddish poet, the master of the Yiddish ballad – Itzik Manger – dedicated to the magical landscape of and around Kittev, an inspired ballad. The ballad is called: "Between Kossev and Kittev".

Between Kossev and Kittev,
Stands a golden well.
In its deep clear water, I found a sun.

Toward the night and grey mountains,
I carry the sun;
In its clear golden brightness,
All the roads bloom.

I am a simple tailor's
Wild lost child.
Gave up my youthful years
To wandering and wind.

Now I have found it.
Now it is forever mine.
The light of the darkened roads.
The thin golden shine.

*[Page 16]*

The bright word upon the lips.
The golden shine in the hand.
I am the last apostle
Of the newly revealed land.

Between Kossev and Kittev,
Stands a golden well.
In its deep clear water,
I found a sun.

## Chapter II

# The History of Kittev

The general history of Kittev and the history of its Jewish settlement began in the year 1715, after the then owner of all the Kiev estates – the Polish general and Kiever, Count Josef Potocki, granted Kittev the right to be a city and with it, he also gave the Jews more rights and even certain privileges. Then, the Jews, among other privileges, also received permission to build a synagogue which was free of tax payment. Thus, the first Kittever synagogue was built early in the 18th century. At that time, masses of Jews settled in Kittev.

For the right to settle and live in Kittev at that time, Jews had to pay the famous "head-tax". It is known that in the year 1719, Kittever Jews paid 330 gulden head-tax. In 1736 they paid 400 gulden and in 1739, 550 gulden head-tax.

The increased head-tax payment did not scare off and stop the stream of Jews into Kittev. Month-to-month and year-to-year, the number of Jews in Kittev increased. The Jews built houses, established and built up various artisans' workshops, opened stores and began to deal with the peasants in the nearby villages.

*[Page 17]*

In the year 1765, Kittev numbered 360 owners of houses. Of them, 166 Polish and Ukrainian: 70 Armenian and 124 Jewish home-owners. There were at that time 136 families of tenants so that, in the year 1765, 972 Jews were living in Kittev.

In the year 1771, Kittev and the nearby villages of Kuti-Stareh, Slabudka, Kabaki, Rivna, Tudiav, Rozen-Mali, Rozen -Vielki, Rastaki, Bialaberezka, Bervinkova, Charatsova, Dolhopol, Hohopol, Hrinova, Yablonitsa, Krasnaila, Perechresna, Polanki, Stebne, Fereskool and Ustsierki belonged to the Polish duchess, Ludvika Z'mnishkov Kashtelanova of Cracow. And from May 1, 1782, when all of East-Galicia including Kittev were incorporated into Austria, Kittev and the surrounding villages were added to the estates of Kossav and Pistin.

With the inclusion of East-Galicia into Austria, there opened for the Galician (Galitsianer) Jews and also for the Kittever Jews, a new era – a new time of a free life.

The Austrian monarchy with its Crown-City of Vienna, ruled over various lands and peoples and gave all her citizens and subjects, equal rights, not discriminating or limiting any people or minority. Thus, after the absorption of East-Galicia into Austria, there opened up, for the Kittever Jews as for all Galician Jews, easier living conditions and brighter perspectives. As citizens with equal rights, the Kittever Jews were able to send their children to the higher government schools to develop their abilities and talents in all areas of intellectual and free professions.

Then the Kittever Jews – equally with all other citizens – for the first time in their history, also got the opportunity to work in the municipal and government offices and they made use of this opportunity properly. Jews became teachers in the city's public schools, worked as "bureaucrats" in the city post office; even became judges and in general had access to every position.

*[Page 18]*

The Kittever Jews began ever more to occupy positions in the free professions. They became doctors, lawyers, dentists, engineers and other similar professions. Little by little, Jews began to play a notable role in the social life of Kittev.

Enjoying all rights equal to all Austrian citizens, the number of Jews in Kittev grew. In the year 1849, the city of Kittev had 3700 inhabitants, and in the year 1890, it already had 6353 inhabitants – of them, 3045 Jewish residents.

At the start of the 20th century, in 1900, Jews made up 50% of the population of Kittev. There were then 3197 Jews living in Kittev.

Until 1918, Kittev belonged to the Austro-Hungarian monarchy under the reign of Kaiser Franz Joseph. After World War I, which lasted from 1914 to 1918, ending in the falling apart of the Austro-Hungarian monarchy and the collapse of the Hapsburg dynasty, there was a regrouping of the small nations and countries which previously belonged to the great Austro-Hungarian kingdom. The Czechs became independent and founded the Czechoslovak republic. The Hungarians founded the independent Hungarian republic, and Bukovina became a part of Romania. Kittev and all of Eastern-Galicia were left without guardians and went through various changes. At the beginning, we had a Ukrainian government with a capital city, Stanislav. Then the Romanians took pity on us and occupied our area. Finally, the Romanians withdrew on the order of the League of Nations, and we became Polish citizens.

*[Page 19]*

## Chapter III

# Kittev Between the Two Wars

With the inclusion of East-Galicia into the Polish republic, a great change entered into the life of Galician Jewry and naturally, the life of the Kittever Jews.

Notwithstanding the solemn promises and assurances of the Polish rulers that Polish Jews would enjoy equally with all other citizens the freedoms and privileges guaranteed by the Polish constitution, the Jews in reality were reduced to second-class citizens who had to fulfil all civic duties but had limited rights.

To start with, the Poles began to make their government offices "Judenrein" (devoid of Jews). Those Jews who were working in government offices from the time of the Austrian rule, were dismissed by the Poles. No other Jews were employed in their stead. In order to drive the Jews out of the free professions, the Polish rulers began limiting the rights of Jewish students creating the ill-famed "numerus clausus" which permitted only an insignificant number of Jewish students to enter the universities.

But the Poles didn't content themselves with this. They started a drive to drive the Jews out of their last and strongest position. They undertook to tear trade (commerce) out of Jewish hands. They did it in two ways: First, by making various limitations and all sorts of difficulties and second, by jacking up the taxes; and principally, by setting up against the Jewish trader a powerful competitor – a Polish commercial element that had government support and received help in the form of large loans and tax reductions, etc.

*[Page 20]*

Such was the new situation under the new Poland and in such an atmosphere that the Jews had to live and struggle for their existence.

The number of Jews living in Kittev after the city became a part of Poland was 2605 persons and amounted to 47.5% of the population. And yet, despite the large percentage of Jewish citizens, the Poles did not allow a single Jew into a government or municipal position.

In Kittev, there were two public schools of 7 grades – one for boys and the other for girls. In both schools, there were employed over 20 permanent teachers and auxiliaries – but beside the one Jewish teacher for religion, the Poles did not admit a single Jewish teacher even if the Jew had much better qualifications than their own Polish teachers. The same with the Kittev Circuit Court under whose jurisdiction, 22 surrounding villages fell. The court employed a sizeable number of judges, clerks, bailiffs, guards and other workers. But among all these positions, not one Jew. In the post office there were also no Jews except a couple left over from the Austrian time. The new Polish masters chose to pension off those Jews after dismissing them, just to not allow them to work in a government institution.

It was hard to find a Jew in the other city departments, as for example, in the tax bureau, in community management, in the police, etc.

*[Page 21]*

With their taxes, the Kittever Jews covered more than 70% of the city's municipal budget; Yet, the municipal council did not allow a single groschen for Jewish institutions such as the orphan's home, synagogues, libraries and similar establishments. In the municipal council itself, where Jews – based on population and taxpayers – should have been in the majority, they would get an insignificant number of representatives through an artificial election-regulation. And the Jews were powerless there against the overwhelming number of Polish, Armenian and Ukrainian representatives.

Let us now take a look at the economic standard and living standard of the city. In general, it was a backward standard that found itself in a stage of development. Kittev had no system of piping, and water had to be drawn from the city wells. In the city, there were professional water carriers who brought the water to houses. The water carriers mostly used two wooden buckets, hanging on a wooden "yoke" which they carried on their shoulders. The more advanced water bearers were transporting the water in a barrel with a hand-faucet, and at every house where they stopped, they would measure out the water into the buckets.

To light the houses and the streets at night, it was necessary to use kerosene lamps. It was only in the year 1935 that we obtained electric light. Ice boxes, heaters, gas or electric kitchens were not available. We also did not know of central heating and would heat the oven with wood in specially bricked cooking and baking ovens.

The sanitary conditions were also primitive. Kittever Jews built the only bath-house at their own expense and maintained it themselves. The Kittever bath-house was famous with its steam-baths. There were also a couple of wooden bathtubs and, naturally, two mikvahs – one cold and one warm.

*[Page 22]*

Gradually, even under the Polish regime, Kittev began to make progress, improve its appearance and begin to look like a modern European town according to the style of that time. There was a Polish hall built where every Friday, Saturday and Sunday, various Polish and foreign films were shown. From time-to-time, there were also theatre performances, among them many Jewish ones. Beside the local Kittever amateur group, various famous Jewish theatre troupes would visit Kittev: Sigmund Turkov, Ida Kaminski, Jonas Turkov, Joseph Kamen, Moritz Lampe, Shoshana Rabinowitz, the Stanislaver Goldfaden, etc. There were concerts, lectures, balls and other entertainments and amusements. Weddings and balls were also held in the halls of Shtetner and Plaviuk.

The roads around Kittev were improved; the main streets in the city itself were asphalted and lengthened at both ends. In short, the town assumed a decent appearance. Trees were planted, sidewalks were widened, and life became more comfortable.

Only Jews lived in the city center and at the market-place in the nearby main streets. The longest and most beautiful streets of Kittev, the Sniatiner and Kossover streets as well as the Tudiaver, were only partly inhabited by Jews. In the Dolina, very few Jews lived with the exception of a few Jewish tanners.

Relations between Jews and their Christian neighbours were generally friendly. This was natural because they had grown up together, gone to school together and met every day.

Also, in the sphere of transportation, train connections in Kittev made progress. Swift "fiakers", large and comfortable auto buses, connected the city with neighbouring cities and train stations. From 1932 onwards, we had a direct train connection from Kittev through Romanian transit territory – with Sniatin-Zaltusheh in Poland. The Kittever railroad station was located on the Tudiaver road near the Chermesh. But the train was mostly used for transporting freight to and from Kittev. Through the train, Kittev had a direct connection with all of Poland and this greatly helped toward the blossoming and development of the city.

*[Page 23]*

But the main factor in the development and progress of the city were the Jews. With their energy and diligence, they transformed a backward town into an industrial and trade center which was known throughout Poland.

**Chapter IV**

# Historic Personalities and Spiritual Leaders

Kittev – like all other cities and towns in pre-war Poland, had various classes of Jews. Hasidim and Misnagdim, Orthodox and free-thinkers, Maskilim and Apikorsim (atheists), great scholars and famous teachers, educated Jews and ignoramuses. There were also rich people, middle-class and poor. In general, however, the Kittever were reputed as scholars, good workmen, capable businessmen and also as sensible Jews with a sense of justice. When traders and other Jews from neighbouring cities had a Din-Torah (lawsuit) or a difficult and complicated trade issue, they would come to the Kittever Rabbis, or refer the matter to an arbitration court of Kittever men of affairs.

When one writes about the life and achievement of the Kittever Jews, one must first mention the great Kittever Rabbis and Rebbes (Hasidic), who inscribed themselves into Jewish history with their works and good deeds.

Kittev had a series of great Rabbinic authorities. From the time when Kittev first became a Jewish community until the final destruction, eleven Rabbis sat on the rabbinical chair of the holy community. Eleven generations of famous Gaonim (eminent authorities), capable and talented leaders and righteous men (tsaddikim). Three of the eleven truly immortalized the name of the city because they were called "Kittever. Under this name, they were immortalized in the Jewish world. These were, in the 18thC, R. Gershon Kittever; in the 19thC, R. Moshe'le Kittever; and in the 20thC the old Kittever Rabbi R. Chaim Gelernter.

*[Page 24]*

Kittev is also known as the city of the holy Baal Shem Tov. Before the Baal Shem was revealed, he supposedly lived for a considerable time in Kittev – in the Kittever environs. His brother-in-law was Reb Gersho Kittever who was born in Kittev and passed away in Jerusalem in 1760. He was a great Cabbalist and observed fasts the greater part of his time. How famous Reb Gershon was among the scholars of his time is attested by the Gaonim R. Yechezkel Landau, the "Noda B'Yehuda" and R. Yehonasan (Jonathan) Eibeshitz of Prague, author of "Luchos Ha-Eidus" (Tablet of Witness). Both Gaonim wrote with respect about R. Gershon and praised him as a Cabbalist and rabbinic authority.

When R. Gershon first became Rabbi of Brod, his sister Hannah, daughter of R. Ephraim Kittever, married R. Israel Baal-Shem who then was living in Kittev. After the father-in-law R. Ephraim passed away, the Baal Shem with his wife moved to the brother-in-law's in Brod.

But the Baal Shem could not stay long in Brod because his brother-in-law, the Gaon R. Gershon, considered him an ignoramus and simply drove him out of the house.

The Hasidic fantasy spun a whole legend of how the Baal Shem became R. Gershon's brother-in-law and how the Broder Dayan (rabbinic judge) drove him back to the Carpathian mountains. The poet, Menachem Boreisho, immortalized the legend in his epic poem: "The Walker". This is entitled: "R. Gershon Kittever":

*[Page 25]*

"At R. Gershon Kittever's round the Beth-Din table,
Sit men of affairs with a lawsuit.

Laying out their claims, noisily they argue,
But R. Gershon Kittever keeps thinking of his father.

What happened there, and who is this Israel
That before his death Father should write with him T'naim? (Betrothal contract).

Just plain Israel, not Rabbi or Our Teacher!
How could he betroth his daughter to such a one?

The door opens and before his eyes, there stand
Some sort of person in a torn fur pelt.

Reb Gershon rises to hand him a coin,
The guest whispers: "I need to tell you something".

"If you need so, tell. It's just between us two"
And he leads him into a separate room.

That one digs in his breast pocket, pulls out the T'naim:
I've come to take my wife, my name is Israel.

Barely did they revive the Dayan from his faint:
"Father in heaven, do I deserve such shame"?

He wails to his sister: "How do we get rid of him"?
But she answers: "Dead men don't renege".

*[Page 26]*

The wedding takes place and poor Reb Gershon
Sits as a school-teacher with his brother-in-law.

But the head is dull as a non-Jew's, lehavdil.
Barely he recites the words of the prayers.

His sister goes out to dig clay from the pits:
Seven years pass and the husband is ever dearer.

So you see clearly: it's a curse from God.
"So let him work here as my coachman"!

He harnesses horse and wagon and gets stuck in mud.
He's not even human - - just a wild Tatar!

"Now I've done my duty toward God and toward world.
Go where you wish and live with him as you like".

The story tells further how R. Gershon comes to Brod for his son's marriage and there he reconciles with his brother-in-law who was suddenly revealed as a Tsaddik. R. Gershon becomes a follower of the Baal Shem and starts to spread his Hasidic teaching throughout the world. And this is how Boreisho concludes his poem about the Baal Shem's being revealed:

On a summer day there's excitement in Brod.
The city goes to meet a "Good Jew" (a Rebbe).

Someone found him in in a forest,
And his teaching, they say, shines like seven suns.

*[Page 27]*

> From a far distance, in such heat,
> From branches they weave him a chair to sit on.
>
> He starts speaking Torah, plain good speech.
> Hearts are filled up with love and joy.
>
> And Reb Gershon Dayan's dancing in the midst
> With all the coachmen and blacksmiths of Brod.

Prior to his being revealed, before he became famous, the Baal Shem lived in a small village between Kossev and Kittev and supported himself by digging clay which his wife, Hannah'le carried to Kittev by horse and wagon to sell to the poor people to coat their floors for Sabbath.

There in the village, not far from the Carpathian Mountains, the Baal Shem lived in seclusion for seven full years. Day and night he would wander through the deep Kittever forests and meditate on the deep secrets of God's nature. There he discovered God in Nature, in all creation. There he comprehended the pantheistic and mystical idea that everything that happens above in the higher spheres, is connected in a harmonious unity – is one with the world below, with the earth and its creatures. Here in the endless Kittever forests, he learned the language of bird and worm, the secret of the trees and the grasses. Everything from a cedar in the forest to a tiny grass, does the will of the Creator – everything sprouts and grows with duty and with joy. Here in the magical landscape "between Kittev and Kossev", the Baal Shem would pray to God with joy and devotion. Here was born to him the great idea of Hasidism – to serve God with love and happiness – with pure motives – with love to the Torah and to every Jew – to the scholar as to the Psalm reciter, to the plain man of the people as to the Tsaddik (saintly person). These were the main foundations of the great Hasidic movement whose founder and creator was Rabbi Israel Baal Shem Tov.

*[Page 28]*

A talented Yiddish poet of Easter-Galicia, Baer Horowitz, who gained fame through his poems on Hasidic themes, gave shape in a poetic-artistic way to the folk-legend about Baal Shem and his wife digging and transporting clay to Kittev:

> And I, my Hannah'le, tell you,
> The hut is the prettiest home –
> Pure gold you carry to Kittev,
> Not a wagon of simple loam.
>
> And I, my Hannah'le, tell you,
> That yellow Indian corn meal
> Is dearest manna from heaven.
> There is in it no lack.
>
> And I my Hannah'le, tell you,
> That there isn't in all the world,
> One rich enough to purchase
> Even part of my pleasure of soul.
>
> Not to torture myself have I come here,
> Not to fast week after week.

I've run away from God's splendour,
from the dull day-by-day yoke.

Here I must ripen, dear wife mine,
Solidly anchor my joy,
That I should be able to carry
To brothers far and wide.

*[Page 29]*

How, smashing will be my message!
I'll press into hearts and hands
The great, the joyous fire
Which pent in my bosom burns...

The time is not far off, O wife mine!
To the valley you with me will come - -
With me, the helper, reviver
Of the people Israel.

(The Baal Shem Tov in the Mountains)

R. Gershon Kittever went off to Erets Israel around 1840 and studied Torah taught by the Cabbalist R. Chaim ben Attar in Jerusalem. Afterward, he settled in Hebron. He later became the leader of the Midrash Hasidim which was founded by Yehuda Ha-Hasid. R. Gershon was the first Hasidic pioneer to make Aliyah to Israel.

A second historical personality was the famous Tsaddik R. Moshe'le Kittever whose name is legendary not only in Kittev but everywhere that his name reached.

Among the many wonders that are told about the Rebb R. Moshe'le z"l is the following story: Once, Erev Yom Kippur at Kol Nidre, in the Great Synagogue where the Tsaddik davened – it became crowded – a crush – an actual danger to life. R. Moshe'le ascended the Bimah and commanded all the daveners to cast aside their taleisim. As soon as they took off the taleisim it became roomier in the synagogue and they could proceed with the prayers. Since then, they established the custom in Kittev not to bury the dead in taleisim but in white shrouds.

This story is presented as a historical fact and as confirmation of minhag (custom) in the book "Oneg Chaim La-Shabbos" by the Kittever Rabbi, the Gaon R. Chaim Gelernter z"l, which was printed during his lifetime in Munkatch.

*[Page 30]*

R. Moshe'le's grave is on the old Kittever cemetery. Over the grave stands an Ohel (structure usually marking an important person's grave) where Jews would come in a time of trouble to pour out their troubled heart and pray for good health and sustenance.

The tenth Rabbi on the Kittever Rabbinical chair was the Gaon R. Chaim Gelernter who was famed not only as a deep scholar, but also as a good preacher and author of several important books on Halacha (Talmudic law) and Aggada (Midrash) which interpret and explain difficult matters in the Talmud and Shulchan Orech. The titles are: "Oneg Chaim La-Shabbos, Simchas Ha-Chag, Pri Eitz Chaim". These works are discussions about laws and religious problems.

At the beginning of the 20[th]C when R. Chaim Gelernter became Rabbi in Kittev, a contention flared up. There was an opposing party against the Rabbi who were called the "Levi'yukes" because the group consisted mostly of Levites from the families Huterer, Orenstein, Tillinger and others. They moved heaven and earth that a different Rabbi R. Yanke'le Shor should occupy the Rabbinical seat of Kittev. Naturally, R. Chaim also had his supporters who defended him at every opportunity. They were ready to fight to the end of their strength for their beloved leader, R. Chaim Gelernter. The Levi'nikes were not too picky in their struggle against the old Rabbi – all means were Kosher and the old Rabbi endured plenty of vexations and indignities from them.

R. Chaim was by nature very modest and peaceable. He always sought to avoid arguments, ignored his enemies and tried not to give them an opportunity to cause him shame and disgrace. But once, on a Sabbath, the Levi'nikes went over the line and received their well-deserved punishment.

*[Page 31]*

It happened on a Sabbath after prayers. The old Rabbi R. Chaim with a group of his supporters was at the house of an admirer of his where they had been invited for Kiddush. A bunch of Levi'nikes burst into the house, led by Meir Huterer, and shamed the old Rabbi by throwing stale eggs at him. The Rabbi's followers defended their beloved Rabbi. A fight ensued, and the Rabbi could no longer bear the Chillul-Ha-Shem (desecration of God's name), and he shouted at the Levi'nikes: "God blessed be He will requite you for this insolence!". He turned to the main leader of the group and said: "You know Meir, what is says in the Siddur—Hameir La-aretz"? it didn't take long and Meir Huterer fell deathly ill and died. (explanation: the two Hebrew words mean: "Thou bringest light to earth". But they can also be translated to: "Meir into the ground").

A second trouble-maker, who was one of the leaders at the Kiddush, became paralyzed. Then fear and trembling befell the whole group of Levi'nikes. They came, one-by-one, in their stocking feet to beg forgiveness from the Rabbi. With that, there came an end to the great Rabbinic controversy.

After the decease of the old Rabbi R. Chaim, the Kittever kehillah received as Rabbi the R. Leib Yetches, who despite his youth, was full of Torah. R. Leib was the last Kittever Rabbi and perished on Kiddush Ha-Shem with his entire community of Jews.

Known throughout the whole Kittever region was the Scribe, R. Dovid'l. His scribal work was famous. A pair of tefillin or a Sefer Torah that R. Dovid'l wrote, was accounted as a precious rarity. If a Jew managed to obtain a pair of tefillin, a mezuzah of R. Dovidl's holy work, he kept it as the greatest treasure and left it as an inheritance to his children.

The Kosher ritual slaughterers of the last generation, R. Meir Shochet-Schechter, R. Leibish Cohn and R. Rafael Schechter were great scholars and God-fearing people beside being rare prayer-leaders. R. Meir was a patriarchal personality and often substituted for the Kittever Rabbi and Dayan in answering ritual questions and solving difficult problems of Torah laws.

*[Page 32]*

It would take too much space, perhaps a whole book, to describe the various types of Kittever melamdim (teachers of children in cheder) and also the "rebbitsins" with the various "helpers" in the cheders – the role that they played in the lives of their pupils. I will, therefore, limit myself to a few brief outlines.

The Kittever cheders, houses of study and Talmud Torahs, were also education-institutes for the Jewish children of the surrounding towns and villages. Jewish parents who, to make a living, had to live in the villages among Ukrainians and didn't want their children to grow up among non-Jews, would bring the children to Kittev and enrol them in the cheders and also with private melamdim, where they lived all year.

Among the teachers of the smallest children the outstanding ones were: R. Meir the Red Wolfish and his wife the "Rebbitsin" Sosheh. When she gave a hiccup, not only the children would get scared but the "Rebbe" himself became terrified and awoke from dozing. Other dardakei-melamdim were: Moshe Chaim Tsach and Zalman Hammer.

Among the intermediate-level Chumash-melamdim, the outstanding ones were R. Abraham Mauerer, R. Chaim Zwiebach Bershtelmacher (brushmaker) and R. Leib'ele Horb (hunchback). The melamed Chaim Zwiebach, or Bershtelmacher, when he got angry and fell into hot wrath, would call the pupils dog souls. Leib'ele was known by the name Horb for two reasons: first because he had, God preserve you, a little hunch and second, near his Cheder there was a hill where the children would skate and sled in the winter days. This hill was called "Leib'ele Horb's hill".

Among the high-level Gemara-melamdim, the outstanding ones were R. Abash, R. Itzikel and R. Meir Yupiter with his son Yossel, as well as R. Micheleh Horner. R. Micheleh was already a modern melamed; Beside his knowledge of the Gemara, he was also versed in the modern Hebrew literature and language. Let me also mention my former Rebbe R. Chaim Shatner who was accounted among the best Kittever teachers. He mostly taught privately with individual students and later he also conducted a Kittever Talmud Torah.

*[Page 33]*

The Kittever dardakei-melamdim had their "helpers" whose job it was each morning to bring the little children to the cheder and at noon, to bring each child food from home. Naturally, the helper would first taste the child's food and often his "tasting" meant eating up the biggest portion. In the cheder itself, the helpers would also do "light" work such as saying blessing with the children, teaching them Krias-Shema (the reading of the Shema) and generally taking care of them. In the meantime, the melamed's wife would "borrow" the helper to bring her water, chop wood, go to the market on an errand, carry a chicken to the Shochet, etc. The helper would also help the rebbitsin do business with the children and sell them various candies and other nosh.

The "rebbitsins" would go to the homes and , teach the girls Hebrew (reading the Siddur), say blessing with them and recite the Shema. There were also in Kittev writing teachers who taught, especially girl pupils, to write in Yiddish. Among the writing teachers were Yudl and Velvel the writer.

In the field of Hebrew education system, Kittev truly made a contribution and could serve as an example for other cities. Even before World War I, Kittev possessed a good Hebrew school led by the modern Hebraist and Maskil, R. Jacob Shatner. His students and girl students, first among the Kittever Jews, popularized the Hebrew word and the modern Hebrew literature thereby laying the foundation for the later Hebraization ofthe Jewish youth.

After World War I, there came down to Kittev a young talented Hebrew teacher, Issachar Shpiegel who helped to modernize and organize the Hebrew school in the city. Thanks to his pedagogic talents and his broad knowledge, the school grew and made progress and became a modern Hebrew center in miniature.

*[Page 34]*

It must be recognized that the Kittever Jewish youth had Issachar Shpiegel to thank for their Hebrew knowledge. They often mentioned their teacher's name with great love and respect. After Issachar Shpiegel left for Erets Israel, private teachers took over the Hebrew School and attempted, in the same building and according to his system, to go on with the work but without success – not because they were bad pedagogues but because the Hebrew language was then already a living tongue. It had conquered the Jewish street, and the students and girl students increased in number. It was necessary to have more teachers and a thorough revamping of the old school system; there was a need for a larger normal school and a kindergarten to satisfy the requirements of hundreds.

We then had perhaps the finest epoch of our life. The national consciousness of the Jewish youth had awakened and reached its highest peak. The Jewish youth had the will to live in a Jewish environment using the old-new Hebrew language, through Hebrew song and "Hora" dances. A partial revision in the education system was called for, which would be adapted to the new generation. It was necessary to replace the crowded, stale Cheder by a large, bright and airy normal school with trained and modern pedagogues. It was necessary that the Jewish youth should, beside the "Tanu Rabanan" (our Rabbis taught) and the "Daf Yomi" (daily page of Gemara) become acquainted with the modern and secular Hebrew creators and literature – with the values of the Haskalah and the great Zionist leaders – the modern prophets who taught us about the great Return to Zion movement, about Jewish renaissance in our old-new land. We needed to be the pioneer-chalutzim, pointing the way for a new generation which would be able to go up to its own land and live there as a free and independent people.

*[Page 35]*

There was then established in Kittev a citizens' committee in which were represented all the Zionist parties. We also founded a large four-class "Tarbut" school with a big kindergarten supported by the tuitions paid by the well-to-do parents. We rented a large building with the necessary number of classrooms, a garden for the kindergarten and most important, we brought in trained and modern Hebrew teachers and important pedagogues who made it possible for the Kittever Jewish youth to get a hundred percent Jewish national education.

From 1930 onwards, Kittev also had a Beth-Jacob school, a religious school for girls conducted by trained Beth Jacob teachers from Warsaw. The Beth Jacob school took the place of the old Cheder with the melamed. As already mentioned, Kittev also had a Talmud Torah where most children of poor parents who couldn't afford tuition went. The income of the Talmud Torah came from support, from monthly free-will contributions and also from a subsidy from the Kittever religious community. The Kehillah was an independent institution, an autonomous body – anyhow it was supposed to be such – and it was supposed to manage the Jewish funds, be in charge of education and generally, coordinate and assist the organized Jewish religious and social life in Kittev.

Each year, under the supervision of the district government, there were elections held to the religion council and naturally there were elected only such councilmen as were kosher in the eyes of "Starosta" (governor of the province). If it happened through an oversight of the government that the will of the people found expression and a Jewish national people's representative was elected, his speeches did not resound in the ears of the rulers. A national representative would usually explain that the community should not just concern itself with the Rabbi, Kosher-slaughter or cemetery. It should also deal with the daily problems of the community such as Jewish education institutions, the national funds and social problems of a broader nature. Such explanations did not please those in power and they would find ways to get rid of such a representative and appoint a government commissar to run the religion council until "new" elections.

*[Page 36]*

The regular income of the religion council came from the religion tax – a levy that everyone paid according to the council's decision – from Kosher slaughter, from the cemetery, the bath-house and similar. From this income, the community covered its budget, paid wages to the Rabbi, the Shochtim, Dayanim (judges), cantors and other religious functionaries and also employed a permanent staff of people who worked in the office and directed its various divisions.

The Jewish community in Kittev, that is the official organized Kehillah with its long-term president, the assimilationist Dr. Savarin Hartenstein, did not redound much honor on the Kittever Jews and was of little use to them. Besides being an obedient tool in the hands of the Polish headman of the district, he accomplished very little in the social, organizational or cultural areas.

## Chapter V

# Kittever Synagogues and Houses of Study

The Kittever Great Synagogue, its houses of study and the various prayer-versions which were used there, form a separate chapter in the history of the city.

*[Page 37]*

The Great Synagogue was the largest and most beautiful building in town; around the synagogue there was a spacious area that served as a gathering place for the Jewish youth at various local and national gathering and celebrations. On Sabbaths and holidays, the place would be filled with worshippers from the Synagogue and the nearby study-houses who gathered and discussed things there during the Torah reading, removing the Torah from the Ark and before and after prayers.

The architecture and structure of the synagogue building, the large, broad interior columns on which the colossal structure was supported and also the magnificent paintings in the most glorious colours and hues, aroused a reverence, a holy trembling in everyone who entered the magnificent holy place. The Kittever Great Synagogue was accounted as the most beautiful synagogue in the entire district and was able to take in all the Jews of Kittev.

From two sides, north and south, stairs led up to the women's balcony of the Great Synagogue. This was so constructed as to resemble a deep and handsome balcony in a large modern theatre. At the front of the Great Synagogue, at both sides of the main entrance, there were two small synagogues: at the right – the butchers' synagogue and at the left the tailors' synagogue. And as the Great Synagogue was "cold", it had no ovens and very few worshippers would daven there in the frosty winter months. They would daven in the nearby smaller butchers' and tailors' synagogues.

Not far from the Great Synagogue, opposite and around it, were located the other Kittever houses of study: the Chasidic bet-midrash, the high bet-midrash and the peltsen (fur-pelt) bet-midrash. Not far away was the Kossover house of worship (kloiz)[2], the new bet midrash and the Visznitser kloiz.

*[Page 38]*

Between the Court Street and the Tailor Street was located the Chortkover kloiz. The Kittever Rabbi also had his own minyan which was in his own quarters in the house of the religious community. The Kittever Rebbe (Hasidic) also had his own minyan.

Nearly every kloiz and bet-midrash had its permanent gabaim, prayer leaders and singers. At this opportunity, I wish to mention three Kittever batei-midrashim (houses of study) and their prayer leaders and singers:

The finest gentleman and permanent gabai of the Chortkover kloiz was my father–in–law, R. Shmuel Liebergall,may his memory be for a blessing. He was a religious aristocrat, a great scholar and one of the best prayer leaders and singers of the preceding generation. He was endowed with a sweet and hearty voice. Whoever had the privilege of hearing his sweetness-filled prayers and songs, on holidays and days of awe, will remember him always. Till this day, my memory retains his heartfelt renditions of the "Yaalos" (a piyyut sung after Kol Nidre), his "Avodah" (during Mussaf on Yom Kippur), his "Va-yeesov kol l'avodecha" and the other prayers, piyyutim and chapters of the Machzor and of the High Holidays (days of awe) prayer service. The leading people of the city used to come to the Chortkover kloiz and during the service, would listen with the greatest reverence and with bated breath to the sweet prayers and heartfelt singing of R. Shmuel Liebergall.

The permanent gabai of the Visznitser kloiz, also a splendid prayer leader and singer, was R. Zaide Hutterer. Those who davened at the kloiz and his friends respected him like a rabbi. He was a great learned man and worldly Jew. When his youngest child Ephraim Hutterer died in his early youth and R. Zaide would stand at the cantor's desk on the High Holidays, and with a tearful voice sing out the "Ha-ben yakir li Ephraim", all the daveners wept rivers of tears. ("Isn't Ephraim my beloved child, - in Yom Kippur Mussaf).

One of the finest gentlemen and the permanent prayer leader of the New Bet-Midrash was R. Yeshayahu (Isaiah) Bergman. Not only was he himself a good singer but the talent was inherited by his two younger sons, Berel and Leib'ele. Often on a Sabbath or holiday, the neighbours would stand themselves under the windows and listen to Yeshayahu Bergman's heartfelt songs and z'mirot, accompanied by his sons and daughters.

*[Page 39]*

Among the prayer leaders and singers of the last generation, I want to recall R. Rafael Shochet and his only son, the Talmudic genius (eelui, in Hebrew) – Shmuel'ik and last but not least (he uses the Hebrew expression meaning "the last is dearest"), Yakir Knall, the only one of the Kittever singers who was saved from perishing and is now in Israel. Yakir Knall was the last song-master and also the elegizer of Kittev. Going together with Kittever community on her final way, he sang out mournfully the Neilah prayers of Yom Kippur.


# Chapter VI

# Jewish Livelihoods in Kittev after World War I

During World War I, in the years 1914-1918, Kittev and all Eastern-Galicia was occupied by the Russian armies. The majority of the Jewish population, fearing the Cossack hordes, took flight to Hungary, Czechoslovakia and Austria before the Russian army came in, and there they remained until the end of the war.

When they returned to their former homes, the Jewish inhabitants of Kittev found everything utterly laid to waste. Not only were all the stores emptied by the robbers but even the doors and windows of the houses were torn out. Generations of Jewish effort and toil, the Russian occupiers robbed, tore apart and destroyed. Every Jew had to build himself a house anew and work to assure his survival.

There were Jews who, in view of the great destruction, considered if it was worth to begin rebuilding on an uncertain base or to emigrate. The far-sighted ones began to emigrate at that time. A sizeable emigration to America and other lands across the sea began. By the way, there were already Kittever landsleit in America who had immigrated there before the first World War.

*[Page 40]*


# World War I

Still, most of the Kittever Jews quickly forgot the War and its dreadful results and again addressed themselves to rebuilding the ruins and creating new sources of livelihood. Jewish shopkeepers stood themselves at their tables in the market-place and sold their wretched goods; Jewish wagon-drivers and carriers began to carry on push carts sacks of flour from the Kittever mills to the stores and the houses of the city and the surrounding town. Jewish tanners began, in a primitive way, to produce thick leather from which Jewish shoemakers sewed boots and shoes. New textiles were not available so Jewish tailors sewed clothes out of military cloth and made suits and coats. In short, every Jew according to his trade and profession and, under the most primitive conditions, began to find a source of livelihood, and they made progress.

Jewish work and Jewish energy and diligence once again brought the expected good results. After a couple of years of strenuous Jewish labour, Kittev was built anew even more beautiful and modern than before the War. Commerce in Kittev began to bloom like never before. Jewish tradesmen rebuilt fine businesses and filled them with the best goods. The wagon-drivers threw away their push carts and bought large wagons with strong horses and carried goods from and to Kittev. On the Kittever plaza now stood a row of new, gleaming fiacres (hackney coaches), hitched to hee-hawing horses, swift as eagles which connected Kittev with the surrounding cities and villages. In time, the Jewish coach-men sold their horses and wagons and hackney coaches and acquired autos and taxis and established a regular motor traffic from and in Kittev which functioned with exemplary punctuality, departing and arriving at the scheduled hour and minute.

*[Page 41]*

In and around Kittev, the Jews built a large number of sawmills which gave employment not only to a large number of Jews and non-Jews in Kittev, but also to the Poles and Ukrainians of the nearby cities and villages. The finished material from the sawmills was sold for the surrounding cities and villages and a large part of it was exported abroad and shipped through the Polish port of Danzig.

The large Kittever mills which were also in Jewish hands, used to sell their flour for the surrounding cities and villages which had no mills of their own.

The Kittever Jewish fruit dealers used to buy up all the produce of the orchards from the Kittever peasants and the peasants of the surrounding villages, which they would then sell the various famous Kittever fruits all over Poland and thereby created a good and steady market for all Kittever fruits.

Beginning in the year 1930-1931, Kittever Jews developed a large new source of livelihood, the rug industry, which brought much profit and prosperity to all Kittever Jews and also to many non-Jews from the surrounding villages.

The rug industry first developed in Kossev, about ten kilometres from Kittev. From there it spread to Kittev and the surrounding area, in the cities and villages. The carpets were woven from wool on large wooden looms in a very primitive manner, all by hand, not mechanized. Hundreds of Kittever families made a nice living from the rug industry, and many of them became rich and their wealth grew from day-to-day.

In connection with the rugs and carpets that Jews produced, there sprang up a new, until then unknown trade. Large warehouses opened which sold a variety of wools and strings for rug-making. Kittever artisans quickly learned the skill of building weaving equipment and worked day and night to deliver more and more looms for the manufacturers. Non-Jews also learned the trade and became experts. In time, the rug industry branched out so that nearly every Jewish house in Kittev was directly or indirectly involved and drew profit from it. Kittever Jewish young men would go forth all over Poland as agents and peddlers of rugs and handwoven items such as tablecloths, bedcovers, curtains, etc.

*[Page 42]*

The working class in Kittev also made progress. There arose an organized Jewish worker who began to play a role in the public life. There was founded a professional organization of the rug-workers which fought for their interests and carried out a successful strike in 1935. As a result of this, other workers – those of the mills, sawing and tanning industry were also organized and in time won better conditions and higher wages for their members.

At that time, there was also founded in Kittev a government fund for the sick from which the workers and their families would benefit. Through the sick-fund, one received free medical help, dentists and doctors; even the medicines in the apothecary shops and prescribed by doctors were obtain free by the workers. Besides this, workers who were sick received a stipend from the fund which enabled them to support their families during the time of illness when they could not work.

In the last years before World War II, Kittev gained a reputation as a good watering place, a pleasant vacation spot. In the summer months, thousands of guests would come to the city to enjoy the air and spend their summer vacations. In and around the city, a large number of guest-houses were built as well as beautiful villas for the cure-seekers which also, naturally, enlarged the source of income for the city and its inhabitants.

*[Page 43]*

In conclusion, it is worth remarking that, in general, commerce, industry, trades and the free professions were almost entirely in Jewish hands. This has to be ascribed entirely to the energy and abilities of the Kittever Jews who transformed the city into an industrial center and thereby raised the standard of living of the Kittever population and that of the surrounding cities and villages.

## Chapter VII

# Jewish Life in Kittev After World War I

The Jewish community life in Kittev after World War I, until the great Hitler destruction, mirrored, in miniature, that of the overall Jewish community in Poland. Kittev like all Jewish settlements in Poland, possessed a multicolored life with all shades of color. An important role in the forming of the Jewish life was played by the Jewish youth and the national conscious Jewish intelligentsia which grew up on the one hand in an atmosphere saturated with anti-Semitism aiming to degrade the Jews and rob them of human and civil rights and on the other hand, grew up in the years of Jewish national awakening – after the Balfour Declaration, when the great Zionist movement began to captivate the Jewish masses and taught them to become the generation which would be "the first to redemption and the last to enslavement" to realize the 2000-year aspiration, the dream of the Return to Zion.

*[Page 44]*

The first and oldest Zionist organization in Kittev was the General Zionists, which was founded before World War I and was led by such Kittever personalities as Dr. Menasheh Mandel, Moshe ben-Chaim Gottlieb, Dr. Marcus Alesker, Wolf Mer and others. The founders and leaders of the first Zionist party in Kittev were the pioneers of the Haskalah movement who wished to fulfil the Haskalah slogan: "Be a Jew in your home and a human being outside". {This slogan is given in Hebrew}. They demonstrated that one could be a Jew with a warm Jewish heart even without beard and side locks, and one might go to Shul (synagogue) without a fur-cap and long coat , but dressed in modern European clothing; that one could study the Bible and a page of Gemara (Talmud) not only on the hard bench of a Bet-Midrash but also in a modern Hebrew school, and that one may also learn and study the general sciences.

The founders and leaders of Zionism in Kittev were the first standard-bearers of Herzl's thought and thereby laid the foundation for a great Zionist movement in the city which branched out after World War I and took in the majority of the Kittever Jews.

When writing about the earliest Zionist activity in Kittev, one must mention the personality of the beloved and recognized leader of Kittever Jews, Dr. Menasheh Mandel who was, not only the leader and ideologue of his party, but always found in the front line of the struggle for Jewish honor and Jewish rights.

This fighter for Jewish interest in every time of trouble, R. Menasheh Mandel, was a talented speaker, a seasoned polemicist and debater, a Talmudist and a modern Hebraist, and in general a proud national Jew whom everyone who came in contact with him, respected.

The first Zionist youth organization in Kittev was "Hashomer Hatsair" and it was also the first group of the Halutzim movement in Eastern Galicia.

*[Page 45]*

However, the strongest and dominant Zionist youth organization in the city was the Zionist-Socialist youth movement, "Gordoniah" founded in 1926.

The writer of these lines was a member of the Committee of Gordoniah and led its Secretariat until the last day of its existence.

In Kittev, there was also a strong Poalei-Zion (Labour-Zionist) party which, after the world-wide merging of Hitachdut with Poalei-Zion, also united with Gordoniah and together formed the "Echod" party. Among the meritorious members of Echod, I want to mention the names of our presidents who perished for the sanctification of the Name and sanctification of the Nation: Hillel Gaster, Elathar Buller and Isaac Grebler.

In the years 1930-1931, Chaim Gottlieb and Joseph Leib Urheber founded the Zionist-Revisionist youth organization, "Betar", which subsequently developed and attracted a sizeable number of young people.

Also active in Kittev there was a Zionist women's organization, "Wizo" which carried on the charitable and educational work of the women and greatly helped in conducting the various Zionist fund drives for Jewish National Fund and others.

In the local committees of Keren Kayemet (Jewish National Fund) and Keren Ha-Yesod, all Zionist parties were represented as well as the Women's Zionist Organization, Wizo.

The headquarters of Keren Kayemet and Keren Ha-Yesod in Lemberg would establish yearly quotas for the cities and the local committees would conduct collections. Every month, they emptied the K.K.L. collection boxes which were found in nearly every Jewish home. Besides this, there were special collections which were mostly held on Hanukkah, Purim, Pesach, Lag B'Omer and 15th day of Shvat. Also, synagogue pledges (nedarim) and Yiskor contributions were dedicated to the Keren Kayemet.

*[Page 46]*

Additional income for the Zionist funds came from the dances and other entertainments which brought in certain amounts.

The Keren Ha-Yesod had quarterly payers, a voluntary tax from every Zionist.

A charitable institution which was the pride of the Kittever Jews was the orphans' home. Right after World War I, when the impoverished population received a large number of orphans and the situation was heart-wrenching, a group of Jews, under the leadership of Dr. Marcus Alesker and Isaac Grebler, decided to help solve the tragic problem and succeeded – with great effort and exertion – to fund the Kittever orphans' home.

This orphans' institution was a comfortable home for the poor orphans and provided all their necessities. It gave them a suitable upbringing and prepared them to become good and useful citizens. The main income for the orphans' home came from the Kittever raternal organization of landsleit in New York and the rest was covered by the Jews of Kittev themselves.

A second important charitable institution from which the Kittever Jewish poor as well as the middle class benefited was the free-loan (gemillus chesed) fund which was managed by a committee in which all the Jewish parties were included. The fund would give small interest-free loans to artisans and small businessmen, and they had months and sometimes years to repay.

The Kittever Bikkur-Cholim (sick assistance) supported itself thanks to the monthly donations of the Jewish population and greatly helped the sick of the poorest classes. Kittev also had a Jewish people's bank beside the city bank which assisted the Jewish artisans and the small businessman.

The Jewish population made use of the Gordoniah library. Under Joshua Nachman and my unimportant self, the Gordoniah library grew to be the most popular reading institution in the city. The library had the newest Yiddish, Hebrew and Polish books.

*[Page 47]*

The Kittever Hashomer Hatsair and Betar had their own libraries.

It should be emphasized that the Zionist parties of Kittev and their institutions were famed throughout Galicia. This was thanks to their socially and politically trained leaders and their high cultural level and the lofty national educational work which brought honor and prestige to the name of the city.

In 1925-1926, a Jewish chamber of commerce was founded in Kittev which took in all Kittever businessmen and artisans, from the smallest storekeeper to the great manufacturers and industrialists.

Founder and permanent secretary of the Kittever chamber of commerce was the capable and hard-working young man, Wilhelm Mach, who was also active in many other communal areas. Thanks to his organizational talents, the chamber grew and became the largest non-partisan organization in Kittev. The chamber always stood on guard to fight for the interests of the businessmen and artisans before the tax bureau and all other government bureaus.

The chamber of commerce would always inform and explain to the businessmen and artisans about government laws and orders. It would do paperwork and tax forms for them for free. This was of great importance for every tax payer.

Kittev also possessed sport groups. The first organized sport club in Kittev was the "Maccabi" founded by Butsieh Tillinger and Wilhelm Mach in 1925. The sport club had two football teams and a gymnastic division under the supervision of a trained instructor who would conduct various gymnastic exercises.

*[Page 48]*

The Maccabi sport club attained the highest satisfaction and recognition in the years 1927-1930 when it defeated all sport clubs of the surrounding cities and thereby became the recognized football champion of Pakutsia.

In later years, the Kittever Zionist youth organizations, Gordoniah, Hashomer Hatsair and Betar also began to organize their own sports clubs and carried on various sport activities such as football, ping-pong and so on.

## Chapter VIII

# Sabbaths, Holidays and Life-Style

Sabbath and Yom-Tov in Kittev could be seen and felt in every street, house and in every nook and cranny. All businesses were closed, all workshops were silent, all transport and communication was halted and the market place was empty and cleaned up. The whole city rested and on everything and everyone, there was an outpouring of the repose and tranquillity of Sabbath.

The day before each Sabbath and Yom-Tov, the hairdressers were very busy, the bath-house was full. Jews went to the bath-house to immerse themselves, to steam themselves and to sweat. Erev Shabbos at dusk, the stores closed, and Jews hurried to the synagogues. The houses were neat and clean and though all the windows, there gleamed the candles and one could see the white-covered Shabbos tables with the Challahs and the goblets of wine.

On Sabbath morning, all the synagogues were filled with worshippers. As soon as prayers ended, nearly at the same time in all the houses of prayer, the streets were flooded with homeward-bound men, women and children. Many Jews provided themselves with newspapers. Some bought the "Heint" (Today), some the "Morgen" (Tomorrow), or the "Freieh Vort (Free Word, the "Moment" or the "Radio". The semi or truly intelligent youth would provide themselves with the "Chvilla" – a Jewish paper in the Polish language.

*[Page 49]*

On coming home, you would find the busy home-makers who would serve the delicious Sabbath foods. Everyone sat reposeful at the table and enjoyed the special dishes. Often there would be guests at the Sabbath table. After the relaxedly sung Zemiros (Sabbath melodies) the courses of food would be brought in. Kittever Jews did not know from any "diet": we ate chopped onions, fish, soup, all sorts of meats, jellied beef-foot, various kugels and tsimmeses and after eating our fill, we napped for a couple of hours. And even though we lay down with a full stomach, we woke up healthy and fresh and ready for a glass of tea, Shalosh-Seudos (third meal of the Sabbath) and so on.

Among Kittever Shabbos-fruit, sunflower seeds took first place. One could simply not imagine one Shabbos in Kittev without cracking seeds. There were Jews who specialized in drying the seeds and flavouring them with salt and oil. On Friday and Sabbath, these Jews had sustenance aplenty. The seeds were sold by measuring them out in a lass, at five or ten groschen per measure. The seeds posed a problem for the community management which was responsible for keeping the streets clean; but they were helpless and had to watch, gritting their teeth, as Jews, sitting on the benches in the market-place or strolling on the sidewalks, cracked the seeds and spat out the shells at every step. Kittever Jews got great pleasure out of cracking seeds.

On Shabbos afternoon, the older generation used to return to the synagogues and study-houses to recite Ethics of the Fathers and listen to a good discourse from the Rabbi or a preacher. The youth used Sabbath afternoon differently. During the summer time they went on outings to the surrounding woods – on the Oidiush, on the Levadeh or on the Shzaribish, and took pleasure in the Sabbath enjoying the beautiful Kittever nature. If the weather was not suitable for a stroll, the young people would gather in the various clubs and meeting-places, dance and sing or listen to a good lecture or recitation or participate in various political or Zionist discussions. Others played a game of chess or rummy. Those who preferred Olam Ha-Zeh (things of this world) to Olam Ha-Bah (things of the spirit) went to the women's society and spent time there with good looking, attractive girls and young married women.

*[Page 50]*

Every holiday in Kittev had its separate charm and lustre. Anyone who grew up in Kittev and absorbed the traditional Jewish Days of Awe with their customs, the patriarchal customs, will never forget them. He will yearn all his life for those solemn days.

The Days of Awe (High Holidays) began with the Selichos – nights in Elul. Every Jew felt a trembling then, and even the greatest unbelievers felt it their duty to rise up for Selichos on those awesome nights. On Rosh Hashanah and Yom Kippur, all the synagogues were packed with daveners (people praying). It was necessary to place extra benches in every bet-midrash for the worshippers.

A couple of weeks before Yom Kippur, the market price of chickens had already risen. Jewish home-makers began to purchase sacrificial fowls (kappores) for their households. Especially high the price rose for white roosters and hens because every Jewish mother wished to buy a bright sacrificial fowl (lichtige kapporeh) for her husband and kids. When the time came for the ceremony (waving the chicken around the head) the poor ritual-slaughterers (shochtim) had to labour day and night to slaughter and pluck hundreds of roosters and hens.

Our mothers, of blessed memory, of bright remembrance, would make a point of personally preparing the large Yom Kippur candles that were lit in the synagogues. A couple of days before Yom Kippur, they would go to the wick-makers, women who would thread the wicks for the large tallow-candles.[3] This happened as follows: every Kittever home-maker used to make two large tallow-candles, one for the dead and one for the living members of the family. As the woman who put in or drew the wicks from the individual threads inserted each wick, she would call out the names of the family members – a name for each thread. And with it, the wick-drawer said various prayers and incantations.

*[Page 51]*

The finished large tallow-candles were then stuck into wooden boxes or large pots filled with sand and set up in the synagogue Erev Yom Kippur before Kol Nidre.

Erev Yom Kippur at Mincha there stood long tables in the synagogue on which were arranged bowls with inscriptions: for example: House of Study, Shamess (sexton), naphtha, Bikkur Cholim (Help for the Sick), Talmud Torah, Jewish National Fund and more and more. Every Jew who came to daven threw his contribution into the bowls.

In a corner of the synagogue, the Shamess stood with a leather strap and waited for the penitents who would lie down on the synagogue floor and he would give them lashes.

Erev Yom Kippur, after the pre-fast meal, every Jew began to prepare for the great Day of Judgment. The older Jews dressed themselves in white robes (kittel) and white stockings. Before going to the synagogue, they would assemble the children and grandchildren, lay their hands on their heads and with great fervour, bless them with the traditional Jewish blessings.

Yom Kippur at Kol Nidre, all the streets appeared empty. Even non-Jews, on Yom Kippur night, feared the Jewish God and did not show themselves in the thickly populated Jewish streets. All kith and kin were in the synagogues for Kol Nidre. The girls who stayed home also did not engage in idle pursuits on this holy night – they understood the seriousness of the Judgment Day.

*[Page 52]*

The streets around the Great Synagogue and around the Houses of Study were strongly lit by the flames of the hundreds of large tallow-candles in the windows of the full houses of prayer. Inside it was hot and stuffy from the large crowd of worshippers. The air was thick and suffocating from the smoke and the tallow of the burning and smoking candles.

After the Kol Nidre prayers, the older Jews remained in the synagogue until midnight and recited Psalms and Hymn of Unity (Shir Ha-Yichud). An impressive picture was the picture of the Musaf Avodah service on Yom Kippur. At the words: "They would kneel and prostrate themselves" – the worshippers went down on the floor, kneeled and recited the prayers. At Neilah time, the girls gathered outside the synagogues as they had fasted all day and were waiting for the Shofar-blowing so that they would not, God forbid, transgress the Law and eat before the time. Yom Kippur night after Maariv, if the weather was nice, all the Jews coming from the synagogues stood in groups on the street and blessed (renewed) the moon.

Right after Yom Kippur, they began to prepare for the joyous Succos days. On the Jewish streets, the self-built Succahs appeared covered with green branches and hung about and decorated with colourful covers and decorations. Sometimes, two or three families would eat in one Succah. When one family finished eating, another home-maker came into the Succah, blessed the candles and served her family the meal. There were also pious Jews who slept in the cold Succah regardless of the danger of getting a cold.

Not everyone could afford to buy an Essrog so the members of two or three synagogues would join together and buy an Essrog in partnership. After Hallel or Hoshanos, the Shamess would quickly carry the Essrog with the Lulav to a second synagogue. After the service, the Shamess or his wife would carry around the Essrog from house-to-house to allow everyone to fulfil the mitzvah of bentshing Essrog.

*[Page 53]*

For Hoshanah Rabbah, the poor Jewish boys would cut green willow branches which grew by the water and weave Hoshanos. These they sold on the day of Hoshanah Rabbah near the prayer-houses and synagogues to all the worshippers.

Simchas Torah was the happiest day, and the Kittever people celebrated it in a unique way. After noon on Shemini Atseres, there was already a Simchas-Torah atmosphere in the city. The worshippers gathered in their synagogues where the Gabaim had prepared beer and wine, various fruits, broad beans, kidney beans and cakes. All afternoon they enjoyed themselves; ate, drank and sang hymns until there came the hour of Hakafos (parading with the Torahs). At Hakafos, everyone was already quite tipsy and the dancing and singing could be heard through the streets. There were also respected gentlemen who invited the common people to their homes and prepared a royal spread for them. This custom was followed by my father-in-law, R. Shmuel Liebergall, may he rest in peace, and R. Zaide Hutterer. My father-in-law would invite the worshippers of the Chortkover Klaus and they celebrated at tables with roasted ducks, holubches (stuffed cabbage leaves – which we call prokkes) and other dainty foods. They sang hymns and the most beautiful prayers until late in the night. I shall always remember the jolly Simchas-Torah Kiddush that R. Laib'tshe would make (recite) Shemini Atseres night in my father-in-law's house. The Kiddush was a masterpiece! A mish-mash of words and Biblical verses where each phrase began with the last word of the preceding phrase. The Kiddush would start like this:

The sixth day …were finished the heavens[4] --- the heavens tell of His glory --- His glory fills the world. His attendants ask "Where[5] --- Where is Sarah your wife?[6] --- your wife is like a fertile vine in the precincts of your house --- your house and in your gates[7]--- It shall come to pass if you hearken diligently to my commandments which I command you today[8] --- today You will strengthen us, today You will exalt us[9] --- and so on and on.

Every phrase was sung with the appropriate tune of the prayer. The Kiddush lasted half an hour and fitted into the joyous mood of Simchas Torah. Not until late at night did we proceed, singing and dancing to the synagogues and the ardent Hakafos ceremony began.

*[Page 54]*

The same went on in the Wizshinitzer Klaus. The worshippers would celebrate at the house of their Gabbai Zaide Hutterer until midnight, embrace each other and danced calling out "Long live our Rabbi and Teacher" (in Hebrew).

We, the Zionist youth, observed Simchas Torah morning in our meeting hall. The purpose of the separate minyan was to collect money for the Jewish National Fund. At every Aliyah, the person called up to the Torah would pledge (neder) for the Fund. The entire service was sung out and drew a large crowd. The prayers were led by the brothers Berel and Leibel Bergman who were noted as good prayer leaders and singers and a chorus of young boys helped them. After the service, the Committee treated every worshipper with honey-cake and whiskey, and everyone enjoyed themselves.

The Zionist youth also sponsored a ball on Simchas Torah evening at which we spent the whole night.

When Hanukkah came, the Jewish organizations would arrange Hanukkah evenings in various ways: A tea, a show about the miracle of Hanukkah and similar shows. Mainly, Hanukkah was a holiday of the young. There were lectures about the Maccabean revolt, about the heroic deeds of the Maccabees and the meaning of Hanukkah as a parallel to the present-day heroic deeds of the Chalutzim in the diaspora and in Israel.

When Purim approached, preparation began for this joyous holiday. In the streets, one would meet the professional Purim-walkers who disguised themselves and went to collect alms in the surrounding towns. On the Fast of Esther, at night, it was already lively and jolly in the city. There appeared masked groups who visited the homes of their friends disguised as various romantic figures. In the homes of their boyfriends and girlfriends, they sang appropriate songs and declaimed verses, or played theatre-scenes and every house received the masked visitors happily and treated them to drinks and snacks. In the Jewish houses, it was indeed joyous and bright, as it says in the Megillah: "The Jews had light and joy". The houses were full of eager onlookers who wanted to guess who the masked ones were. When a girl's squeal was heard, you knew already that a young man had tried to guess who the girl was and had pulled the mask or the veil off her.

*[Page 55]*

In all generations, Purim was a day for Jews to send Shalach-moness (Purim portions) and give Tzedakah. This custom was strongly observed by the Kittever Jews. In the morning at prayer service, they began to give out charitable donations. All day, until late in the evening, children and grown-ups disguised and not disguised, also representatives of local charitable institutions and pro-Israel committees, visited Jewish homes where they were received in friendly fashion and treated to tasty foods and liquors. All were given the Purim donation with a generous hand.

Purim afternoon began the process of sending Shalach-moness to relatives and friends, from groom to bride, to the in-laws and so forth.

In the streets, one would meet children with little covered baskets covered by plates full of Purim Shalach-moness. Oranges were a rarity in Kittev and they had to be brought from larger cities, so it happened that someone got a couple of oranges and used them to adorn the Shalach-moness package he was sending to his relative or a friend. The Kittever Jews were very polite and friendly and knew how to treat company. The never sent a tray or a platter back empty. The Kittever women were also good housewives and showed great skill in baking. Thus, you could see on the Shalach-moness trays and plates the most various sweet pastries that supplied the homes from Purim to Pesach. Fruit cake, honey cake and other sweet dainties which the Kittever women baked had a reputation.

*[Page 56]*

The Purim holiday ended with the traditional Purim masquerade ball which was arranged by the city committee of the Jewish National Fund.

A popular figure in Kittev on Purim day was Chaim Peshe-Roize's. All year, he dealt in fruit making and made a living from it. He was a pious Jew and the permanent Shamess (sexton) of the Great Synagogue. Every Purim and for many years, Chaim made himself up as a gypsy with long hair and a dark face. He put a large sack on his shoulders and took a long thick stick in his hands and went out with a helper boy of his (also dressed as a gypsy) and all day he would visit the homes of the more prosperous Jewish householders and obtain sizeable contributions from them – mostly in the form of signed chits for 20 or 50 kilos of potatoes or matzos which he, Chaim Peshe-Roize's would distribute among the poor and needy Jews for Pesach. At each house, he was entertained with a couple of glasses of whiskey and something to eat so that by night time, he was very drunk and they had to bring him home in a horse-drawn wagon. Before he went home, Chaim made an appearance at the masquerade ball and danced the first dance while the music played his favourite melody: "Mein shtetele Belz".

Shabbos Hagadol (the Sabbath before Pesach) in Kittev had a special character. If there were Jews who forgot when Shabbos Hagadol (the Great Shabbos) fell, they were soon reminded that today is the Shabbos of the bald men and the smooth-headed Jews were sent off to Egypt to heal their baldness. In truth, on Shabbos Hagadol, it was not enviable to be a Jew whom a Master of the Universe favoured with a bald spot.

The smaller "scabs", with bald spots on their heads, got off relatively easily. It was worse with the older men. If a bald man came into the synagogue – and in every synagogue there were jokers – the jokesters surrounded him and began to kid at his expense. Firstly, they would give him a jovial "Sholom Aleichem" and then began to quiz him on how it went with his trip to Egypt and back – if the operation on his scalp went easily, and similar questions. Instead of answers, there were slaps in the face and there was no shortage of trouble.

*[Page 57]*

Worse yet, it went with the big-shots with large bald spots on Shabbos Hagadol. First thing in the morning, young jokesters would hang red flags on the roofs of their houses and blow trumpets. Often the police had to intervene and help take down the flags. It happened once that a Gabbai, a joker, honoured a bald Jew with an Aliyah – gave him the 5th Aliyah so the jokers all around would start to sneeze and smack their lips. The Gabbai had to insure his head (the meaning of "insure" in this context is unclear) there was nothing to envy him for and the prayer house lost a worshipper.

Shabbos Hagadol in the afternoon, the Kittever Rabbi gave a sermon to teach the people the laws of Kashrus of Pesach. During the week of Shabbos Hagadol and Pesach, the Jews would make great preparations for the holiday.

Kittev had no machines for baking Matzos – only a few modern individuals got Manishewitz matzos – most of the Jews were busy baking oven matzos --- Shmurah matzos and ordinary matzos. The Kittever Rabbi and Shochtim were very watchful that all should be done with the highest level of Kashrus. They took care of the large mill which ground white flour for matzos and koshered the special stones which ground the flour for the Shmurah. They also watched the wagon-drivers, who carried the flour, and saw to it that their wagons would be clean and would not, God forbid, carry Chametsdig flour together with the Pesach'dig flour.

*[Page 58]*

They took care the flour was well covered so it could not get wet, God forbid, by even a drop of rain!

The Rabbis and Schochtim also inspected the Kittever flour-merchants that sold flour for Pesach. They should have separate storage and they would see to it that the scales and weights would not have even a crumb of Chomets on them. But the hardest job which the religious functionaries had, was during the baking of the Matzos in supervising the Matzo bakeries so that all would be Kosher to the highest degree.

Kittev had no equipped Matzo bakery. Before Pesach, a few Kittever respectable householders such as Chaim Mendel the tailor, Sholem Rotter, Sarah the black, Chaim Peshe Roize's, Moshe Yankel Krendel's and others who had large kitchens with large ovens and big rooms, transformed their houses into bakeries. They hired kneading-women, heated the ovens to glowing red, set up a row of women who rolled out the Matzos and perforators who pierced the Matzos with a wheel and setter-ins who, for fourteen to eighteen hours, stood on their feet at the hot oven setting in and baking the Matzos. The rabbinic supervision over the places where Matzos were baked was under the strictest supervision of the Rabbi and the Shochtim. They saw to it that the boards on which the Matzo was rolled out were smooth and freshly planed; they saw to it that the helping-women wore clean white aprons; that the oven would be koshered and that no one, God forbid, should stumble into a suspicion of the presence of Chomets during Pesach.

As previously mentioned, there were enough Jews in Kittev, perfect in the fear of Heaven, who guarded themselves against the tiniest transgression. Those Jews, with their own hands, brought the Pesach into the house. As an example, we will mention such a pious Jew as Joseph Rappaport who had a separate piece of field where he personally sowed the wheat; cut the ears and threshed the grain; personally picked over every grain for Shmurah and these people were the first to grind the flour on the koshered stones – first to bake the Shmurah-Matzo which they personally kneaded, rolled out and set in the oven.

*[Page 59]*

Naturally, Kittever homemakers had Chomets'dig and Pesach'dig utensils, cans for water. Even the water-carriers used to wear white linen robes; a non-Jewish water-carrier was just not entrusted with drawing water from the well, but someone would accompany him and make sure that he didn't touch a piece of Chomets while carrying the Pesach'dig water.

The Jewish storekeepers and their employees, all Jewish artisans, tailors, shoemakers, were very busy in the pre-Pesach weeks and worked day and night to be able to fill the orders. It was the ambition of every Jewish mother and father that they, or at least their children should be supplied with a new garment for Pesach. When the Pesach days arrived and everyone would go out for the holiday stroll around the Synagogue and the prayer-houses, everyone looked over each other and admired his new wardrobe, the material, the tools and the workmanship of the tailor in sewing up and finishing the article of clothing. They also discussed the cobblers who sewed the shoes, and so on.

Lag B'Omer (33rd day of the Omer) was a holiday for the young people. All Cheder boys were off from school that day. The Rebbes and their helpers from the Cheders marched out together with their pupils into the woods and gardens around Kittev and thus, the Cheder boys got the chance to enjoy a few hours in the open air. The Cheder boys would jump and play and the Rebbes (teachers) would tell them the history of Lag B'Omer – about the life and accomplishments of the great Tanna (sage of the Mishna) Rabbi Simeon ben Yochai.

On Shevuos, all Kittev looked like one great aromatic green garden! The colorful flower gardens and the various colorfully blooming fruit orchards intoxicated with their fragrant odours. In honour of Shevuos, every Jewish home and the Synagogue and the prayer houses were decorated with odorous flowers and green Shevuos leaves.

*[Page 60]*

Kittever Jews celebrated in their own specific way, not only the Days of Awe and all the Jewish holidays but observed even the national days of mourning in a responsible and traditional manner.

Tishah B'Av, for example, could be recognized at every step. On Tishah B'Av night, all the synagogues and prayer houses were dimly lit: the lamps were extinguished as a sign of sadness and mourning. The worshippers sat down on inverted book-rests, lit their books of lamentations with a small tallow candle, bowed their heads and listened to the mournful "How doth the city sit solitary" of the prayer leader. It never happened that on the night of Tishah B'Av they should play Yiddish theatre in Kittev or schedule any other entertainment. The Polish owners of the cinema hall, who did show a film on Tishah B'Av night, had an empty hall. In this national night of mourning, every Kittever Jew mourned with the entire Jewish people for the destruction of the nation and its land.

## Chapter IX

# Family Festivities of Kittever Jews

Kittever Jews lived out their lives in a unique style. Their happy occasions (simchas) and their funerals – everything bore the specific Kittever stamp.

*[Page 61]*

When a male was born in a Jewish family, they celebrated a Sholem-Zocher on the first Friday night in the following way: After prayers, the Shamess stood himself on the platform or at the prayer-house table and announced "Ploni-ben-Ploni" (equivalent to John Doe) is giving a Sholem-Zocher this evening and all worshippers are invited. At the Sholem-Zocher, they served liquor, fruits, nuts, cooked kidney-beans and broad beans. On the 7th day, before the Bris, they held a reading of the Shema. The Rebbe, with the Cheder boys, would come into the room where the childbirth-woman lay with her new born and read the Shema as a protection against demons. Before leaving, the Cheder boys would get honey-cake and whiskey. The father of the new born would stand at the door with a bottle and glasses in his hands and give every child a swallow of whiskey. Another person would hand them honey-cake. The Rebbe's helper would receive double. The circumcisions were often performed in the same prayer-house where the father davened.

When a female was born, they would make a festive meal and children would take candies out of the little girl's cradle.

When a little boy began learning Chumash, they also made a little Seudah to which they invited the teacher and the older pupils. They dressed up the Chumash boy and put on him a watch with a chain. He then held his first speech for the assembled people. At the Bar-Mitzvah, the boy naturally was called up to the Torah and everyone was invited for Kiddush and to the Bar-Mitzvah festive meal.

At a betrothal (T'naim) a plate was broken to confirm that the coupe are bride and groom and after this, they struck hands and wrote the T'naim (articles of betrothal).

On the Saturday before the wedding, they held a Forshpiel (merry entertainment on the night of the Sabbath preceding the wedding") – the bridegroom, at his home, and the bride at hers with her girlfriends. Sabbath morning, the groom was called up to the Torah. The women who davened in the women's section, would throw candies at the groom. After prayers, the groom would invite the worshippers for Kiddush. Also, in the bride's house, they held a Forshpiel.

Kittever weddings used to take place in a hall or a house, if one had a large house. Others held the ceremony (Chuppah) under the sky near the Great Synagogue. Often one would meet a wedding procession in the Kittever streets. The musicians went first playing a wedding march followed by the best man and bridesmaids with lighted candles in their hands. After them, followed the groom and bride and in-laws. They marched to the Great Synagogue where the Rabbi and Shamess and guests were waiting for them. In addition, Kittev had its own wedding tune: tra-la-la – with the Shamess sang while the in-laws circled the groom and bride seven times.

*[Page 62]*

The Sheva-Broches party in Kittev was celebrated on the 1st Friday after the wedding. At covered tables, people would gather. At the head sat the newly married couple and everyone made merry.

In the case of a funeral, God preserve us, the Shamess would announce on the streets by calling out: "Go to a funeral obligation"! When he was stopped and asked, he would tell who the dead person was and when the funeral would take place. The funeral had its set route of march through the Jewish streets and would pass by the prayer house where the deceased used to daven. If the deceased was a scholar his bier would be carried into the prayer-house and was eulogized there. The bier was always followed by a member of the Chevrah Kadishah (burial society) carrying a large tin collection box (pushke) and everyone threw contributions into it. The (Chevrah Kadishah) Jew would constantly rattle the pushke and sing out in a wailing monotone: "Charity saves from death"! "And who doesn't want to be spared from death"! So, they threw into the pushke.

Kittev had no professional grave-diggers. But there was in the city a Chevrah Kadishah organization to which the Kittever artisans belonged and they carried out their work to perfection. The money they received from the wealthy families was used for the Jewish artisans' fund.

Thus, the Kittever Jews lived according to their customs and traditions at happy events and at funerals in sadness and in joy. The customs and traditions would pass from generation-to-generation and became as holy as the laws of the Torah.

### *Translator's footnotes:*

1. The Yiddish word "shafn" connotes work that is creative and productive.
2. A shul is a synagogue. A bet-midrash is a small house of prayer and study. A kloiz is a small synagogue and study-house, frequently restricted to some occupational or social group.
3. They made the wicks for the ritual candles out of the threads used in measuring graves.
4. This first phrase is the start of the Sabbath eve Kiddush.
5. From the Kedushah.
6. From Genesis.
7. The end of the first paragraph of the Shema.
8. Beginning of 2nd paragraph of the Shema.
9. Yom Kippur Musaf.

*[Page 63]*

## Chapter X

# Kittever Heroes

One should particularly mention the heroic Jewish youth of Kittev which, on many occasions and with self-sacrifice, defended Jewish honour and sometimes also the life of the Jews of Kittev. In this way they taught the enemies of the Jews a lesson in how to live with their Jewish neighbours in peace.

I wish to mention just a couple of incidents which serve as an example on how Kittever Jewish boys repelled attackers and took away their appetite for messing with Jews.

Right after World War I, Kittev was, as mentioned before, occupied by the Romanians. The Romanian soldiers had a little fun at the expense of the Jewish population, beating and pulling Jewish beards. One time, on a Sunday afternoon, a Romanian started chasing after a Jew, caught him, beat him and whipped him with a long whip and insulted him as well. Two Jewish boys arrived – Moshe Klinger and Israel Hechler, and not fearing the strength of the Romanian tuft of hair, they dragged him into the hallway of Rachel Tillinger's house in the market square – beat him up really good, took away his weapons and then threw him into the dark cellar. The soldier who scoffed at the Jew begged the Jewish boys for mercy, to spare his life. After he got out from Jewish hands, barely with his life, he learned a lesson and didn't bother a Jew any more.

As mentioned, the Kittever Jews always strove to live peacefully with their Polish and Ukrainian neighbours. It seldom happened that a non-Jewish neighbour should show his ugly anti-Semitic side openly and attack a Jew just so. The Jews used various methods to pacify their non-Jewish neighbours and try to sober them out of their anti-Semitic hate. With the formation of the Polish republic, the Polish anti-Semitism grew. This anti-Semitism penetrated into such towns as Kittev and gradually poisoned the long-lasting peaceful relations between the old neighbour peoples.

*[Page 64]*

In the year 1926-1927, the Polish anti-Semitism passed from words to deeds. When the local Polish students, sons of the Polish local government officials, would come home on vacation, they brought with them the anti-Semitic spirit of the universities and wanted to plant it in Kittev. But they received such a lesson from the Jewish boys that they had no further desire to express their anti-Semitic doctrine through deeds.

In public, the anti-Semitic "heroes" were afraid to practice their anti-Semitic deeds so they tried to do it at night when everyone was asleep and nobody could hinder their black work. Once, they broke the windows of a Jewish house that was in a non-Jewish neighbourhood (in the Jewish streets, these anti-Semitic mouth-heroes were afraid to show themselves) another time, they pasted anti-Semitic propaganda on the telephone poles – hatred and enmity to Jews – calling on the Christian population to boycott Jewish businesses and artisans. Afterward, they also started to attack physically helpless older Jews whom they met in the street. It came to this that Jews who lived in Christian neighbourhoods were afraid to go outside at night especially during vacation times when the students had returned home.

*[Page 65]*

The representatives of the Jewish community naturally turned to the police requesting that they arrest and punish the nocturnal attackers. They pointed out that it was against the law of the Polish constitution to incite one part of the population against another. However, the police didn't hurry to catch and punish the guilty ones, who among them were their own sons; perhaps they enjoyed seeing how the Polish students amused themselves at the expense of the "Zshides" (derogatory terms for Jews). Then the heroic Jewish youth of Kittev determined to take the law into their own hands, drove the anti-Semitic "darlings" away from the Jewish streets.

The most popular heroes of the Kittever Jewish street were the three sworn comrades and friends: Zaide Mandel, Gedaliah Landvehr and Shlomo Moskowitz. They were fearless heroic young men, swift and clever so that even the Ukrainians and the Hulutzes of the surrounding villages, who respected a Jew in proportion to his "hands of Esau" – trembled with the fear of death before the three comrades who were called "the team". It was woe to the "sheigets" who fell into the hands of one of the team. The team organized the Jewish self-defence and thereby put an end to the attacks and the anti-Semitic propaganda in Kittev.

The defence was organized in this matter: A few nights each week, several Jewish boys watched over the Jewish houses that were located in the Christian section. Once the anti-Semitic night-heroes broke the windows of a Jewish house on the Sniatiner Street and began pasting anti-Semitic placards on the telephone poles, the Jewish boys would appear and treat the students to such a beating that the next day, they were ashamed to show their black eyes and bruises to their comrades. This was their reward for their anti-Semitic deeds.

In the summer of 1934, Kittev was famed throughout Poland as a spa and a pleasant vacation spot. Each summer, thousands of guests would come down here with their families. In that year, there were a sizeable number of students among the guests who belonged to the Endekes – the Polish anti-Semitic party. Kittev was a town where one met Jews at every step.

*[Page 66]*

This bothered the Endeke students very much. The Poles, therefore, at every occasion when coming across a Jew, in the summer places, at the Chermesh and similar places of amusements – sought to provoke and insult the Jews. At those times, the Kittever Jewish youth would appear and teach the anti-Semites properly, responding to their provocations appropriately and (repay them) even with per cent.

There comes to mind a Sunday. The Polish spa guests and the anti-Semitic students gathered at the Sokkol hall for a Polish ball. When they were well lubricated and happy from the extra glasses, they set out into the street and hollered: "Beat the Jews". They demonstrated their heroism by beating up two Jewish little boys who were playing in the street. After this heroic piece of work, they ran back into the hall. But it didn't take long before all Kittev knew about the attack on the two Jewish boys. Jewish young fellows gathered on the streets and held a consultation on how to teach the anti-Semites that Kittever Jews were not helpless and could strike back. They worked out a whole strategy and a number of boys volunteered for the "job". The rest went quietly home because they knew they had left the matter in good hands.

Next morning, it became known that the Endekite students had been found lying in the gutter, beaten up, more dead than alive. When they subsequently came to complain to the police, the police advised them to pack up and go back to where they came from because Kittev was not Warsaw or Lemberg and that they should well understand and remember. And indeed, the Endekes remembered this for a long time.

The anti-Semitic attacks did not cease completely especially in later years when the anti-Semitism increased

*[Page 67]*

throughout Poland. Some attacks on Jews still took place on the part of the anti-Semitic spa guests but each time, the Jews fulfilled the verse: "an eye for an eye" and drove off the attackers.

On many occasions, the Kittever Jews, especially the Jewish youth, exhibited heroism, bravery and courage in defending Jewish rights and not allowing Jews to be degraded as second-class citizens. Later I will talk about the role of the Jewish youth in Kittev in guarding the city from an attack by peasants from surrounding villages at the beginning of World War II when the Polish military, along with the police, retreated and left the city wide open.

## Chapter XI

# Kittever Nicknames and Types

Just as in other cities, there were a number of Jewish families in Kittev who were called by the names of their occupations: Chaim Hersh the Shuster (shoemaker), Mechl the Shneider (tailor), Moshe the Stolier (carpenter,) Abraham the Buchbinder (bookbinder), Dov'tshe the Shamess, Zaide the Chazan, Joseph the Cohen, Meche'le the Katzav (butcher), Leib'eniu the Muller (mason or bricklayer) Moshe Meir the Kalch-Jew (whitswasher), Berish the Becker (baker), Velvel the Becker, Zindel the Bershtelmacher (brush-maker), Shlomo the Krupnick (barley dealer), Rachel the Boobeh (a regional word not in my dictionary), Itzie the Rophe (healer), Anshel the Frizirer (hairdresser), Yankel the Treger (carrier), Meir-Hersh the Baal-Agolah (wagon driver), Eisig the Katzav, Alter the Kirshner (hatter), Yossel the Zeigermacher (clock-maker), and many others. All the artisans who were called by their trades took it as self-evident and felt as though this was their second name. Therefore, in time, their children were called the same way, for example: Min'tshe, Berish the Bekker's daughter, Moshe Leib'une the Muller's son, Moshe Mechele the Katzav's son, Ethel, Itzie the Bedder's daughter, and so on.

*[Page 68]*

Another category of Kittever Jews who were called by special names were men and women who were called by their parents' names: Chaim Peshe Roize's Yankel Chaim Mendel's, Moshe Yankel Crendel's, Feivel' Chananiah's, Itzie Yossele's, Feige the Raphael'iche, Moshe Hannah's, Shlomo Shime'les, Gedaliah Mirele's, Moshe Choneh Adelle'. My own mother, may she rest in peace, was called Sheindel Roize's (the name of my grandmother who in her old age went to Eretz Israel to die there).

The third category of Kittever names were the nicknames that were attached to people for various reasons such as their origin, character, occupation or because of an unusual happening in their life. Among this group, the names were of a tragi-comical nature. There were in the city various characters and personality types. There were Jews with a sense of humour who loved to poke fun at themselves and other who joked at the expense of their neighbours and friends. But there were Jews without any sense of humour who would get very insulted and angry when they were called by their nickname. Often, the use of a nickname would cause anger and enmity. As mentioned before, there was no dearth in Kittev of jokesters who liked to wise-crack at another's expense. If a sensitive Jew fell into the company of jokers, he had no lack of troubles. Very often a joke would end in a fight.

The children of Yehudah Leib Klinger were called the Shneiderukes (an insulting form of the word for a tailor) even though they were all businessmen. The family Druck was designated as Shkrabes (worn-out shoes). Mechele Ungar, who was a tailor, was called Mechele Katz (cat). When he met children in the street, they would hide and holler: "Mechele Katz" and meow like a cat. Mechele would chase them and throw stones . . . Mechele was afraid to pass by the meat-markets because as soon as they saw him, the butchers and market-youths would start a caterwauling: one would meow, a second would holler "mitz, mitz" and a third would holler "prush". A fourth would sneeze and poor Mechele would swallow it all because he simply was afraid to start a fight with them. His only weapon was the curse and he used to curse them with might and main.

*[Page 69]*

Chaim Windrech was called "Chaim what time is it". If one asked him for the time he replied with curses.

Abele Shnitzer was called Abele Hooze and some even thought that that was his real family name.

Itzik Booler was called Itzik Tson (tooth); Meir Socher – Meir Tsitsele; Chaim Sender was called Chaim Ketzele (pussy-cat); Gedaliah and Elihu Shatner – Gedaliah and Elihu Pletnick; Feivish Solomon and his son were called Zazaule; Meir Tsirel – Meir Fuftsiger and Yossel Ehrlich –Knapper.

Zaide Shatner was called Zaide Tukeh because of an actual happening. Once, going down into the cellar, he fell down the steps and dragged down with him various wooden utensils with which he dealt. The fall made such a noise that his wife came running and asked breathlessly: "What happened Zaide?" Zaide could only mumble: "Tu-tu-tu, I'm feeding the chicks". His wife, who was quite a Cossack, answered: "A black dream upon you, your chicks are in the attic, not in the cellar". The neighbours who heard this comical colloquy between husband and wife, gave Zaide the name Zaide Tukeh.

In Kittev there was also a Jew named Chaim Shnitzer who was called, Chaim Ya-Chaitse: a true story. This is how it happened: His wife's name was Chai'tse and she had a cow which only she, Chai'tse would milk. It happened once that Chai'tse got sick and Chaim had to milk the cow. The cow, being used to Chai'tse milking her, would, in no way, let herself be milked by Chaim. She twitched and kicked him with her feet. So what does Chaim do? He got the idea to fool the cow to make her think that he was Chai'tse. Done and done! He put on an apron and a kerchief on his head, imitated a woman's voice and started telling the cow that he was Chai'tse. If the cow believed him, I don't know but I do know that the neighbours saw it all and heard it all. They in confidence told their neighbours as a secret. It became a "secret for all Brod". Chaim was nicknamed Ya-Chaitse (Russian for: "I am Chai'tse").

*[Page 70]*

Moshe Strauss was called Moshe Shostick; Shmuel Ornstein – Shmuel Zaveruche (hurricane); Monieh Ornstein – Monieh Buziak; Abraham Hutterer – Abraham the corpse; the families Ezra and Yossel Grau and Velvel Grau – the Tshuchanes and the Shmertz family – the Pertsiukes.

Leizer Tillinger, a dark-complexioned man, was called the "double-eight" (in dominoes the black stone is the double-eight because it has sixteen black dots on a white background). Moshe Foigel was called Moshe Ganev (thief). Actually, he was a Jew with a long beard who went to Kossev for High Holidays to be with the Rebbe.

Elasar the hatmaker was called Alter Plooz; Aaron the carrier – Aaron Trimbe; Shimon Foigel – Shimon Kuzshme; Totke Tannentsop – Totke Niuch; Hersh Leib Chasid – Hersh Leib Shniapkes; Hersh Tau – Hersh Loksh; Totke Zwiebach – Totke Mitskes; and Yude Klinger –Yehudah Kolbasnik.

There was also in Kittev a Jew of many occupations and few blessings (in Yiddish this rhymes), who was called "Yoske the Moid" (maiden). Among the wagon-drivers there were types who provided much humour and fun.

We had a wagon-driver called Shmuel Kluger. He was called: "The Youth". He always looked healthy, with a ruddy face and his horses were also big and strong, reddish with gleaming hides. The Youth loved his horses very much. He never touched a whip to them. If someone insulted the Youth, he just got angry but if a horse of his was touched, he was ready to commit murder.

*[Page 71]*

There was another wagon-driver, Moneleh Shustick, an extremely poor man. From time-to-time, the Kittever Jews took up a collection to buy him a horse to allow him to earn his wretched livelihood. As Moneleh was bitterly poor and barely earned bread for his family, he showed the horse hay on in the Siddur (a pun on the Hebrew letter H, called Hay). Naturally the animal couldn't last long and would "stretch out its hooves". Moneleh always explained using the words of Grandfather Mendele (the Yiddish writer Mendele Mocher S'forim) in the story "The Mare"." I worked long and hard to train the horse not to eat, so now, for spite, it goes and dies."

In Kittev there was also another wagon-driver, Shemaiahu Sander who was called the Shtomper (stumbler). The story of the "Shtomper" is as follows: One Friday morning, Shmuel Kerner, a Kittever tanner, had a lawsuit scheduled in the court in Kossev. He hired Shmaiah to drive him to Kossev for the trial. On the road, driving step-by-step, Shmuel Kerner realized that at this rate they would never get there on time. But Shmaiah didn't even answer – he just kept on driving slowly and even started singing a Rosh Hashanah tune. Then Shmuel Kerner in his irritation let fall a word which made him lose the lawsuit. In excitement he called out to Shmaiah: "Such a lazy horse, such a stumbler, I wouldn't even give him straw to chew". When Shmaiah heard this, his wagon-driver's pride was aroused and since

Shmuel had insulted his chestnut and called him a stumbler, he turned the wagon around and drove back to Kittev. Shmuel's pleading and threatening had no effect: "You called my chestnut a stumbler so he won't take you to Kossev". That was Shmaiah's decision and Shmuel Kerner lost his lawsuit.

*[Page 72]*

It's worth mentioning another category of names of Kittever Jews who were given nicknames because of their skin and colour. Such for example were: Yehudah Leib the Blue; Meir the Red; Sarah the Black, Bobbe the Red, Shmuel the Yellow, and so forth. Others had the "privilege" of being named for their physical defect: Shmuel the Blind, Yossel the Deaf, Moshe the Mute, Hersh the Crooked, Leibele Hunch and others.

Finally, I want to mention a special type of Kittever Jew – the Jewish village-walkers – Jews who went into the mountains at the beginning of the week, from village-to-village, seeking to buy something – a little cow, a goad, a lamb or a slab of cheese or butter. For Shabos, these Jewish village-walkers would return to their families and sell the livestock to the butchers and the cheese and butter to their neighbours. These Jewish village-walkers who lived so much among non-Jews in time began to use non-Jewish words in speaking. Altogether, they spoke more Goyish than Yiddish.

I recall a case of two brothers, village-walkers, who returned to the city to observe Yahrzeit for their father. The older brother knew a little Hebrew and went up to the reader's desk.

It was then the time of counting the Omer (between Pesach and Shevuos). He didn't know which day of the Omer it was so he turned to his brother and asked him in Ukrainian "what number is it today?" The next day, this brother went to the reader's desk again. It was a Thursday when the Torah is read. When it came time to close the Aron Kodesh (the Holy Ark), he turned again to his brother and called: "lock the gate.

*[Page 73]*

This kind of Jewish village-walker and village inhabitant, simple but upright Jews who struggled their whole lives to earn their piece of bread and nourish their families, provided plenty of material for Jewish humour and folklore. These were Jews who were ready to sacrifice their lives for their faith.

Let me be permitted to close this chapter about Kittever Jewish folklore by noting that I have not covered all the Kittever folk types. For example, I have omitted the various types of Hasidim who belonged to the various Hasidic courts (each Rebbe's establishment is like a royal court) – the Misnagdim who scoffed at the Hasidim. Also, Kittever Jews who gave Tsedakah or gave in secret, and ordinary Kittever people who had Jewish hearts of gold and were ever ready to fight for Jewish honour and Jewish rights. I also didn't dwell on the various types of Jewish artisans – women who sat in the market-place, and others. This would require an entire separate book.

## Chapter XII

# Polish Jewry Before World War II

It would not be right to depict the social and cultural life of the Jews of Kittev; the awakening of their national consciousness; their cultural and education institutions – all that they created- without an overview of the great pre-war Jewish community of Poland as a whole. After all, Kittev was but a small link in the chain of Polish Jewish cities and towns – a microcosm of Polish Jewry in general.

*[Page 74]*

The Jewish community in Poland was a living and productive organism. There was a pulsating active Jewish life in every city and town, in every village where Jews found themselves; an energetic Jewish communal life, full of a spirit of enterprise and initiative, whose energy brought prosperity and wealth for all of Poland.

Trade, industries and the free professions lay, on the whole, in Jewish hands. Jews conducted the Polish export and import in an organized fashion. Polish industry continually grew and developed thanks to the capable Jewish industrialists of Lodz, Billitz-Biale, Bialystok, who were famed for their textile and goods factories; for their linen and cloth fabrics.

Jewish community life in Poland was a colorful rainbow which encircled the whole country. Polish Jews had various organized movements, parties and institutions; professional societies and cooperative enterprises. Poland had her religious Jewish parties: Hasidim and Misnagdim, Orthodox and Maskilim, Agudas Israel, Mizrachi, Hapoel Hamizrachi, the youth organization Bnai Akiva, Revizionists, Brith Hanoar named for Joseph Trumpeldor (Betar), the Judenstat party, General Zionists, Hitachdut, Gordoniah, Bosliah, Hechalutz, Right Labour Zionists, Left Labour Zionists, Ha-Shomer Ha-Tsair, the socialist Bund party, the leftists and the professional societies.

Among all these parties and groups, there was a competition and a struggle which often overstepped the bounds of their local chapters and became a public issue. The struggles were especially noticeable before elections, elections to the community council, the Seyim (Polish parliament) or the Senate and also before elections to the Zionist Congress.

Every one of the parties issued propaganda and put forward their programs as the best and most equitable. Each party and group had pretensions of being the only one able to solve all Jewish problems.

*[Page 75]*

To gain the support of the community and of the Jewish masses and popularize its thought and ideology, each party had its propagandists, preachers, lecturers, speakers, who travelled around all the cities and towns. Each party also had its written organs, daily papers and weekly and monthly periodicals.

The Polish Jews especially excelled in the cultural-educational sphere. Poland possessed networks of general and trade schools, Hebrew kindergartens, elementary schools and also high schools, orthodox and secular teachers' schools as well as great and famous Yeshivos and Beth Jacob schools for girls. All of them helped to educate and raise up a proud Jewish national type of which World-Jewry could be proud.

It would take too much space to write about the contribution of Polish Jewry in the fields of journalism and literature. In the first instance, the press, which had a circulation of many thousands: The Heint (Today), the Moment, Tageblat (Daily Page), the Morgen (Tomorrow), the Radio, Neies (News), the great Jewish-Polish daily the "Chvilla" and the periodical publications, literary gazettes, Vochenblatt (Weekly Page), the various other literary journals and the Hebrew press.

Jewish Poland possessed a whole group of world-renowned writers, poets and prose writers, romance writers and novelists and dramatists, composers, conductors, musicians, theatre stage-managers and directors. From the Polish-Jewish publishing houses, all of World Jewry drew as from an inexhaustible well. The Polish-Jewish printing presses were famous the world over. And who can forget the Yiddish theatre in Poland; the famous Vilna company, the actors Zigmunt Turkov, Ida Kaminski and Jonas Turkov, Maurice Lampe and Shoshanah Rabinovitch and others?

Polish-Jewish genius was also noticeable in the field of the free professions. The most prestigious attorneys in Poland were Jews; famous Jewish professors, surgeons, pharmacists and dentists filled every city and town in Poland. Jewish talent, genius and initiative was evident throughout the country. Naturally Jewish participation in the free professions and in all branches of the economy elicited plenty of jealousy and enmity from the Polish population and strengthened the anti-Semitism.

*[Page 76]*

In regard to Zionist activity and pro-Israel action, Poland surpassed all of World Jewry. Polish Jewry was the backbone of the world-wide Zionism – both as a reservoir of Chalutzim and in the area of raising funds. Polish Jewry furnished huge sums for the Zionist funds, Keren Hayesod and Keren Kayemet. The Polish Zionist youth organizations provided an idealistic human-resource which had no equal in many generations. All over Poland there spread networks of Hachsharah (preparatory training) points where Jewish boys and girls productized themselves and prepared to live as workers in the historic Jewish homeland. It is surely no exaggeration when we state that Polish Jewry prior to World War II had the biggest share in preparing the way for the rise and the establishment of the State of Israel.

With the rise of Hitlerism, the Jewish horizon in all of Europe and particularly in Poland began to cloud up. The black anti-Semitic forces in Poland raised their heads and prepared for open strife against the Jews. The Poles used all methods to push Jews out of their economic and cultural positions. Not only did the Polish government not hinder the anti-Semites, but it strongly encouraged their anti-Jewish actions. Various anti-Semitic laws were enacted which increasingly degraded the Polish-Jewish community and robbed it of its civil rights.

*[Page 77]*

The Endeke (National Democratic) party carried out a systematic propaganda aimed at driving Jews out of public life. They incited and organized pogroms and attacks against the Jewish population in many cities and towns. At first, the Endekes contented themselves with boycott-propaganda against Jewish businesses and goods. Then they started to "picket" the Jewish factories and stores. They terrorized the Polish customers of Jewish businesses; beat them and drove them away with violence. They also especially before the Christian holidays, tried to compete with the Jewish storekeepers. When the Jewish businessman would resist this competition, the Endeke students would incite the anti-Semitic mob to look the Jewish stores and murderously beat the Jewish merchant as well.

The pogrom in Pshitik is sadly notorious. In this Polish-Jewish town, the anti-Semitic ruffians attacked the Jewish stores, robbed and murderously beat the Jewish storekeepers. They also murdered a Jewish storekeeper. The Polish police who watched it all, did not lift a finger to stop the bandits, and did not make the slightest effort to catch and punish the murderers.

The Polish regime also did everything possible to ruin Jewish commerce and industry. They stopped the credits for Jewish commerce, raised taxes while encouraging the general economy by reducing taxes and issuing credit at minimal interest rates. The Poles also turned over to their co-religionists an exclusive monopoly on tobacco and cigarettes, liquor, salt and other articles.

Setting themselves a goal of wresting the free professions out of Jewish hands, the government established the notorious "numerus clausus" for Jewish students in the Polish universities. In general, they admitted only a small percentage of Jews to the high schools and universities. Finally, to completely embitter the life of the Jewish student, they came up with this drastic method of insulting and degrading him.

*[Page 78]*

They would force the Jewish student to sit on special benches. The benches on the left (they wanted to show that all Jews were communists). If a Jewish student refused to sit on the left-hand bench, the anti-Semites would jump him and murderously beat him. At the Lemberg Polytechnic, the Endeke students murdered a Jewish student because he defended himself when they tried to force him to sit on the left-hand bench.

The Polish government also forbade Jews to buy real estate. Ostensibly, the law said that Jews may not be landowners in areas bordering the neighbouring countries. Since nearly all of Poland bordered on neighbouring countries, it made it almost impossible for a Jew to buy a house or a field or a garden or an orchard anywhere. A Jew was only allowed to sell his house or garden to a non-Jew without limitation.

The depth to which anti-Semitism was rooted in the hearts and minds of the Poles may be seen in the fact that a few weeks before the War broke out with Hitler, regardless of the fact that they days of Polish independence were numbered, the Polish Seyim still let itself be swept along with the anti-Semitic wave and passed the "Shechita" law which forbade Kosher slaughter. This law was introduced in the Seyim by the member of parliament, Mrs. Pristar. Instead of unifying all the forces in the country against the enemy's attack and forging a united defence, the Poles, even in the face of the greatest peril to their nation, would not free themselves of their in-grown hatred of Jews and pushed through this law.

Kittev was no exception. Here too Jews suffered from the various anti-Jewish limitations and anti-Semitic laws. The richer Jewish parents could still afford the luxury of giving their children higher education and sending them to universities although they knew well that no matter how they excelled in knowledge, they would never have a chance to get any government job, not even that of a chimney sweeper or a street cleaner.

*[Page 79]*

The taxes pressed more and more heavily on the Jewish merchant, artisan and house-owner. Those who enforced the tax law acted cruelly against Jews. It happened more than once that a Jew who could not pay the tax on time lost his whole inventory which was liquidated by the tax collectors. In this way, many Jews lost the ability to earn a bit of bread for themselves and their families. From the Jewish house-owner who could not pay the tax on the property, they would take away the furniture, even his clothes and the pillow from under his head. Jews often had to borrow a suit for Shabbos so that they could go to the Shul to daven.

A short time before Hitler's attack on Poland, the government which had finally begun to comprehend the danger, began to make preparations for defense. They then issued a call to all inhabitants of the country in which they appealed to their patriotic feelings and asked them to respond generously to the government loan which they proclaimed.

In the face of the peril which threatened the whole country, the Jews tried to forget all the glaring injustices perpetrated against them and they were the first to respond generously to the appeal and made a large contribution to the government loan. In Kittev, the Jewish population contributed more than 90% to the collection for the voluntary government loan.

The chief of the District of Kossiv, Fiola, established a quota for the entire Kittever community. The Council was to collect the sum from all citizens. The Kittev Jews were the first to hurry to pay the voluntary tax while the other citizens, Poles and Ukrainians, took their time. This slowed down the loan process in the city.

*[Page 80]*

When the chief of the Kossever District, Fiola, saw that the collection in Kittev was in trouble, he came up with an idea. He came to Kittev and ordered that, within 24 hours, the Kittever Jews should make up the amount that the Ukrainians and the Poles failed to contribute. Not all the Kittever Jews were able to contribute again, so the chief ordered a few Jews to be arrested. Those who were arrested were kept in prison until their families produced the money.

This is how the Polish authorities treated the Jews. It should also be noted that among the anti-Semites were many former socialists and revolutionaries alongside of whom Jews had fought for social justice. Poland also forgot that Jews had often fought and shed their blood for independence and freedom of Poland. The former socialists and revolutionaries also forgot all the ringing slogans of "Liberty, Equality and Fraternity", the ideals for which so many Polish patriots and Jewish revolutionaries had sacrificed their lives. Polish chauvinism gained the upper hand. The Jews were the first victims of the raging Polish nationalism and chauvinism. The chauvinists united with the most virulent anti-Semites and together degraded the Jews to the status of second-class citizens who had to fulfil all responsibilities and bear all the burdens of citizenship and yet suffer from limitations and discriminations. When Polish

Jews tried to protest against these crimes and demand justice from those in power, they were met with the well-known anti-Semitic refrain: "If you don't like it, go to Palestine". " Poland for the Poles"!

In such an atmosphere and under such conditions of anti-Jewish excesses and discriminations the Polish nation made its final preparations to fight against the Nazi enemy; in such a pestilent and poisoned atmosphere of blind hatred toward Jews, did Poland seek to unite all its citizens in the last battle for its future.

*[Page 81]*

## Chapter XIII

# The German Invasion of Poland

Friday, September 1, 1939, the Nazi blitzkrieg invasion of Poland occurred. The war began with such swiftness and brutality, form air, land and sea, that the Polish army was unable to endure the first blows of the German attack and began to collapse.

On land, the German mechanized divisions; the heavy tanks and armoured cannons, quickly broke through the Polish forward defence lines and began their destructive march on Polish soil. On the sea, the German fleet which was supported by the German Luftwaffe, attacked the Polish fleet and bombarded the Polish port cities of Danzig and Gdynia. From the air, the Germans sowed destruction on all Polish cities and villages. All- important Polish industrial centers and factory cities, all important railroad stations and bridges, military camps and staging points, all aerodromes and military storehouses, went up in flames.

The Polish air force played a pitiful role during the short period of the German-Polish war and was practically unnoticeable. Already on the first day of their attack, the Germans damaged all the airfields and crippled the greatest part of the planes that were on them. The Polish planes and their fliers became helpless immediately after the first blows from the enemy.

The Polish soldier actually did exhibit a great measure of heroism and patriotism in defending his homeland. They had to stand against a gigantic armoured force with the most modern weapons. Polish soldiers threw themselves upon German tanks with bottles of gasoline. With incendiary grenades in one hand and a gun in the other, the Polish infantry tried to stand against the enemy's mechanized divisions, but defeat was inevitable. It was impossible to defeat such a mighty and overwhelming army as the Hitler war-machine which trampled, burned and destroyed everything in its way.

*[Page 82]*

There were other reasons for the quick collapse of the Polish army beside the German bombardments. No small part was played by the rottenness and demoralization in the ranks of the Polish military which weakened their defensive power. The demoralization had an especially strong effect on the districts of Poizn and Upper Silesia. A large number of Polish officers hailed from the German areas: (Pomerania, Poizn and Silesia. They showed themselves as traitors on the first day of the war, put obstacles in the way of the defense. There were even cases when the ordinary Polish soldiers recognized the traitors and shot them on the spot. This fact can serve as an example of the inner demoralization of the Polish army.

Right after the invasion, in the first hours of the blitzkrieg, the Polish government ordered a general mobilization and called up all reserves. When the soldiers reported, many officers kept them waiting several days before they were taken into the military barracks. There were also cases when some were admitted to the barracks but sent away after a few days because it developed that there were no uniforms for them or enough weapons to send them to the front. After the collapse, when Hitler-Germany and Stalin-Russia divided Poland between them, entire warehouses packed with uniforms and various kinds of weapons, enough to equip whole armies, were found!

*[Page 83]*

In Kittev as in all of Poland, the Hitler invasion filled every inhabitant with dread. The Jewish population found itself in a state of fear and panic. Every Jew took account of the atmosphere in which he found himself and trembled at the danger which was coming. With terror in our hearts and anxiety in our souls, we awaited the dreadful morrow.

In the first hours of the general mobilization, there were, in Kittev, among the Poles and Ukrainians, Jewish young men that were mobilized and who never returned from the battle. All means of transport: automobiles, wagons and even bicycles were confiscated by the army. Every few hours, transports of mobilized Kittever youth left Kittev for Kolomei. Many of them fell in battle.

In the first hours of the war, hours of despair and despondency, when all the Polish nation stood face-to-face with the greatest enemy and fought a life-and-death battle with the aggressor – even then they did not forget the Jew. The police confiscated the radios from all the Kittever Jews and thus robbed them of the only means of knowing the news of the world and the happenings in Poland. We had to live in the dark during every Jew's most fateful hour. After many pleadings and interventions, the rulers deigned to return a few radios to certain Jews – this after a promise that they would give back the radios.

In the first weeks of the war, Kittev, which lay not far from the Romanian border, became a place of refuge for thousands of refugees – a passage for tens of thousands of Polish government officials and, for a large part, the Polish officers-corps which fled to Romania.

*[Page 84]*

After the first week of the war, there began to stream into Kittev large transports of Jewish refugees from Upper Poland and Upper Silesia who had left their homes, businesses and factories to save their lives from the German murderers. From these refugees, we learned the first frightful details of the Germans' scandalous deeds. They told how the Germans had shot at members of their families with machine guns; how the Germans had bombarded the defenseless cities and burned thousands of houses together with their inhabitants; how the Germans had bombarded railroad stations where thousands were waiting for trains, and above all, how the German fliers had zoomed low and strafed the railroad cars filled with refugees, brutally destroying thousands of men and women.

In the second week of the war, there also arrived members of the Polish government in Kittev who had first sought refuge in Baranovitch near the Russian border and came to Kittev from there. Here, for a short time, was the Polish capital with all the foreign embassies, quartered in the richest houses of Kittev. On the Oidiush hill, they set up a radio station to broadcast various government decrees and orders.

These fateful days, the numbered days of the Polish government in Kittev, the end of Poland's independence and the start of the Hitler occupation, happened to coincide with the Jewish Days of Awe which etched themselves deeply into memory.

All the Jewish synagogues, kloizes and prayer-houses were filled with thousands of worshippers. In these truly awe-filled days, we forgot all the traditional heartily-sweet Rosh Hashanah tunes and recited the prayers with wailing and weeping which came from broken Jewish hearts.

*[Page 851]*

On the first day of Rosh Hashanah, in the midst of the service, the Polish military and police appeared in all the houses of prayer and demanded that the daveners (worshippers) go home and open their stores to enable the Polish refugees to supply themselves with all their needs on their way to Romania.

Right after Rosh Hashanah, the Government left Kittev and retreated to Romania. Along with the Government, all the foreign embassies also left Kittev except the Soviet embassy.

In the days between Rosh Hashanah and Yom Kippur, long formations of Polish soldiers, brigades of tanks, motorized anti-aircraft and thousands of trucks filled the roads leading from Kittev to Romania. These accompanied the higher government people and their families.

For the Jewish refugees, it was very difficult to flee and cross the Romanian border. There were Jews who had provided themselves ahead of time with valid Polish passports and, therefore, crossed the border without difficulty. However, most had to steal across the border because the head of the Kossover district, the Jew-hater Fiola, refused to provide them with the necessary papers. Among those who sought refuge in Romania was the President of the Jewish Seyim club, Dr. Shwarzbard of Krakow, who also had to smuggle himself across because Fiola would not issue him a passport.

It's interesting to mention how this Fiola, before his departure to Romania, sent for the wealthy Kossover Jews and demanded a cash contribution. His excuse was that Poland had no interest in fighting Hitler and that the whole war was carried on by the Jews and on behalf of the Jews.

On September 17th, the radio reported that the Soviet army had crossed the Polish border with the objective of occupying the Polish White Russian and Ukrainian areas, which meant Kittev and all of Eastern Galicia. Then, Hitler and Stalin divided the Polish country between themselves, according to the treaty signed by the Hitlerite foreign minister, Von Ribbentrop and the Soviet foreign minister, Molotov. After 29 days of war, the 35,000,000 population of Poland was divided, not for the first time in its history – between the two neighbouring major powers – this time, Hitler Germany and Communist Russia.

*[Page 86]*  *[Page 87]*

**Second Part:**

# **<u>The Destruction</u>**

*[Page 88]*

*Blank*

*[Page 89]*

## Chapter XIV

# Kittev Under the Soviet Occupation

After the Polish army, the police and the border-guard left Kittev, the city was left abandoned without any protection or defense. But the Jewish inhabitants, especially the young people, did not remain helpless but found an answer to the threatening situation. Jewish young men created a Jewish self-defense, armed themselves with a little outdated weaponry which the Polish police did not manage to take along, and armed the young men who posted themselves on all the roads that connected Kittev with the surrounding villages. They prepared to defend the city in the event of an attack by the Ukrainians and the Hutsuls of the nearby villages.

Every morning, a Polish battalion would come from Vizshnits to guard the city and in the evening, it returned to Romania. Toward evening, the Jewish self-defense took over the defense of Kittev. This went on until the first Soviet patrols occupied the city.

The first Soviet patrol that came to Kittev consisted of four tanks with their crews. They rolled into Kittev in the early morning hours. There were then, in the city, an insignificant number of Polish soldiers. As soon as they saw the Soviet tanks, they hit the road to the Romanian border. Upon crossing the Romanian border, one Polish officer, a Major, drew his revolver and shot a bullet into his head.

*[Page 90]*

Among the last group of Polish military that left Kittev at the arrival of the Soviet tanks, was the Polish poet Dolega-Mastavitch. He was probably preparing to write a Polish poem of lamentations, an elegy upon the destruction of his country. He wanted to carry with him into exile the impressions that the Soviet tanks had made on his spirit. He was in the last row of soldiers and kept looking back to glimpse again, perhaps for the last time, his conquered homeland. A bullet from a Russian tank struck him and he gave up his poetic soul on Polish soil. On his grave in the Polish cemetery in Kittev, the Polish population of the city deposited, each day, great wreaths of fresh white-red roses, to colour of the Polish flag.

The next day, after the tanks, there entered the first units of the Soviet occupation army. The initial fear of the Kittever citizens passed over and they came out of their houses and gathered on the Ring-place to look over the "liberators" and at the same, learn something of life in the Soviet-land. A Red Army man got up on a table in the middle of the market square and gave the population of Kittev their first lecture in the style of the well-known Communist propaganda. He sang hymns to the Soviet Union, boasted that in Russia all the people were equal and that there was no difference between Jew, Ukrainian and Pole. All have the same rights and privileges. He stressed that we should rejoice at the privilege of being freed to begin enjoying the same freedoms which all Soviet citizens enjoyed. All of it is thanks to, he said, the great leader and friend of all the oppressed – the great Comrade Josif Vissarinovich Stalin.

*[Page 91]*

Our home-grown communists were overjoyed at having finally lived to the house of the "great liberation" and, after the first lecture of the Red Army man , they became so enthusiastic, as though they were sure that the Messiah had come, but instead of a white donkey, he had ridden in on a Soviet tank. The local revolutionary committee immediately organized a provisional city-government and a city militia and made plans for reorganizing life according the law of Marx and Engels (this is an ironic take-off on the wedding ceremony when we say "according to the law of

Moses and Israel") as interpreted by Lenin and Stalin. The first step was supposed to improve the condition of the poor classes. For this purpose, they called a mass meeting to which 90% Jews and only 10% of the Armenians, Ukrainians and Poles came. In the name of the revolutionary committee, a speech was made by Meshulam Zeidman a scion of the richest member of the Kittever bourgeoisie Reb Yekeleh Zeidman Meshulam himself was always a wastrel and a neer-do-well, incapable of earning a broken groschen or gaining a steady livelihood on his own. Only his envy and hatred of the friends of his youth who had worked themselves up, drove him into the ranks of the malcontent Communist fellow-travellers.

In his programme speech, Meshulam declared fervently: "Gone is the time when a small segment of the population had all the good things and the other part, the greatest part, suffered hunger. With the help of the victorious People's Army, we will take the superfluous wealth away from the rich and turn it over to the poor classes of the population".

In soviet practice, however, Comrade Meshulam and his revolutionary committee comrades were unable to realize their programme. A few days later, there arrived in Kittev a Soviet city-commissar who only accepted the first part of the programme, that is, to take from the rich everything they owned. But not the second part, that is, to turn the wealth of the rich over to the poor, because that would contradict communist teaching which combats all philanthropic help and support. According to their teaching, this delays the maximal realization of the Communist idea and the world-wide social revolution.

*[Page 92]*

With the arrival of Comrade Kushtsh and his assistants, the capitalist face of Kittev changed and everyone tried to appear more proletarian in order to find favour in the eyes of the foreign and home-grown Commissars. The men started to wear boots and short caps and overcoats, just like the Russians. The women hid away their expensive dresses and fur coats and started to dress plainly so as not to draw the attention of the Comrades.

Commissar Kushtsh, for his part and with the help of his adjutants and also the home-grown Jewish and Ukrainian communists, immediately started to reorganize the city economy in line with Soviet methods, forcing their life-style upon Kittev.

Every day, the Commissar would make public new decrees which had one aim, though various open and disguised means, to achieve the nationalization of every type of private property. In order to equalize the population, at the very first, they forced all storekeepers to open their stores and sell off all the goods at the old pre-war prices. They forced them to exchange the old Polish zlotys for the new Soviet rubbles – a zloty for a rubble. The population had not much confidence, neither in the Polish zloty nor in the Soviet rubble, so they simply besieged the stores from morning to evening and bought up everything they could just to get rid of the saved-up zlotys and the rubbles that they had.

But the merchant could not buy any new goods with zlotys and rubbles which he had received for his goods. So, he began, in the nights when nobody would notice, to carry a little of his goods out of his store and hide it for later. For the zlotys and rubbles, he had earned, he tried to buy a few dollars which would be useful in time of trouble. The worth of the dollar, therefore, rose on the black market. From five zlotys (the pre-war price of a dollar) the dollar rose to 80 and 90 zlotys and more.

*[Page 93]*

In the larger businesses and industries, the workers, according to communist instructions, organized workers'-council and sent representatives to meetings where they were taught how to be on the watch for owners that would not remove finished goods from the factories. They were also taught to mislead the factory owners into thinking that everything would remain as is and that they would not be nationalized so the factory owners and merchants would invest more and more and buy raw materials.

By the end of October, 1939, Kittev had not only a military occupation management but also a civilian management. Soviet schools, courts, police, NKVD, a food supply headquarters, a bank, post office, etc. The chiefs of all these agencies were Soviet Ukrainians, communist party members. Over all the agencies, even of the secret police (NKVD) stood the local communist party committee led by a Party Secretary appointed from Kiev, who was the actual dictator over all the Commissars in the city. Before the Party Secretary, every trembled with the fear of death. His word was law and nothing went through without his approval.

In the beginning of November, the nationalization (Soviet term signifying plain robbery) began.

They nationalized all the Kittever factories, all the industry, the mills, the tanneries and all businesses. They forced the owners to turn everything over to the Soviet and they gave the keys to a worker who was appointed as director or manager of the particular nationalized enterprise. There were also nationalized, the larger houses and hotels, or dwellings having ten or more rooms. The owners of the factories and businesses were driven out of town as enemies of the working class. All these Jews who were branded by the Soviet regime were warm-hearted Jews who were always ready to help out a Jew in time of trouble. Now, they had to wander from city-to-city, from village-to-village, until they could get a permit from the military, for a significant payment, to settle somewhere and remain under constant surveillance by the NKVD.

*[Page 94]*

With the nationalizing of the Kittever industry, businesses and houses which were in large part Jewish property, came the end and the total liquidation of private enterprise and initiative which had been built up by the Kittever through years of great effort and hard work.

The new supervisors and directors of the businesses divided among themselves the remaining goods and sold or liquidated it all. The communist city-bosses left only two restaurants and two large stores which had to supply the population with bread, clothing and other necessities. The artisans were also organized according to the Soviet manner, in cooperatives. They worked eight hours a day and divided up the earnings.

The food supply looked puny – especially in the first days of the new order in the city. The peasants stopped bringing their products to market. The poor masses who had not had a chance to store food, got up at 3a.m. and lined up outside the bakery to get a black, clay-like loaf for their families. They sold only one bread per person. The stores were mostly empty without goods and without customers. When a shipment of goods arrived (summer articles in winter and winter things in summer), the populace stood in line before dawn and in two hours, the goods were all sold out. They bought everything – everything in sight, just to get rid of the few rubbles.

*[Page 95]*

The restaurants, the eateries, however, were always full. From dawn until late into the night, things there were cheerful and happy. These were places where on could get drunk on cheap whiskey, drink up and forget one's troubles.

The Jewish communal and religious life in Kittev came to a standstill upon the entry of the Red Army. The various parties and organizations, all secular and religious institutions, liquidated themselves and their officers and activists, secretly hid and buried all record-books and party archives, the pictures of the Zionist leaders and other documents.

The communist culture committee took over the city and the Zionist libraries. The books were transferred to the Polish Sokol House which was now called Kittever people's house in the name of Joseph Stalin. There, the home grown literature experts studied the books and rejected those which were un-kosher and unsuitable from the Communist viewpoint. The "treife" (not kosher) books were used as heating fuel for the Josef Stalin House.

Overnight, all the Kittever Cheders, Hebrew schools and kindergartens were dissolved. They were replaced with a Jewish public school run by a Kittever young man, a communist who had not even completed six grades of public school. Overnight, he was transformed into a pedagogue, became the leader and director of the Soviet-Jewish public school. The teachers and women teachers were also, with two or three exceptions – not pedagogues.

They were supposed to inculcate into the Kittever Jewish children, the communist teaching in the Yiddish language according to a method dictated from Moscow in line with the Soviet school books.

The Prayer-houses began to lie vacant, half empty at least – not one younger person was seen at a Minyan. The only worshippers were elderly Jews who were not fit for any kind of work. The young and the middle-aged were afraid to show themselves in the street and, even more afraid to go to daven. They didn't want to be noticed by the home-grown informers who might, God forbid, consider them as idlers and religious hypocrites.

*[Page 96]*

According to the communist system, everyone – man and woman – had to work and do his part for the communist state and the new society. Those men who had not previously provided themselves with work in a factory or in an office were sent by the Soviet commissars for forced-labour.. They were sent out into the surrounding Kittever woods where, under Ukrainian youth supervision) they chopped trees to fill a certain quota. With the "large" wage they received for this labour, they barely had enough to pay the wagon-driver who carried them to-and-from work.

It was impossible to elude the eye of the new rulers. They surrounded every citizen with a thick net of informers and spies – secret and visible – and nobody could escape them.

Every house had to have a book in which were set down the names, ages and occupations of each inhabitant. A copy of the book with the recorded names was turned over to the NKVD. If anyone of a house's inhabitants went away or somebody came for a visit, it too had to be recorded in the book and turned over to the NKVD.

In order to keep tabs that the recordings were accurate and that nobody would be able to hide, they appointed, for every ten houses, a official who visited the appointed houses nearly every day and found out what was going on in each house. He knew who would come and go, what they talked about and how they lived. Most important, he knew who was working and where. In this way, the NKVD was informed about every person and had a say over everyone's fate.

*[Page 97]*

Before long, the NKVD began to carry out house arrests in Kittev. One Friday afternoon, a row of trucks was seen in the main streets of Kittev. In these trucks, a lot of Ukrainian and Polish men, who were removed from their houses in the middle of the night, were loaded. These were forcibly exiled to Russia.

Munieh Socher and Yonah Sender were the first Kittever Jews who were arrested on that dreadful night and were never heard of again. Despite the most varied efforts to find out about their fate, no one could learn what became of them.

Fear and terror befell every Jew in Kittev. We feared relatives, perhaps they were informers; we didn't know whom to trust and whom not to trust. The former businessmen, Zionist activists and Jewishly-conscious people suffered the most. They were afraid to spend the night within their four walls and would hide out with relatives or friends where they could be more or less secure. Many risked their lives to smuggle themselves across the border into Romania. Not a few were caught by the Russian border-police and shot on the spot.

After the first few months of Communist rule in Kittev, came the disappointment in the new "saviours", in the communist deliverance. The local Jewish communists, some of them intelligent idealists who truly believed that the realization of the communist idea would bring the solution of the Jewish question, now, seeing how and with what means the idea was being realized, became bitterly disillusioned. They saw with what disrespect the Soviet rulers treated the Jew; how they referred to Jews as speculators, which to them was as insulting a term as "zshid" to the anti-Semite. These Jewish communists now experienced one disappointment after another. They saw how the rulers were making a reality of the ideas of Karl Marx and Friedrich Engels.

*[Page 98]*

The local communists experienced their first disappointment in December, 1939, when the new directors of the nationalized factories paid the workers and employees in Polish zlotys. The day after the first payment, a decree was issued that the Polish zlotys had lost its value. The workers could not even use their wages to buy a piece of bread for their hungry families.

This produced deep bitterness in the ranks of the workers and more so in the ranks of the communist idealists who could not forgive the communist functionaries for their anti-proletarian action against their own comrades – the poor workers.

Before the War, the reports about Soviet Russia were contradictory. According to reports from the Soviet radio and press, life in Russia was paradise. The foreign radio and press reported that the Soviet citizen lived in great poverty and had not the slightest personal freedom. In other words: life under the Soviet dictatorship was a life of slavery.

From October, 1939, when the Soviet armies occupied Poland and Galicia, the iron curtain was slowly raised. One could really become convinced that the entire 20 years of propaganda about the communist paradise was one big lie. The Soviet reality appeared as one huge concentration camp where people worked and slaved for a starvation wage and possessed only one shirt and a pair of shoes.

Right after the entry of the Russian military into Kittev, the Jews, particularly the communist idealists, began to inquire about the life of Soviet citizens – their working conditions, the prices of living quarters, food, clothing and so on. For all questions, the soldiers had the one familiar communist answer: "In Russia, we have plenty of everything. The living quarters are cheap and comfortable. Food products and clothing are plentiful and everything is as cheap as borscht". But soon, these lies began to burst like soap-bubbles when civilian Soviet functionaries and their families appeared in the city.

*[Page 99]*

Aside from the servants of the NKVD and the leaders of the communist party-committee which constituted the Soviet aristocracy, the other Soviet citizens who came to Kittev looked hungry and were barefoot and naked. A large part of them wore galoshes instead of shoes. Husband and wife shared on coat which they passed back and forth…

When the civilian officials came to town, they went from store-to-store and bought everything in sight. It was obvious that, for the hard-won rubbles that they earned in Russia, they had nothing there to buy. Goods were doled out over there for each person and could only be obtained with a (ration) card. A suit, a shirt, a pair of shoes or a coat were obtained only once every couple of years and at a high price. Not every worker could afford the luxury. Thus, the inhabitants of paradise were happy in Kittev where they had the chance to purchase things which they could not get in Russia. I remember how, at the New Year ball, the Russian women came attired in Polish night-shirts, attractively embroidered and adorned. The Russian women could not imagine that in poor capitalist Poland people slept in such shirts.

In Russia, they did not even dream of having a night gown. When the new Soviets came into a restaurant and found out that they could buy everything their heart desired, they were surprised. One Russian ordered forty boiled eggs at one time!

*[Page 100]*

These hard and stubborn facts still could not convince the local communist idealists that all the propaganda was completely false. They believed in the propaganda like a religious Jew in the Torah of Moses. They could not imagine that they had deceived themselves all these years. Until there came a time when they finally opened their eyes. In the first weeks of 1940, notices appeared in the city saying that in Donbass, Ukraine, they had a need for workers. The young people who would volunteer and were ready to leave would receive travel expenses and the best working conditions. On the basis of these promises, a few young communists reported for the Ukrainian Donbass and were seen off with great fanfare.

It did not take long, perhaps a couple of weeks, and letters began to arrive from the *meraglim* (biblical word meaning spies) who had gone to inspect the communist paradise. These letters acted like a thunderbolt on a bright day on the spirits of the Kittever communist sympathisers. The letters confirmed that in Donbass the people did live like angels in paradise. They ate like angels and go about clothed like angels... The *meraglim* were afraid to spell out their bitter experience and their disappointments openly because their letters might fall into the censor's hands. So, they wrote with hints and allusions, as for example: The people here eat like in our town on Yom Kippur, they dress like on Purim ... Adam and Eve were driven out of the Garden of Eden after they opened their eyes and saw that they were naked. ... They also wrote that Rabbi Eliezer and his comrades, who opened their eyes and saw the whole truth, were not allowed to leave the Garden of Eden. By Rabbi Eliezer, they meant a certain L. Shmeterer. They wept through these letters and begged their parents and relatives to do everything possible to save them from Paradise and bring them back to Hell in Kittev.

*[Page 101]*

The parents employed various means and tricks to enable them to bring their deceived sons home and a few months passed before the meraglim slipped back into town, secretly, one dark night. They now looked more dead than alive: pale, wan, skin and bones. For a few weeks, they did not show themselves out of doors, for shame.

When the Soviet courts began to function in Kittev, there the whole nature of Soviet justice, Asiatic cruelty and brutal justice was revealed. The judges and prosecutors revealed themselves as savage brutes who did not concern themselves about the condition of the poor working people. The first victims of the proletarian justice were the proletarians themselves. The proletarians who waited daily for the new saviour now recognized the Messiah as a false saviour – a devil masked in red.

A wave of trials crashed onto the heads of the *procrastinators* and saboteurs. But the real speculators got off with light sentences or were freed altogether because they had enough money to bribe, buy off the judges and the prosecutor.

As in all occupied areas, in Kittev there was a great shortage of retail goods and especially essential foodstuffs. The local production was minimal. The quality got worse day-by-day. The quantity didn't even reach 25% of pre-war production. This was all the result, firstly, of the shortage in necessary raw materials and secondly, the poor management and use of unqualified workmen. The Communist commissars who could not cope with the pitiful production, found a scape-goat – the poor neglected worker whom they branded as a *47aughter4747ator* , a saboteur, a speculator and on whom they threw all the blame for the permanent crisis; for the hunger and poverty which the population suffered. The masses naturally knew that the hunger and poverty were inflicted by the robbery and plunder policy of the commissars but they were helpless against the might of these commissars and their evil assistants, the NKVD. They were even afraid to protest and, with clenched fists and gnashing teeth, often had to applaud after the speeches of the deceiving occupiers.

*[Page 102]*

The first *procrastinator* who was convicted in Kittev was a poor Jewish shoemaker who went, one morning, to the bakery and got in line to buy a black bread. He was late getting to work and was sentenced for tardiness.

Among those convicted of sabotage were also Jewish youths and young Communist sympathisers who were previously appointed to responsible posts because of their Communist convictions. Since they lacked the appropriate schooling and technical training, and their work was not successful, they were accused of sabotage and sentenced to years in jail.

The way and means that the Communist commissars employed in establishing their rule in Kittev, revealed the truth about the slave-life of the Soviet citizen, and finally the corrupt anti-proletarian approach of the Soviet people's court in Kittev. All of this called for great resentment and bitterness in all classes of the Kittever population. Especially embittered against the Soviet occupiers were the poor classes of the population. The poor, who for so many years, awaited the social revolution, now became the first victims of its tyranny.

But the most to be pitied were the deceived Communist idealists – boys and girls from both rich and poor Kittever Jewish homes who, for so many years in the times of Polish rule, suffered and were persecuted for their convictions and now experienced bitter disillusionment. At first, they still didn't want to admit that the Communist idea, in the shape of Communist commissars, was a fiction. But in time, they had to acknowledge that their ideal was bankrupt. The Communist commissars began to suspect the Jewish Communists of Trotskyism and started to dismiss their Jewish comrades from responsible jobs and replace them with Ukrainian nationalists from Kittev.

*[Page 103]*

Because of the great disappointment, many Jewish Communists became penitents (turned back to Judaism). As an example of their repentance, the following occurrence can serve as an example:

The Rosh Hashanah-Yom Kippur season was the time when the people's court would carry out mass convictions of Kittever Jews as punishment for tardiness. Their purpose in this was to frighten off the Jews who would go to daven and might thus be late for work. Nevertheless, not one Kittever Jew failed to go to the Synagogue services on Rosh Hashanah and on Yom Kippur. The Jews of Kittev hoped for the day when they would be freed from the Communist yoke and, therefore, did not want to provoke the rulers – to give them the least pretext for persecution and imprisonment. On Rosh Hashanah in 1940, therefore, all the young men and boys, with the exception of elderly Jews, gathered in the Synagogues at two o'clock at night and conducted the High Holiday prayers and in the morning, they ran to their work. When one looked around in the Prayer houses, one was astonished to see among the worshippers who had come to shul at two in the morning, many former Communists who had never before crossed the threshold of a prayer-house. Now they came to the Beis-Medrash (prayer-house) to demonstratively express their solidarity with the Kittever Jewish community and at the same time, to hold a sort of protest-demonstration against the barbaric anti-religious actions of the Communist rulers.

*[Page 104]*

In the spring of 1940, Kittev was a military camp. The Soviets concentrated military forces here and made preparations to invade neighbouring Romania. On the advice of Hitler, Romania gave in to the Soviet ultimatum to let them annex Bukovina and Bessarabia and voluntarily turn over these regions to them. As soon as the Soviet army occupied Bukovina, they started carrying out their "liberation-work". During the nights, they raided the homes of the enemies of the people: Zionists, Socialists, Bundists, and drove thousands of Jews out of Chernovitz and surrounding towns. They confined them in cattle cars, 40 persons to a rail-car, and sent them to Siberia.

In the spring of 1941, the Soviets began to build, in Kittev and nearby areas, various strategic positions and fortifications such as bunkers. They also prepared underground depots of explosives and other sorts of war materials. They were already preparing for war with Nazi-Germany. But these preparations helped very little. Sunday, June 22, in that year, the Germans began their long-prepared blitzkrieg against the Soviet Union. The Soviet rulers abandoned the city within a few days fearing that their only retreat passage to Russia, the River Dniester, might be cut off and that they would thus fall into the hands of the Germans.

*[Page 105]*

## Chapter XV

# The Destruction

After the invasion of the Soviet Union by Hitler, all of Poland, the former Russian or Crown-Poland, Galicia and all of Ukraine with their large Jewish communities, fell into the hands of the German mass-murderers. The S.S. and the Gestapo immediately began to carry out their pre-planned bestial destruction of Polish and Ukrainian Jewry.

In no other European country were the German murderers able to carry out, so completely, their planned devilish program of murder and bring about the total destruction of the Jews as in Poland and the Ukraine. In the Poles and Ukrainians, they found many voluntary assistants who gladly participated in the mass extermination. This could only have happened in countries where large proportions of the populace were already deeply infected with anti-Semitism and were only waiting for the first opportunity to begin practicing and realizing this poisonous hatred.

The German cannibals carried out the total destruction and extirpation of Polish Jewry in a systematic and pre-planned way. At first, they degraded and enslaved the Jews. Jews were made to wear a symbol of shame – the yellow patch or star – a white armband with a sewn-on Star of David and the inscription: "Jude". The Jews had to do a variety of forced labour for the German occupiers and their local Ukrainian under-lords or errand boys. After seven o'clock in the evening, a Jew was not allowed to show himself outside and, in general, he was not allowed to come into contact with non-Jews. For breaking these laws, the punishment was death.

*[Page 106]*

Little-by-little, in stages, the Germans also ruined the Jewish population economically. At first, the Jews were forced to turn over to the Germans all their foreign currency; their gold and silver articles; all woollen and fur clothing, etc. Afterward, they were forced, and all under the threat of the death penalty, to pay various taxes (more accurately, "tribute") for the Gestapo, for the militia and for the Judenrat (Jewish committee) and other evil inflictions. After they had thoroughly robbed the Jews "by law", there began a new series of robberies. The German criminal police robbed; the district gendarmerie robbed; the border guards went from house-to-house and robbed for themselves. The Ukrainian militia also robbed, robbed without end. No use talking about the Judenrat. The life and property of every individual Jew, according to German law, belonged to the Judenrat which was a tool in the hands of the Gestapo. The Judenrat robbed for the Gestapo and stole for the militia. Not seldom did the Judenrat members murderously beat Jews who did not want to furnish certain materials which the Judenrat believed had been hidden. When they had completely squeezed out and emptied the Jews, the hideous physical destruction began.

The German S.S. and the Gestapo, with the aid of their Polish and Ukrainian murderers, began to carry out the first "Judenaktion" (as they called their murder campaigns). They went from one Jewish house to another shouting: "(Jew, come out!. They murdered many Jews on the spot; others they led out of town and shot. In every city, the campaign (action) was carried out in a different manner.

After these actions, the Jewish population in every city and town diminished. Then the Gestapo drove together the remaining Jews and pressed them into ghettos. The ghetto consisted of a few fenced-off streets which were guarded by the militia so that no Jew could steal out of the ghetto. After they concentrated the mass of Jews in the ghetto, it was not hard to raid the ghetto suddenly and carry out the special actions. First, they liquidated the "shmelt", a technical and degrading term for the older Jews. The next time, they carried out a separate "children's day" when they tore children away from their parents and killed them. A third time, it was the "women's day". They would take the men away to their work in the morning and when they returned home in the evening, they no longer saw their wives.

*[Page 107]*

Then would come the day when the Germans decided that the time had come to make the city or town completely "Judenrein" (free of Jews). They then, with the help of the Poles and Ukrainians, surrounded the ghetto – set fire to it from all four sides, and murdered all the Jews.

In this way and with other methods, as in the death camps of Majdanek, Treblinka and Auschwitz, the bestial Germans at first plundered, then murdered and destroyed six million of our brothers and sisters in Europe.

**Chapter XVI**

# Kittev After the Departure of the Soviet Army

Before dawn on Sunday, 22nd June, 1941, the entire Kittever population was awakened by the strong roar of motors and bomb-explosions. On running outside, fearful and astonished, we saw the German planes bombing the fortifications which the Soviets had built in the city and the whole of the surrounding area. They then began to attack Soviet-Russia.

On Monday, 23rd June, the Soviet military began withdrawing from Kittev together with the Soviet troops, all technical groups with their families, those who had built the fortifications for defense, left.

*[Page 108]*

The commissars in charge of the civilian population began preparing to leave the city right after the troops. Thursday, 25th June, the Soviet militia and the NKVD went around nearby villages and requisitioned the houses and wagons from the peasants, brought them to Kittev as means of transport for the Soviet civilian officials as well as for the party-functionaries and the NKVD.

The Soviet officials withdrew all the money from the banks; from all cooperatives, warehouses and stores. They also emptied the food out of the store houses and loaded it to take along to Russia.

Tuesday, 1st July, the Soviet civilians, the Communist party activists, the NKVD and all officials, left the city. They left furniture, housekeeping goods and other conveniences. The rode off in the requisitioned peasants' wagons.

Before their departure, the Soviet commissars appealed to the Jewish population to flee to Russia with them. They foretold that as soon as the Germans would come, they would annihilate the Jewish population. The Kittever Jews did not want to listen to the Soviet commissars. No one could imagine that the Germans would murder people just because they were of Jewish descent. Not one Jewish family agreed to go along with the Russians except a couple of young people who were afraid to remain in Kittev.

The Kittever border-guard left the city on Tuesday afternoon and at night, the last of the Soviet border-guards ignited the stores of ammunition, the military materials and all that they could not take with them.

*[Page 109]*

The following morning, the Ukrainians of the whole area flocked to Kittev and began looting the remaining Soviet storehouses. Having finished with looting, they then gathered opposite the community house and with great noise and uproar, made a gala occasion of pulling down the Soviet flag with its large five-pointed start from the tower and hoisted the Ukrainian flag. Those who were the ring-leaders at this ceremony, were yesterday's ardent Communists who had held various offices in the Soviet administration.

The Kittever Jews stayed in their houses during this time of parade and the ceremony of raising the flag, being afraid to go out.

Friday, 4th July, a Hungarian cavalry detachment arrived in Kittev, ready to take over the city. Before they arrived, the Ukrainians on the road by which the Hungarians came, built a large tower, hung a Hitlerite swastika on it, and on both sides of the swastika, the Ukrainian and Hungarian flags. The whole tower was decorated with Ukrainian and Hungarian greetings and slogans.

When the Hungarians entered the city, they were met by a Ukrainian committee which treated the cavalry men to wine and cigarettes which they had looted from the Soviet stores. With the approval of the Mayor of the Hungarian occupation force, the Ukrainians immediately began to organize a civilian administration. They organized a Ukrainian militia, which enlisted the same men who, until a few days earlier, were in the Soviet militia and were such big Soviet patriots. The first action of the newly-formed Ukrainian national militia was to loot Jewish homes and drag Jews away to forced labour.

On 13th July, a Romanian infantry regiment came to Kittev and the Hungarian cavalry departed. The Jews immediately tasted how it was to be abandoned and left to the mercy of every anti-Semite and enemy of Israel. Right after the Romanians took over Kittev, there came grievous reports about the murderous deeds of the Romanians in the neighbouring towns and villages against the helpless Jewish population.

*[Page 110]*

## Chapter XVII

# The Pogrom in Yablonitse

The first report that struck the Jews of Kittev like a thunderclap was the horrible news of the killing off of the Jews of Yabloniste.

The village Yablonitse was situated on the Polish-Romanian border at the Chermosh River, half of which belonged to Poland and the other half to Romania.

In Yablonitse, between 80-100 Jews lived. These were honest and upright people in their private life and in business. Relations between the Jews and their neighbours, the Hutzuls, were very friendly. They grew up together, knew each other from childhood and always assisted each other.

Yablonitse was surrounded by large and deep forests. From the forest-wood the Jews and Hutzuls made their living. The lumber at which the Hutzuls and Jews worked together was used in the sawmills of the nearby cities and towns. Weeks at a time, the Yablonitser Jews and Hutzuls lived in shacks in the woods and peace and friendship existed between them. It never happened that a Hutzul would attack a Jew or take anything from him.

But as soon as the Soviets left, the Yablonitser priest gave an incendiary sermon and urged the Hutzuls to murder all the Yablonitser Jews and not to leave a single one! In this way, the priest assured them, they would do a holy work and God would reward them for it. The Hutzuls carried out the "mitzvah" of the priest, thoroughly and in one day, they killed at the Jews in Yablonitser and in a savage manner.

*[Page 111]*

The pogrom was led by the brothers Skotshuk who drew their whole living from Jews and by a Kittever, Ukrainian, Berniuga, who worked in Yabloniste sending the lumber down the Chermosh. Under their leadership, the Hutzuls set out and went from one Jewish house to the next, dragged the Jews to the Chermesh, shot them and threw their bodies into the stormy waves of the river.

The river swelled from the rains and carried a few of the bodies of the Yablonitser martyrs down to Kittev. Kittever young men, who were then working on a bridge, pulled the bodies out of the river and brought them to Jewish burial in the Kittever cemetery.

In Yablonitse, there was a family, Steinbrecher, which numbered ten strong men, real mountain Jews. In normal times, they feared no one and were able to resist any attack. During the Yablonitser pogrom the Hutzuls led the whole family to the water; stood them against a rock; tied them up in barbed wire and thus, bound to each other, threw them into the river.

Of the entire Jewish community of Yablonitse, only one Jewish woman, the wife of Pinchas Surkes, was saved. The murderers threw her, together with all the Jews, into the stormy current but the bullet they shot, missed her. She was a good swimmer and she swam down below the village, got out of the river and went through the woods to Zshabie. Mrs. Surkes perished in December, 1941 along with all the Jews of Zshabie.

After the Yablonitser pogrom, the Jewish inhabitants of the surrounding hill villages such as Hrinove, Stebne, abandoned all their possessions, houses and fields to the Hutzuls and fled to Kittev barefoot and naked.

*[Page 112]*

In Bukovina on the Romanian side and in the nearby city of Vizshnitz as well as in the surrounding cities, towns and villages, the Romanians, straight after they had marched in, murdered the majority of the Jewish population. They loaded the rest on trucks and deported them to Transnistria, where most of them perished from hunger and hard labour. After the sad reports that reached Kittev, one can already imagine the feelings of the Jews in Kittev when the Romanians occupied the city.

## Chapter XVIII

# Kittev Under the Romanian and Hungarian Occupation

As soon as the Romanian soldiers quartered themselves in the city, they started in on the Jews. They would beat them in the streets, cut off the beards of old Jews and constantly rob and take everything that came to hand. They were altogether not very picky; they took everything they came across.

The Romanian captain came up with a new idea for pressing money out of the Jewish population. He issued an order to arrest the richer Jews, as pointed out by the Ukrainians and accused them of communism, kept them locked up for a few days then treated them, each day, to beating in the Romanian style. After this, he called them, one-by-one, into his office and told them he would hold them until he received ransom money. The family of those arrested were forced to pay the Romanian captain from 50 to 100 dollars or else gold watches and rings and other valuables.

*[Page 113]*

After about ten days of beating and robbery, the Romanians left the city and a Hungarian regiment returned to Kittev.

The Hungarians acted more friendly toward the Jewish population. Their officers lodged themselves in Jewish homes and when they were told about the horrifying murder of the Jews of Yablonitse, the Hungarian mayor sent to that village a punitive-expedition which took along two Jews from the nearby village of Hriniave. They didn't punish the murderous Hutzuls but they did manage to take from them part of the looted Jewish possessions such as cows, horses and other things. Only a small portion of the loot was returned to the Jews, the largest part the Hungarians kept for their efforts.

The Hungarians were also, in general, not choosy on the subject of loot. They knew that they would not stay long in Kittev so during their short stay, they grabbed like mad from the Jews and also from the Ukrainians. The upshot was that the latter complained about the Hungarians to the German district commander. Before long, the Hungarians left the city and a German military troop, commanded by S.S. Sturmfuhrer Vachman, took control of the city.

[Page 114]

## Chapter XVIX

# Kittev Under the German Occupation

As soon as the Germans occupied Kittev they instituted a ghetto-type situation for the Kittever Jews. They immediately began carrying out their devilish plans to exterminate the Jews. At first, they robbed and starved the Jewish population. Every day, new anti-Jewish decrees and laws were issued and for not obeying a command or a law, one got the death penalty.

All Jews without exception, from the age of 10, had to wear a white band on their arm with a sewn-on Magen-David and the large inscription: "JUDE" (Jew). From 19hr to 07hr a Jew was not allowed to leave his dwelling. A Jew was also not allowed to come in contact with the Christian population. We were not allowed to go out to the market-place to buy provisions and, in general, not allowed to step outside of the marked area. If a Jew was caught outside his dwelling, he was shot on the spot. By a certain date, Jews had to deliver their gold and silver as well as foreign currency, their woollen and fur clothing. After the deadline, if a Jew was found to have gold, silver or a fur coat or a woollen garment, he was shot.

To make sure that all these laws and decrees were strictly enforced, the Germans organized the Ukrainian militia as an auxiliary to their police and gave them unlimited authority and power. As chief of the militia, they appointed the Ukrainian Vladimir Cholevchuk who had been the chief of the Soviet militia.

[Page 115]

In order to organize the Jewish forced-labour and help carry out the despoiling of the Jewish population of Kittev, the Germans created a Judenrat (Jewish council). The job of the Judenrat was to carry out the commands of the local Ukrainian and German rulers. Mainly, the Judenrat had to serve the Gestapo. The local council stood under the supervision of the Kolomei District-Judenrat and was supposed to carry out all its orders. The stores were empty and when the Germans required furniture, leather goods and other products, or wine, whiskey and other alcoholic drinks to become drunker, as well as "women" for their soldiers, the Judenrat had to buy all these products from the Ukrainians and Poles at high prices.

As soon as the Soviets left Kittev, the Kittever Jews began to suffer from a scarcity of essential foodstuffs. As long as one could still go to the villages and buy products from the peasants for dollars, or barter certain things for food, one could manage somehow. But when the Germans came in and issued the anti-Jewish decrees, the Jews were cut-off inside a narrow limit and no longer had any contact with the peasants. There then began, for the Jews of Kittev, a long period of starvation.

The Germans forbade any trade in grain. If they found a Jew or even a non-Jew dealing in grain, they would confiscate the grain from the non-Jew and sentence the Jew to be shot.

The peasants and landowners received an order to turn over the entire crop to the German authority and leave for themselves only enough for their own use. For the grain which the peasants brought to the appointed collection places, they received 18 zlotys per 100kg (pre-war price). On the black market, one could get 400 zlotes per 100 kilos and even more.

Also, other food products such as milk, butter, eggs, chickens, cows and similar things, the peasants had to bring to the authorities and receive payment in zlotys on the basis of the pre-war price. For an egg, they received 5 groschen while on the black market, an egg would cost 1.5 zlotes.

*[Page 116]*

The Germans instituted food rationing. The local Ukrainians were allotted one ration. The so-called folk-Germans received double rations. The folk-Germans were a mixed multitude, a mixture of Poles and Ukrainians who suddenly remembered that they stemmed from the "master race", that they had a great-great-grandmother or grandfather who was German, or that they had a German name and thus called themselves Germans. By means of unchecked documents, they became pure Aryans overnight which gave them the privilege to receive double rations and the right to work and take Jewish property. But even the folk-Germans with these rations could die of starvation.

The Jews were condemned to a starvation death from the start. Not having ration cards, the Jew had to risk his life, steal out of the heavily guarded streets and somehow get to the peasant. The poverty levels which the Jews of Kittev and a large part of the middle class, had nothing left to trade for food to keep life going. A starvation epidemic started. In January, 1942, 140 Jews died of hunger out of a population which numbered 2500. Necessity breaks iron and hunger has no shame; therefore, tragic scenes were enacted near Jewish homes. Entire Jewish families, hungry father and mothers with their starving children, would stand in the streets and beg for bread, weep for a morsel to keep body and soul together. Poor people and middle-class people, former businessmen and artisans – all would go house-to-house begging. When they obtained one potato, a little bran or even the peel of a potato, it was a celebration because they could cook up a little something to warm up their frozen insides. And thus, starving and barely able to stand on their feet, the Kittever Jews had to do forced labour. Each day the Judenrat sent out between 150 to 200 Jewish men and women for forced labour. One group worked at the German border defense in Kittev – Slabudke, Tudiav. The men chopped wood, carried water and cleaned the privies; the women and girls washed the floors and did various kinds of housework. There were also men who worked at paving the streets, building bridges, repairing and rebuilding the bridge over the Chermosh leading to Vizshnitz. This bridge had been blown up by the Soviets before they left the city. This was hard labour – truly "avodas porech" (the term for hard labour used in the Bible in the story of Israel's slavery in Egypt). They had to drag the heavy lumber from the water and lift heavy beams. More than one Jew was killed at this work. The Ukrainians would also beat the Jewish labourers murderously. Many keeled over from hunger; the whole meal consisted of an onion and a radish. The luckier ones were those who got a "dzer" a kind of soup of boiled water sprinkled with a little flour, maize grains or barley.

*[Page 117]*

## Chapter XX

# The First Kittever Judenrat

The first president of the Kittever Judenrat was Dr. Menashe Mandel. As mentioned in a previous chapter, Dr. Mandel was a proud nationalist Jew, the recognized leader of the Kittever Jews of the last generation. Not only was he beloved by the Jews but even the Poles and Ukrainians treated him with great respect and paid attention to his opinion.

*[Page 118]*

During the short time that he served as head of the Judenrat, he tried to comply with the demands of the German and Ukrainian rulers and carried out his service diplomatically and with great tact. The materials and products that he was obliged to obtain from the Jews and the forced labour, he tried to get from the Jews voluntarily and without the drastic measures. To characterize the method of his work in the Kittever Judenrat, it is enough to cite the following fact:

When the Germans came into Kittev, they started straight away to restore the great municipal courthouse and furnish the building as quarters for the German border-guard. In the nearby villages, the Germans also refurbished the former Polish border-guard buildings. For this purpose, they needed various building materials such as paint, lime, cement, nails, locks for doors and windows, kettles and baking pans for the kitchens and other similar materials. They also had to pay the Ukrainian workers, masons and locksmiths, carpenters and house-painters. The artisans demanded their pay not in worthless zlotys but in produce. At that point, the officer of the German border-guard in Kittev came to the Judenrat and commanded the Judenrat to supply him with all the necessary raw materials and produce for the wages of the Ukrainians. He demanded this within a few days otherwise he threatened the well-known German consequences.

Dr. Mandel, the President of the Judenrat, immediately called a meeting of the more well-to-do Jews of Kittev. He held a lecture before them in which he pointed out the perilous situation of Polish Jewry in general and of Kittev in particular. He appealed to all present to take to heart the danger hovering the Jews and advised them to act according to the Biblical verse: "Give me the people and take the goods to thyself" (Genesis XIV, 21), and in this way, maybe we can save our lives, ransom our lives for a future hour. All those present immediately contributed whatever they had. They gave paint, nails, pipes and other building materials; others contributed money which was used to buy from the Poles and Ukrainians the rest of the building supplies as well as the produce to pay the Christian workers for their work in building the quarters for the German border-guard.

*[Page 119]*

The Jewish men and women who worked at the restoration and remodelling of the living quarters did the hardest forced labour and received their pay in beatings and degradation from the Germans and the local Ukrainians, who once made a living from the Jews and now, under the German regime, turned their former employers into maltreated slaves. The Ukrainians completely forgot about the long-enduring friendship and good relations with the Jews and began to show their enmity, becoming the Germans' most faithful helpers in destroying the Jewish population.

The Germans were not satisfied with all the materials which the Judenrat had supplied. If a part of the raw materials such as iron for nailing doors and windows, or kettles for cooking, were made of cheap material, the Ukrainians pointed out to the Germans those Jewish houses which had the best materials and arrangements. A German officer of the border guard and the Ukrainian locksmith Kovaliuk, would then go around to all the newer Jewish houses and rip the brass off all the doors and windows. They broke up the kitchens and tore out the heavy brass kettles and pipes and used these for the remodelled dwellings for the border guard.

When the remodelling ended, there started the business of furnishing the separate dwellings for the guard and their officers. When it came to providing furniture, the SS man, Vachner[1] didn't depend on the Judenrat. He himself wanted to choose the furniture for the rooms. Accompanied by the German border guards and the Ukrainian militia, he went around to the Jewish homes and stole everything their hearts desired: furniture, utensils, bedding, clothing, shoes and furnished and decorated their dwellings. Certain items such as clothing and shoes were sent back to their families in Germany. There were some Jews who tearfully begged the men of the "master race" not to take everything but to leave something for them. But the German border guards answered: *"You Jewish swine don't need it anymore because, first chance we get, we'll shoot you all like dogs and the crows will devour you"*.

*[Page 120]*

The writer of these lines had a "privilege". It was then a couple of years after my marriage and I had a beautiful and modernly furnished house. So, the German officer used my furniture to furnish the dwelling of the commandant of the border guard, "Herr" Schmidt. Mine and my wife's expensive clothing, underwear, shoes, tablecloths, curtains, rugs and other valuable things, Vachner packed into the empty valises he found in the house and sent them off to his family in Munich.

Thus happened the first looting of nearly all the Jewish houses in Kittev. If a Jew tried to protest against the blatant robbery, they gave him a good beating and as extra punishment, emptied out his entire house.

The German murderers hurled the most abusive words at the Jew and insulted him in the coarsest way. Nevertheless, the Jew's possessions were kosher for the man-beasts of the "master race" and they slept in Jewish beds, cooked in Jewish utensils and dressed up their wives and sweethearts in Jewish clothing and jewellery.

*Translator's footnote:*

1.    On page 88 of the translation, the name is given as Vachman

*[Page 121]*

## Chapter XXI

# The Tragedy of the Jewish Refugees from Hungary

At the end of August, 1941, the Fascist government of Hungary drove out about 50,000 Polish Jews and placed them in Polish territory, which meant delivering them into the hands of the Germans.

These were Jews that had lived for many years in Hungary and many of them were born there, married, had children there but their parents stemmed from Galicia which became part of the Polish Republic after World War I. At the time, those Jews emigrated to Hungary which, prior to World War I, was part of the Austro-Hungarian monarchy just as was Galicia. The did not need Hungarian citizenship. Suddenly, these Jews and their children and grandchildren were declared to be aliens.

One cursed late-August night, these Jews were brutally forced into trucks and transported to Poland which was occupied by the Nazi. The Jews were only allowed to take along items which could be carried. Their homes, factories and businesses were confiscated by the Hungarians. But even the few household articles that the Jews took along were grabbed by the Germans. The Nazi tore the shoes off their feet and the clothes off their backs leaving them half-naked and barefoot.

Among the Hungarian Jews who were driven out, were a number of apostates (converts to Christianity) who had married Christian women and had raised their children in a Christian environment. They did not know a single word of Yiddish. These apostates belonged to various Hungarian national organizations and considered themselves as 100% Hungarian patriots.

*[Page 122]*

But even their conversion did not help them. They were torn away by force from their families and property and were treated like all Jews – driven out of Hungary and delivered into the Nazi hands. After the Germans used and despoiled them, they dragged most of the victims as far as the Dniester and killed them. One Hungarian Jewish refugee who managed to escape, told me that the Germans had forced the Jews to build bridges over the Dniester. He told how the Hungarian Jews had to carry heavy beams on their bare shoulders. Those who could not carry the load were all hurled into the depths of the river or torn apart by the German guard dogs, or beaten to death with the German rubber whips. The one who got a bullet in the head was already the lucky one. Only a small number of the Hungarian Jews got away and managed to reach our district with the aim of sneaking over the border back into Hungary. What their fate was- whether some of them succeeded in getting back to Hungary- it is not known. But, it is known that certain Jews who had smuggled themselves from Nazi Poland to Hungary were caught by the border patrol and returned to the Polish side. The German border guard would not let them in again and shot them to death on the border.

The surviving remnant of Hungarian Jews who managed to reach the area and district of Kittev were received by their Jewish brethren, quartered in our homes. We shared our last morsel with them. Even in those difficult and fateful days, the Jews of Kittev did not forget the beautiful virtue of hospitality and they took in the Hungarian refugees with a cheerful countenance. (He uses the Hebrew expression from Pirke Avot). There were cases when Kittever Jewish families, who starved all week and lived on a radish and a beet, on the day that a Hungarian refugee was to be their guest, they risked their lives to sneak out to a village to get a few potatoes or a little milk from a peasant for their last shirt or pair of shoes so that they could see that the Hungarian refugee would not leave their house hungry.

*[Page 123]*

This was the fate of the Jews who were driven out from Hungary. They drank the cup of bitterness until February, 1942, when, on a black and freezing night, the Ukrainian militia of Kittev with their accursed helpers, dragged the Hungarian Jewish refugees from their dwellings, took them to Kolomei and turned them over to the Gestapo who took them out into the Sheperovitz Forest and murdered them en masse! Afterward, they threw the bodies into a large mass grave deep in the forest. Thus, was liquidated the remnant of the Hungarian Jewish refugees.

## Chapter XXII

# The German Tax Bureau

In September, 1941, by order of the Nazi occupiers, the tax bureau was organized in Kossev. All former officials of the Polish tax bureau were employed there and their assignment was to collect taxes from the Jews. The other local bureaus were staffed with Ukrainians. Poles were used for the sole purpose of collecting taxes from the Jews.

The tax bureau began demanding from all Jews, taxes on houses, fields and business. They demanded taxes that had already been paid long ago. If a Jew did not have confirmation that he had already paid the tax, he had to pay it again. The tax collectors evinced an indescribable arrogance (chutzpah) which had one aim: to mock the Jews. They even demanded taxes for fields and houses that the Soviets had taken away from the Jews back in 1939. They also demanded taxes from Jews who were formerly traders.

*[Page 124]*

Kittever Jews understandably began a struggle against this travesty of taxation and complained about the cynical tax orders. Jews attempted to prove with facts and figures that back in 1939, they had stopped getting income from their houses, fields or businesses and that they did not have enough for even their most minimal needs. On the basis of these facts, the Jews requested the tax bureau to leave them alone.

Appeals to conscience and requests for fairness and justice could help very little in this matter. But corruption did help a little. The chief of economy and finances for the district of Kolomei was SS Lorenz. Like all German officials, he was thoroughly corrupt. He and his occupying colleagues made use of wartime and the Jewish disaster to fill their pockets and enrich themselves at the expense of the Jewish misfortune.

When Lorenz came down to Kossev for inspection to review the work of the tax bureau, representatives of the Kittever Judenrat approached him with a request for an audience. They complained to him about the unexpected taxes being demanded from a poverty-stricken population that had been despoiled by the Soviets. He promised to see to it that the tax burden would be lightened a little, but for this promise, he demanded to be provided immediately with a large number of rugs, curtains, woven tablecloths and blankets, fabrics and men's suits. When the Judenrat gave him the requested materials, he requested more and more until he obtained plenty of loot. He then, finally, ordered the Kossover tax office to cancel the mockery taxes on the Jews.

*[Page 125]*

The Polish chief of the tax bureau took himself an example from his boss, the German chief or overlord, and without shame, presented the Judenrat with a list of orders before he would permit the lower tax officials to cancel the taxes. Naturally, the Judenrat had no alternative and supplied him as well with the merchandise. But the overlords and under lords did not content themselves with this. Every lower official demanded his share of bribe. Even then, only a part of the tax was written off – the tax on the nationalized property – but the rest of the taxes the Jews were forced to pay.

After this began the second stage of plundering and robbing of the Jewish population of Kittev and its vicinity.

In the first days of the occupation, the Jews, under the pain of death, had to turn over to the German authority al valuable articles such as gold, silver, jewels and diamonds. In the second stage, the Germans began robbing the Jewish homes and beside their Ukrainian helpers, they made themselves new helpers – the Judenrat.

The Judenraten (plural of Judenrat) that the Germans set up in every city and town, in every out-of-the-way village, had the task of restoring and setting up for the Germans houses and dwellings. They had to take care of the border guards, the Gestapo, the criminal police, the Ukrainian militia and other species of hangmen and murderers. The Judenrat men had to set up the hospitals for the German Wehrmacht, the homes for the Hitler youth and all convalescent homes and summer villas for the German murderers and their families.

*[Page 126]*

In the first days of the German occupation, the Germans and Ukrainians themselves helped to set up their headquarters. They simply requisitioned the Jewish houses that had the desired furnishings and three the Jewish owners into the street or pushed them into the ghettos. After there no longer were any Jewish houses for their quarters and offices, the Judenraten that they had established, were forced to supply them with houses and dwellings. As mentioned before, there were no longer any stores where one could buy furniture and other household necessities, materials for refurbishing and furnishing a house. However, the Judenrat had to obtain all these things and provide them on time. If the Jews did not have the needed materials, a money-tax was imposed on them. With this money, the Judenrat purchased the things from the Ukrainians and Poles, naturally at very high prices.

The border guard, Gestapo, Police and Ukrainian militia continually demanded from the Judenrat leather for shoes and boots, leather jackets, canvas, carpets, fabrics, furs, gold watches and rings; various women's dresses, shoes and stockings. Jews did not have these things anymore so the Judenrat had to buy it all for money from the Ukrainians and Poles. When an SS man or a Gestapo man was due to go home on leave, he came into the Judenrat and ordered various gifts for his wife, children and parents. When SS Vachner went on leave, he took with him, besides a large number of packages of valuable things that he had previously robbed from the Jews, also special gifts that the Judenrat provided for him. Among these were diapers for his newly-born heir in Munich. I, myself, witnessed a scene when a Nazi border guard walked into the Judenrat and showed his torn trousers and demanded leather for the seat.

The border guard Pickeisen demanded that the Judenrat provide him, for the Silvester ball, December, 31, 1941, a pretty "fraulein" to accompany him to the ball. The Judenrat could not obtain this kind of goods in Kittev, so they ordered her in Kolomei. The Judenrat of Kolomei provided this living merchandise to the Kittever Judenrat and the "Overlord" was so pleased with his gift that he even forgot to check her descent, whether she was pure Aryan! Before the ball, it turned out that the "bride" – the fraulein – did not have a suitable dress to go to the ball with her German cavalier. In a great hurry, the Kittever Judenrat had to rob a Jewish woman of a gown, a pair of shoes and a lace kerchief to deck out the fraulein for "Herr" Pickeisen .

*[Page 127]*

In March, 1942, the Sturm-Fuhrer Huber came into the Kittever Judenrat and demanded that they get him a lock-maker to clean his machine pistol which he had used to shoot the Jews during the Juden "actions" in other cities and which he used again, a month later, in April, in Kittev.

## Chapter XXIII

# The Judenrat

I would greatly prefer not to write too much about the Judenrat in general and the role it played during our great national disaster. But I feel that to pass over the matter of the Judenrat entirely in silence, would be to commit a great sin against the memory of my dear friends and comrades of Kittev who perished and against the whole community of the Jewish martyrs in Kittev.

According to the Nazi Gestapo, all Jewish property and all Jewish lives were in the hands of and under the supervision of the Judenrat which could deal with the lives and property as it saw fit. But the Judenraten were, for the most part, no more than a blind, obedient puppet in the hands of the Gestapo.

*[Page 128]*

Thus, the Judenrat members used their authority in favour of the Gestapo and against the unfortunate Jewish victims.

The Gestapo, for its part, spared the Judenrat as long as they served and were useful. At the moment when these Jews, whom the Gestapo designated as the "last Jews", ceased to be useful, the Gestapo destroyed them together with the other Jews.

In the first period before the "Juden aktions" began, responsible Jewish leaders stood at the head of certain Judenraten and tried to do their thankless work sincerely because they still hoped that in this way they would manage to save Jewish lives. As mentioned, it was the task of the Judenraten to collect for the Gestapo the imposed money taxes and to purchase for the Germans various materials and valuable items. During the first period, the leaders of the Judenrat made an effort to have compassion with the poor man when collecting the contributions and requested more money and things from the richer Jew. They also appraised people according to their means and situations. If a certain wealthy Jew did not have that which the Germans demanded, he gave money for which they bought the material and articles from a less wealthy Jew who needed the zlotes to buy potatoes for his family. They acted in the same way in assigning dwellings in the ghettos and in recruiting Jews for forced labour.

When the outlook became darker and darker for the Jews and the Nazi began to extinguish thousands of Jewish lives day-by-day, when this bloody fate descended upon the great Jewish community in Poland and Jewish blood flowed like water, the more decent members of the Judenrat were torn away by the murderers and cut down. Some of them committed suicide, not wanting any longer to serve as tools of the German cannibals. They realized that they could be of no use by their service and chose death rather than to work with the Germans and be partners in destroying their own sisters and brothers.

*[Page 129]*

Then, out of the dark, crawled all the lizards, snakes, reptiles and crawly things who fear the light of day and appear only in the blackness of night. The new Judenrat was the offal of Jewish society. There, the word of the great prophet Isaiah was fulfilled: "They destroyers and they made thee waste shall go forth from thee". (Isaiah XLIX,17) - - your despoilers and destroyers will come from your insides. There then arrived people in the Judenrat who used the great Jewish disaster for their personal egotistic interests. The rich relative or the person who bribed them were spared and the poor man they pressed and squeezed. This is how they conducted themselves during the various "Juden-akzions" in taxations and in sending Jews to forced labour. The Judenrat members were transformed into beasts in human form, lost their image of God and Jewish life became *hefker* (a Hebrew word meaning unprotected, but hard to precisely translate).

At the end of October, 1941, the Kittever Judenrat changed and the fate of the plundered and starved Jews became even more tragic. This is how it came about:

The Gestapo in Kolomei demanded the sum of $50,000 from the Jews of that place. Hard to say for sure if the Jews of Kolomei were able to furnish the sum demanded. Possibly the president of the Kolomei Judenrat, Herr Horowitz, simply wanted to use the power he had received from the Gestapo over all the Jews of the Kolomei district and took the opportunity to begin plundering the Jews of nearby smaller towns on behalf of the Gestapo or his own gang. At the end of October of that year, H. Horowitz, with his assistant, H. Jacoby, drove into Kittev in a luxurious automobile which the Gestapo had provided, and demanded from the then president of the Kittever Judenrat, Dr. Menashe Mandel, to obtain from the Jews of Kittev, by drastic means, the sum of four to five thousand dollars.

*[Page 130]*

Menashe Mandel immediately rejected Horowitz's demand. He argued that the Jewish population of Kittev had been plundered by the Germans and the Ukrainians. He also indicated that Kittever Jews had already paid plenty of money in the forced contributions and that goods had been taken from them. The Kittever people had raised all this in their city and did not approach any other neighbouring city. The District Judenrat President hated to be contradicted so he deposed Dr. Mandel from his post and appointed in his place as President of the Kittever Judenrat, Herr Sigmund Tillinger.

Sigmund Tillinger attempted, as far as possible, to obey the commands and instructions of Herr Horowitz. He organized the Kittever Judenrat on the model of the Kolomei Judenrat. He set up various groups in the Judenrat and each group had a separate assignment. He established a group that dealt with war materials, a group that occupied itself with sending Jews to work and a group for keeping order and similar groups for the cleaning work. Tillinger was a capable and disciplined organizer, and he found suitable people for his work.

The order-keeping group was an unarmed militia which obeyed the commands of the Judenrat. It was supposed to watch that every order of the Judenrat should be carried out. In larger cities, the order-keeping group was forced indirectly to participate in the exterminating Juden-aktions.

The group that had to do with forced labour, led by Zaide Hirsh, had oversight over all Jews able to work and who were sent to do forced labour for the Germans and Ukrainians.

*[Page 131]*

Tillinger conducted himself on the model of the Kolomei Judenrat. He even set up a special Jewish jail, in a large and empty warehouse, and the order-keeping service locked up the Kittever Jews who could not or would not pay the sum of dollars which the Kolomei Judenrat had demanded from them.

In normal times, Horowitz, President of the Kolomei Judenrat, would certainly have been a candidate for a psychiatrist. He was a dreadful despot in his own wretched Judenratic kingdom within a kingdom. Because he had received certain rights and means to force the Jews to obey his commands, he used those rights in an arrogant manner. His watchword was: "you need to give the Germans as much until they will have enough to vomit…" He would boast that when the Germans requested 100 pair of boots from him, he would send them 200. When the Germans ordered 250 covers for the beds in their hospital, he delivered 500. This is how he dealt with all their demands. Naturally, all of this was robbed from the Jews.

Tillinger told a characteristic fact which bore witness to the mental and psychic status of Horowitz – his megalomania and his devilish tricks.

Once, when he, Tillinger, was walking with Horowitz through the streets of Kolomei, they met a former prominent businessman of Kolomei, Herr Bank. Horowitz, who was not liked among the Jews of Kolomei, nevertheless expected that Bank should greet him. But the other man passed him by indifferently. Horowitz could not pass over such an insult, especially in Tillinger's presence. He wished to teach the Jews of Kolomei manners; how they must pay respect to the head of the Judenrat. He called Bank over and gave him two resounding slaps. He also called over an order-keeper and commanded him to arrest Mr. Bank. They put him into the Jewish jail and he was forced to there on a cement floor for a full two weeks until such time Horowitz consented to release him for an amount of ransom money.

The entire duration of his imprisonment in the Jewish jail, Bank had to sleep without a pillow and live on dry bread and water.

*[Page 132]*

## Chapter XXIV

# The Extermination of the Jewish Intelligentsia in Stanislav

Rosh Hashanah and Yom Kippur of 1941, we lived under great tension. We had a foreboding that something horrible was coming upon us. Jews were not allowed to travel from one city to another so we could not tell what was happening in other cities. Various unclear reports reached us by post and reading them filled us with fear and terror.

The daughter of my neighbour, Shmuel Laub, wrote from Tarnopol that she very much wished to come to Kittev with her child. Her husband, she wrote, was already transferred. This meant that the Germans had already taken him away. The daughter of Moshe Druck wrote from Chortkov that her father (who had died six years before) was her steady visitor. Under the impression of such horrible letters, the Jews of Kittev assembled on Rosh Hashanah and Yom Kippur in the synagogues. We had no need of Machzors (High Holiday prayer books) because the prayers burst from everyone's heart – a single prayer to Heaven: "We are perishing, we are cut off, O Lord send us help to redeem us. Pity us and let us not be destroyed".. Ever since the Jewish people were driven out of its own land and scattered and dispersed in every corner of the Galut (Exile), no generation experienced or could imagine what we felt in the Days of Judgment in that year. EveryWorshipper – from the richest to the poorest, children, men and women, among them many Jewish refugees from Hungary – were bathed in tears. Every Jew took account of the dreadful situation in which he found himself. We knew well that our lives were in the greatest peril. Not only the individual, but the entire community, the Jewish nation, was hovering between life and death. Only a miracle could save us as we could find no other prospect of saving ourselves.

*[Page 133]*

Regrettably, our heart-rending prayers and pleas did not help. Our calling upon the merits of our fathers also accomplished nothing. No miracles happened. The major portion of the Polish Jewish collective was destroyed. The great and proud Jewish community of Poland along with the small Jewish community of the old city of Kittev was cut down with the greatest brutality.

On Yom Kippur in the Chortkover Klaus, there was a fruit dealer from Stanislav who had come down here to buy fruit for the Stanislav Gestapo. He told the horrible details of the first Juden-akzion in Stanislav, the action against the Jewish intelligentsia.

Shortly after their entry into Stanislav, the German SS and the Gestapo, with the help of the Ukrainian militia and working from a previous prepared list, dragged from their homes, all Jewish doctors, engineers, lawyers, dentists, technicians, teachers, professors and all the more important Jewish merchants and industrialists, intellectual persons and secretly killed them. The families of the Jews who had been dragged away at first had not the slightest idea of what had happened to their fathers, husbands, brothers and sons. Nobody could imagine that even the Germans were capable of dragging out innocent Jews and destroying them just because they were Jews. They tried, by various ways and means, to find out from the Gestapo what had happened to the arrested Jews, where they had been taken to. But the efforts were in vain. It was impossible to find out from the Gestapo and their assistants what had happened to the Jews.

*[Page 134]*

Several days later, the Gestapo announced that the families could send the Jews who were taken away, packages of food, clothing and money. Understandably, the Jewish mothers and wives hurried and brought the best things they owned for their dear ones because they took the announcement as a sign that they were still alive. But there were no longer living!

Later, a few weeks after the first Juden-akzion in Stanislav, the Jews learned the bitter truth that the Gestapo and SS had murdered these Jews right away and then cheated their families out of packages and money, pretending that it was for the people who had been dragged away.

## Chapter XXV

# The First Juden-Akzion in Kolomei

The first Juden-akzion in our district was carried out by the Germans in Kolomei. It was on Hoshana Rabbah, October 12, 1941.

On Simchas Torah, Tuesday, October 14, we received unclear reports about the akzion in Kolomei. Erev Hoshana Rabbah Isaac Grebler came to Kittev on a mission from the Judenrat of Kolomei to obtain boards from the sawmill in Kittev. On Hoshana Rabbah, he drove back. He was riding on a tractor. On the way, between Pistin and Kolomei, he ran out of gas. He tried to contact the Kolomei Judenrat by telephone but the telephone

*[Page 135]*

lines were cut. On the days the Gestapo carried out the Juden-akzions, they would cut the telephone connections between the Judenraten so that the neighbouring cities would not find out about the akzions. But the switchboard girl in Kolomei warned Grebler not to come into Kolomei because the Germans were murdering Jews in the streets, and the Great Synagogue was in flames.

Hoshana Rabbah morning, the time of mercy, the synagogues in Kolomei were full of worshippers. Suddenly, the Gestapo, SS and Ukrainian militia surrounded and blocked all Jewish streets. The Germans and Ukrainians swarmed over the Jewish homes like hunting dogs. They threw the Jews they caught into trucks and took them to the Sheperowitz forest – shot them all and threw them into prepared mass graves. The Jews who tried to flee were shot on the spot. The murderers set fire to the Great Synagogue, and the Jews who tried to escape from the fire and flame were shot. In this first Juden-akzion in Kolomei, about 6,000 Jews of Kolomei were burned to death or shot.

## Chapter XXVI

# The Juden-Akzion in Kossev

The first Juden-akzion in Kossev took place on Thursday 16th and Friday 17th, October, 1941. Although Kossev lies only 10km from Kittev, we – Kittever Jews, first found out about the horrible destruction of the Kossover Jews the following morning, the 18th of October.

On Thursday morning, a Kittever Jewish young man came from Kossev and told that on that very morning at about eight o'clock, there drove into Kossev several autos with Gestapo and SS men from Kolomei and stationed themselves at the Ring Place. The German forces then blocked and occupied all the roads leading to and from Kossev and did not allow any Jew from the city to leave. The boy managed to jump onto a passing truck and thus saved himself.

*[Page 136]*

On Thursday morning, a rumor spread in Kittev that the Germans were putting all the Jews of Kossev into a (concentration) camp. They allowed each person to take along only one small package. Nobody was interested to find out where this rumor had come from. The report made us all depressed. Weeping and wailing was heard from each Jewish house. Everyone said farewell to everybody, hugged and kissed and waited for the Gestapo's destroyers to come and take us all to the camp. We prepared ourselves for certain death. If the Gestapo had come into Kittev then, they would have captured everyone. Not one Jew would have been able to hide or escape. We found ourselves in a state of complete despair and resignation. It is hard to describe our condition. I sat down on the ground and took my little child into my arms. The child did not understand why she was being torn away from her toys, from her little crib and the big doll. I nestled the child, wept and asked the Master of the World: "Why?" Thus the day passed and dark night crept in. Darker than dark.

Late at night, a Ukrainian youth – Tarnovitski – came to Kittev. I had paid him, earlier, to ride into Kossev to find out what had actually happened there. He brought the frightful news which sounded unbelievable. He told that the Gestapo was rounding up all the Jews and taking them, en masse, up on the Pistin Mountain where two huge pits had been prepared, shooting them and throwing their bodies into the pits.

*[Page 137]*

On Friday, these reports were confirmed. The slaughter of our unfortunate sisters and brothers in Kossev last two days. We went through this horror and shed rivers of tears.

On Saturday, October 18th, we had direct reports of the bitter fate of the Jews of Kossev. We received brief letters from a few Jews who had miraculously saved themselves from the murderers' hands because they had fled to the forest in time or hid with Christian friends.

Now it became clear to all the Jews of Kittev that the same fate, as that of our Kossever brethren, awaited us. When this would happen, no one could know. We just learned from the Kossever akzion that we must try to hide out in any way possible. We began to work out plans and seek means by which to save the Jews settled in Kittev.

I thought of a plan: In Kossev, everything was over so perhaps it would be a plan to move there and hide and wait till the bitter fate would descend on Kittev. I went in to my neighbour, the Polish Doctor Tustanovski, told him of my plan and asked him to give me a note saying that my little girl is sick in her appendix and that I would need to take her to the Kossev hospital for an operation. With the doctor's note, I went to the Ukrainian community authority and obtained the permit. I hired a horse-and-wagon, took along a little food and, on the third day after the horrible mass-murder, we entered the "City of Slaughter". (In Hebrew, this is the title of Bialik's great poem).

A steady rain was falling from the sky in Kossev. The drops fell like hot tears, as if the heavens were mourning the innocent blood that was shed. The streets were empty – everything dead. No living soul was to be seen. The houses were in ruins. The doors and windows smashed. The murderers had despoiled everything. From the middle of the city, one could see the great mountain with the two large, swollen mass-graves, which will remain forever as mutely-screaming witnesses to the greatest murder that the German Huns of the 20th century perpetrated in the very heart of Europe – a crime that had no equal even in the dark Middle Ages.

*[Page 138]*

In Kossev, we drove to a sister-in-law who miraculously was saved by accident from the first Kossever Juden-akzion. From her we learned the horrible details of the mass-murder. I will try to relate the particulars in the order in which they occurred:

The Jewish settlement in Kossev would not have been exterminated in that way had it not been for the local Ukrainians. As the Nazi Sturm leaders told later in the Kossov Judenrat, the Ukrainian national committee of the city, led by Vinitski, Mrs. Gardetska, Mrs. Shtepurak and others, submitted a memorandum to the Gestapo in Kolomei in which they talked about the great disaster; that they have in their city such a large Jewish population who are mostly former traders, parasites. Because of them, the Christian population is suffering from such a shortage in food supplies. They requested, therefore, that the Gestapo should free Kossev from this Jewish plague.

In connection with this memorandum on instructions of the Kolomei Gestapo and in line with their understanding with the Kossov national Ukrainian committee, under the command of the Ukrainian district commandant, Dereshitsky, two huge graves were dug on the night of Wednesday, October 15, on the Pistin Mountain just opposite the house of the Kossover Rebbe, which was now the office of the Judenrat. The diggers were all Ukrainians.

On Thursday, October 16, the Kossover Ukrainian committee called together in Kossev a large number of Ukrainians and Hutzuls as well as the Ukrainian militia from nearby cities and villages. They also lad on a supply of whiskey and other strong liquors. In the morning when the Kolomei Gestapo and SS men arrived and blocked the streets, they started hunting down the Jews.

*[Page 139]*

The Jews of Kossev thought that the Germans had come to take the young men for forced labour so their wives practically forced the men to run away and hide in the woods. The women and children thought that they would manage to remain in their homes and the men would, somehow, hide out in the woods or be hidden by the Christians.

The Jews who were in the homes of gentiles of their acquaintance were mostly turned over to the Gestapo who shot them.

Naturally, Jews ran to hide in the houses of those Ukrainians and Poles with whom they had a long-standing friendship. They had a certain trust in those Christians because had hidden their few remaining possessions with them. These "friends" now got an opportunity to get rid of the owners of these possessions and a chance to inherit them, so they immediately turned over the Jews to the Gestapo. Also, in places where Jews lived in the same building as the Ukrainians, the Ukrainians drove them out of the houses and delivered them into the hands of the murderers so that they could then rob their remaining property.

Such a case happened with the family of David Joseph Buller of Kittev. In 1939, the Soviets took over David Joseph Buller's business and drove out his family. As a family who had been nationalized, they could not find lodgings anywhere. Having no alternative, they moved in with their daughter in Kossev and roomed in a Ukrainian's house in Maskulivke.

On the day of the Juden-akzion, the Ukrainian landlord chased the whole family out of the house and put them into the hands of the murderers.

*[Page 140]*

On the day of the Juden-akzion, the Germans were not even in the village of Maskulivke to hunt for Jews. But the Ukrainians, on their own, turned the Jews out and threw them into the mouths of the murderous fire-spitting machine pistols. The Ukrainian owners of the house in which the Buller family had lived, drove them out of the house and turned them over to the commandant of the Kossov Ukrainian militia, Direzshitski, a former clerk of a Jewish attorney who lived for many years in Kittev. Direzshitski was elevated to greatness when the Nazis entered Kittev. They appointed him as head of the Ukrainian militia in Kossev.

Joshua Gertner who was an eye-witness of the scene, told me how Direzshitski, who knew David Joseph Buller well in Kittev, beat them murderously while escorting them to be shot. He didn't even spare the old grandmother and grandchild of the Bullers.

In the morning and afternoon hours of that Thursday, the murderers drove all the captured Jews into the Kossev court building, locked them into the jail cells and the jail courtyard. The leaders of the Kossev Judenrat attempted to ransom Jewish lives. They offered the leaders of the SS and the Sturm groups ransom in the form of valuables. A special delegation of the Judenrat brought, as price for the lives, a large number of men's and women's furs and other items. The murderers took the costly gifts, but not only did they not free one single Jew, but they arrested the mitzvah messengers, the Judenrat delegation who had put their own lives on the line to rescue Jews, and destroyed them together with the community of the Jews of Kossev.

At noon, the Ukrainian national committee set up a regular banquet for the Gestapo, the SS and the Ukrainian militia. The Ukrainians held venomously anti-Semitic speeches. The whole mob of murderers – Germans and Ukrainians, drank and ate voraciously. Provoked and incited by the venomous speeches, they set out after the cannibalistic feast. They led the Jews forth in groups, forced the victims to strip naked, shot bullets into their brains and necks and threw them into the great pits.

*[Page 141]*

Among the first Jewish vicitms of the Kossev Jewish women, was a beautiful young girl, Shimon Letich's daughter. She was wearing a leather jacket. The murderers commanded she take off her jacket. She answered that she would not give up the jacket voluntarily. Let the murderers take it off her bullet-riddled body later. With hard-bitten obduracy and with her head held high, without a word of pleading as befits a proud Jewish daughter, the girl jumped into the grave and a murderous bullet smashed the skull of the blooming young life.

Among the first male victims was a young man, a son of Leizer Gertner of Zshabie. He had come to Kossev together with a few other Jews sent by the Zshabier Judenrat. They were caught and shot. The young Doctor Gertner managed, before jumping into the mass grave, to call the murderers by their name. He asked how the Germans, the nation of "poets and thinkers", a nation that spoke the language of Heine, Goethe and Schiller, how could they be capable of extirpating innocent men, women and children? He called out that the German people that would tolerate such barbarism would be responsible and in the Day of Judgment which would come, would be tried by the world's conscience and pay dearly.

The murderers hee-hawed like horses, laughed resoundingly, mocked and accompanied their laughter with bullets which they shot into his brain.

*[Page 142]*

The murderers also "saved" bullets. They thus did not shoot the children of five or six years old but grabbed them by the hair with one hand and banged them with the other, or, threw them like a ball or pounded them with their boots and threw them into the pit. The murderers killed and drank, got drunk, slurped and shot and heaped up the large and broad pits. Among the victims in one women's transport was a Jewish woman who was the cook for the German gendarmerie in Kossev – her name was Steiner. The commandant asked the Sturm 65aught to spare her life but the Sturm 65aught said, sarcastically, that he would give this cook two bullets as a bonus. This was later told by Denk Meiner of the gendarmerie who took part actively in the Juden akzion.

Together with the above-mentioned Ukrainian murderer Direzshitski, two more Kittever Ukrainian militia men participated in the mass murder. During the time the slaughter was in progress and the shots boomed out as the German murderers were throwing Jews into the mass graves, these creatures set up a radio loudspeaker and continuously played lively music. When a German or Ukrainian murderer ran to bring a victim, the president of the Ukrainian national committee called him over and treated him with whiskey and wine. He also shouted that he gave another 100 zlotes for whiskey, a zlote for each Jewish head, 100 zlotes for 100 Jews.

On Friday, October 17, the Germans continued the slaughter. The Ukrainians brought the Jews and the Germans and Ukrainian militia did the shooting. The Kossever Jews did not weep or plead for mercy from the murderers – with heads held high they went to the slaughter.

As illustration of the proud behaviour of the Kossever Jewish martyrs, how they acted in the last hours of life facing hideous death, I want to recount the following two examples:

*[Page 143]*

There lived in Kossev a young Jewish doctor Goldstein who was, at that time, the fiancé of Haim Hersh Drucker's daughter. At the pits, the murderers realized that it was worthwhile for them to let the doctor live for now because the city needed him. The doctor laughed at them and declared he chose to die together with his beloved bride rather than live by the grave of the murderers who were killing all his innocent Jewish sisters and brothers.

Moshe'le Feier was considered in Kossev to be a holy Jew – a true *lamed-vav'nik*..(one of the legendary 36 secret righteous people who enable the world to exist). He fasted every Monday and Thursday and sat day-and-night in the Bet Midrash studying Torah. At the time of the Juden akzion, all the Jews ran from the Bet Midrash to hide and called to Reb Moshe'le to flee. He answered that if this was an evil decree from Heaven, he would not hide himself. He put on his white kittel, wrapped himself in his great *tallis*, opened the Holy Ark, buried his head among the Torah scrolls and said the Confession . . . Whoever witnessed the scene in those minutes, how the holy Jew, wrapped in the tallis, his face white and pale as lime from the constant fasts, how his lips whispered a prayer or perhaps a curse upon the murderers of the Jews – that person had to feel that they were not taking an ordinary Jew to the slaughter but a holy figure – an Angel of God. The murderers brought Reb Moshe'le up on the hill to the open pits. Everyone expected that a miracle would occur and the holy one would be saved from death. But no miracle occurred. The murderous bullet did not spring back, no angel appeared from Heaven, no thunder or lightning bolt struck the murderers, the earth did not swallow them up. The mouth that recited God's Torah day and night was silenced; the body wasted by fasting until it was more spirit than substance, was together with the bodies of all Kossever Jews, cast into the huge grave and his blood mingled with the blood of the other holy and pure ones, with the innocent blood of little Jewish children who had never sinned; the blood that boils and will continue to boil like the blood of the Prophet Zachariah, until the great Day of Vengeance will come.

*[Page 144]*

The sum-total of the Juden akzion in Kossev which lasted two days, Thursday 16th and Friday 17th, October, 1942, was 2500 Jewish victims. Of them, some 1700 old people, women and children and 150 refugees from Hungary. There remained in Kossev about 1000 Jews; very few whole families, mostly men without wives and children without parents. The remaining ones were frightened and mixed up, some of them went out of their minds completely. Religious Jews, former Hasidim of the Kossever Rebbe, became the biggest atheists. I don't want to put on paper the words and the blasphemies that fell from their lips, as for example, the eruption of wrath of the former Hasid Biller when he heard someone mention the name God. Another Kossever Hasid, Letich, said that of all the prayers in the service in the Shmoneh Esrai (the Amidah) he understood only the benediction: "Thou favourest man with understanding", because after all these experiences, if one retained his understanding (remained sane) it would appear that there is a Higher Providence, but in the rest of the benedictions, he no longer believes.

The Ukrainians torched the Great Synagogue in the city. Some of the Jews who had hidden in the Synagogue attic were unable to escape the flames and were burned to death. Those who ran from the hellish fire into the street were shot and their bodies thrown into the flames, among them many children. Among the martyrs who perished in the flames was the Kittever Jewish woman, Chaya Hosenfratz, a daughter of Elasar Hutterer together with her husband and child.

## Chapter XXVII

# Juden-Akzions in the Nearby Cities and Towns

Following the slaughter in Kossev, one dark night, the Ukrainians of the village of Ritshka attacked the Jews of that village and murdered them all. The German police came down into the village with bloodhounds to find out if the Ukrainians had used weapons (guns) to murder the Jews. Killing Jews with axes or knives was not punishable; the Ukrainian got the priest's assurance of going to Heaven. But for killing Jews with weapons, the Ukrainian was subject to punishment, not for the murder you understand, but for illegal possession of weapons!

At the same time, dreadful reports reached us about the Juden-akzions in a whole series of cities and towns in our area such as: Delatin, Nodvarne, Tarnopol, Chortkov and others. In Utenieh, the German murderers came in the middle of the night and dragged the sleeping Jews out of their beds and shot them all, naked as they were. In Delatin, the Germans shot about 2000 Jews during the first akzion. In Yarmetshe, Varachte, Yablonitse, Mikultshin and Tatarov, the German and Ukrainian murderers cleared the whole area of Jews. The few Jews who managed to flee into the woods were slaughtered by the Hutzuls who hacked them with axes and slaughtered them with knives.

In every city, the Germans carried out the akzion in a different way. In Horodenka, for example, they summoned the Jews to be vaccinated. When the Jews gathered, they took them all to the previously prepared mass graves.

*[Page 146]*

After shooting the Jews, they came to the Judenrat and demanded to be paid 10,000 zlotes for the bullets they had used up in the "Juden-akzion". They treated the defenseless Jewish victims with blatant cynicism and mockery.

In the smaller towns, the Germans, with the help of the Ukrainians, liquidated the Jews all at once and made the whole town "Judenrein". In the cities with a larger Jewish population, they employed a different tactic. First they robbed the Jews completely, then they started to carry out various akzions: First, second, third – until they reduced the Jewish population to a minimum. Finally, they imprisoned the small number of Jews in the ghetto and, at their appointed time, destroyed them with no difficulty.

In Kolomei, the murderers established the Jewish ghetto after the first Juden akzion. They appointed a certain time by which all Jews had to be in the ghetto. On the way to the ghetto, they also shot many Jews and if a Jew was caught outside the ghetto, he was murdered immediately.

But the whole ghetto consisting of a few streets, could not take in all the Jews. In every small and crowded room, ten persons were pressed together. In every attic, closet and stable, the unfortunate Jewish souls were squeezed like herrings. But still, many Jews remained outside and had no place to put themselves.

The Germans solved the matter of living-space in their own way. They did not add a couple of streets to the ghetto but every few days, they carried out more actions and day-by-day reduced the number of Jews in Kolomei. They would carry out intellectual akzions, i.e. take the Jewish intelligentsia and people of the free professions and shoot them. Another time they would start to clear out street-by-street such as the Ghetto street, the Makara Street. Among the martyrs of the Makara Street there were the Kossever Rebbe with his beautiful daughter. The Nazis also carried out "Shmeltz-akzions". After the men had left for their work, the murderers would descend on the ghetto and take away the old people, the women and the children.

*[Page 147]*

In Lemberg, the Germans demanded that the Judenrat provide them, for a special purpose, 35,000 Jews. Because the Judenrat refused to deliver the Jews, the Germans, again with the help of the Ukrainians, dragged out 50,00 Jews and killed them in various ways. In the years 1940-1941, some 500,000 Jews lived in Lemberg. In October, 1942, when the Germans liquidated the Lemberg ghetto, there were only around 15,000 Jews there. Upon liquidating the ghetto, they shot all the Jews to death with machine guns. The Germans and Ukrainians kept shooting until, literally, every Jew had fallen.

Better-off were those slain by the sword than those slain by hunger. (Lamentations 4:9) (This is my translation: You will see different wording in English bibles).

After the Juden-akzion in Kossev, the Gestapo and SS officers became frequent and constant guests in Kittev. Every other day they would come to the Kittever Judenrat with various orders. (For goods).

Every time they came into the city there was a great commotion among the Jews. We thought that the final hour was at hand. When a relative from Kolomei warned that on a given day the in-laws were coming to the wedding in Kittev, not a single Jew was to be found out of doors on that day. All, big and small, ran to hide. A few hid with Christian neighbours who were well paid for their hospitality. Most ran to hide out in the surrounding woods.

In early November, the season of rains and frosts began. In the cold, wet and dark nights, the Kittever Jews who were hiding in the woods had to lie on the wet and frozen ground with their little ones and with no food. More than one Jew collapsed and expired from hunger.

[Page 148]

With the arrival of the cold winter, starvation became unbearable. There were cases when Jews wished the Gestapo would come as quickly as possible and release them from the dreadful torture of hunger.

At that time, it was impossible to barter with a peasant for food. After the Juden-akzion in Kossev, the nearby peasants had looted so much Jewish property that for the offer of a man's good suit of clothes, they would not give more than 10 or 15kg of grain. I, myself, saw a Ukrainian in Kossev sell a Jew's Persian fur coat and ask $10 for it. Most of the Jews already had nothing to trade for and hunger increased. People walked around like living corpses. Whoever did not experience such dreadful starvation, could in no way imagine it. When we, as Cheder boys studied the verse in Lamentations: "Better-off were those slain by the sword than those slain by hunger", we simply could not comprehend it. What does it mean that those who died by the sword were better off than those who died of hunger? Now we understood it perfectly. We saw Jews wandering about the streets with emaciated faces, with big bulging eyes. For those people, nothing mattered. Even hunger did not affect them anymore. They body was so weak that the organism could no longer digest food. I saw how one such living corpse swallowed a spoonful of soup and gave it back; his stomach simply did not function any longer. Many Kittever Jews died of hunger at that time. The candidates for death by starvation, awaiting their horrible end, envied the murdered Jews who were resting in the mass graves on the Pistin Mountain.

The price of grain on the black market rose from day-to-day.

[Page 149]

They paid more than $100 for 100kg of grain. It became impossible to bring grain in from the villages because the Ukrainian militia and the Germans guarded all the roads and confiscated every bit of grain that they caught. The black marketers then began to smuggle grain in from Romania. They also smuggled kerosene and were paid $3 a liter for it.

As a way of starving the barely breathing Jew even further, the Ukrainian city management ordered the mills to take 20% for the community every time they ground any grain. If a Jew managed to get a few kilos of grain from somewhere, he could not bring it to the mill. Beside this, there was the danger that the first Ukrainian or German who came across a Jew with a little grain, would immediately take it away. Wishing to avoid these highway-robbers, Jews ground the grain themselves in coffee-grinders or other types of small mills.

I myself, for example, set up a meat-grinder and together with my family, I would, during a whole week, grind the flour for bread. Grinding the grain on this mill took a long time – 1 kilo took a whole hour. The work was hard and one lost one's health at it. Until you saw a little flour for a small loaf of bread, you were bathed in sweat. Upon us was fulfilled the curse in the Chumash against Adam the first man: "By sweat of thy brow shalt thou eat bread".

## Chapter XXVIII

# The Juden-Aktion in Zablatov

At the end of November, 1941, we were terrified by the dreadful report which came from Zablatov, some 40km from Kittev, about the Juden-akzion there.

*[Page 150]*

In the morning of November 25th, there suddenly and unexpectedly arrived from Kolomei a row of trucks with Gestapo and SS men and also a gang of Polish students. With the help of the local Ukrainians, they blocked all the streets and fanned out over the Jewish homes driving the Jews en masse outside the town where the Ukrainian murderers had already prepared mass graves. The Germans, as in other cities, shot the Jews and threw them into the pits. The Polish students helped them in this mass murder.

Just one fact will suffice to allow one to comprehend the great tragedy of the Jewish Holocaust in Zablatov. On the day of the Juden-akzion in Zablatov, many Jewish men were doing forced labour building a bridge. Over this bridge, the murderers drove the victims on their final journey. The Jewish husbands, fathers and brothers who were doing slave labour at the bridge had to look on as their dearest and most beloved were taken to the slaughter and with tightly closed lips and fainting countenance and extinguished eyes, they sent their last glances towards these martyrs.

In Zablatov, the murderers spared the Jews who were working for them, for the time being. In other cities, including Kittev, they even took the Jewish workers and shot them all.

The number of Jews killed during the first Juden-akzion in Zablatov was comparatively "small", about 50%. This is because the Jews expected the disaster and many hid themselves.

After the akzion in Zablatov, the Jews of Kittev expected the coming of the murderers. They could no longer flee to the woods because snow had fallen and the footsteps would betray. Very few Jews had the necessary sums to pay Christians of their acquaintance to conceal them. So the Jews began to dig stealthily, in secret, various hiding places in their own dwellings. Neighbours and acquaintances told one another their plans and helped each other in digging pits and holes. The work was mainly done at night when the Ukrainian militia men and the Judenrat representatives left the Jew alone and did not visit him at home.

*[Page 151]*

## Chapter XXIX

# The Juden-Akzion in Zshabieh

On December 15, 1941, the Ukrainian community leadership of Zshabieh informed the Jews of Zshabieh that, by command of the German forces, they had to set up a ghetto for them. They commanded that all the Jews should, during one day, move to Krasnik – a village near Zshabien. When the Jews went to Krasnik, their possessions were immediately looted by the Ukrainian Hutzuls because the Ukrainians only allowed the Jews of Zhabieh to take along portable items. They also guarded the Jews so that no one could flee.

The Jews of Zshabieh immediately sensed the arrival of their end. Many of them were strong mountain Jews who knew no fear and they broke through the ring of Ukrainian and Hutzul guards and fled into the forests. But only some of them succeeded in saving themselves in the forests. Many of them were caught by the Hutzuls and brutally murdered with axes and knives.

When the Ukrainian militia had driven all the Jews into Krasnik and imprisoned them in the villa of the Jew, Kamill, they phoned the Gestapo in Kolomei and reported that they could now come and do their work.

*[Page 152]*

On the night of the fearsome murder of the Jews of Zshabieh, Feige Shpigel of Krasnik, a brave and beautiful girl, asked permission of the murderers to let the Jewish men, who were separated from the women, bid farewell to their wives and children. At dawn, before they jumped into the pits where they were murdered, the women put white kerchiefs on their heads. Feige Shpigel, who led the column of women, encouraged them and asked them not to weep or scream. Feige was the first to jump into the pit and to fall from the murderous bullet.

Among the Jewish women in Zshabieh was the old Jewish mother, Pelzel. She asked to be surrounded by her five daughters and thus, lying in their midst, the mother and her daughters perished.

The Zshabieh Juden-akzion took place on Thursday the 4th day of Hanukkah, 1941. After the Juden-akzion in Zshabieh, the burgomaster of the surrounding villages got together, drove "their" Jews to Kolomei and turned them over to the Gestapo who shot all of them to death in the Sheperovitz forest.

### Chapter XXX

# The Final Weeks Before the Juden-Akzion in Kittev

After the Juden-akzion in Zshabieh and after all the surrounding villages became "Judenrein", the Kittever Jews sensed that their turn was coming. No miracles would prevent the Holocaust; they would have to share the fate of the other Jewish communities.

Remarkable how, under the shadow of death and those horrible days and nights, part of the Jews of Kittev, especially the religious classes, were ruled by some mystical feeling – a religious psychosis – and started to believe and hope for a miracle. In the very fact that the murderers had spared Kittev thus far, they saw God's hand. Jews began to refer to various dreams and signs which supposedly hinted that our city would be saved from the Nazi Angel of Death.

*[Page 153]*

Every Monday and Thursday, the grave of Reb Moshe'le in the cemetery was besieged by Jews who prayed the Tsaddik to be an intercessor for them and save them from the horrible death. Kittever Jews told one another a bizarre dream that the Kittever Llui (prodigy of Torah study) Shmuelik ben Reb Rafael Shochet had dreamed. Shmuelik dreamt that Reb Moshe'le Feier, the Lamed-Vovnik, appeared to him and gave him the message that the Jews of Kittev should prepare for a great Simchah which would take place on the Chamishah Asar B'-Shevat (15th of Shevat, the New Year of the Trees). Even the Christians had heard about this dream and were awaiting the day along with the Jews.

However, the majority of the Kittever Jews were not carried along by the dream and understood that we were not favourites to the Master of the Universe. And that is what happened to Polish Jewry as whole, would happen to us all. We started to prepare ourselves; to stand guard so that the murderers at least would not catch us by surprise. We built and fortified underground hideaways to hide in when the dreadful hour would strike.

In my dwelling, I dug a pit two cubit square and made wooden benches to seat ten to twelve persons. I prepared a full pail of water and food for two or three days. The pit could be entered through a cupboard which stood above. When the cupboard doors opened and the bottom removed, there was an opening through which one person could squeeze. Under the cover of the opening there was a small ladder by which one could descend into the living grave. Once inside, standing on the ladder, one could close the cupboard from inside. The bottom was then replaced and thus we could secure ourselves. Air for breathing was obtained through a small hole which was hollowed out in the wall and was covered by a prisbe.. This was our place of rescue. When the fortress was completed, I timed, with a clock in hand, how long it took for a person to climb down into the pit. This was done at night. We tested several times how long it took our whole family of twelve persons to crawl into the pit and close the floor and the cupboard doors after us.

*[Page 154]*

We then started to keep watch every night. In daylight, one could see if the murderers were arriving, but at dark when it was forbidden for a Jew to go outside, it was hard to keep watch. Every two hours, a different man posted himself at the window and checked what was going on outside. In this way, we could, at a few minutes' notice, hide in the pit. In this way and in similar ways, the Jews of Kittev made plans for hiding from the murderers.

But, as mentioned before in those horrible winter months of 1941-1942, not all the Jews of Kittev were bound so tightly to life as to look for every means of hiding and saving their lives. There were many Jews who completely despaired of life, who in their great suffering of hunger and cold were waiting for the murderers to come and release them from starvation and suffering. The dreadful hunger and merciless cold cut down lives every day. The fields lay covered with a thick layer of snow and a starving Jew could not even dig up a beet or a radish to fill his empty stomach. From the dwellings, everything had been robbed. There was nothing that could be bartered for with a peasant, for bread or a couple of potatoes. The few pieces of furniture, a table, a bench, a wooden bedstead, a noddle board – all had been burned long ago to warm the emaciated, frozen body and limbs. Of a population of 2500 Jews, in those dreadful winter days, five or six Jews expired daily from hunger and cold.

*[Page 155]*

As in other cities, the Judenrat in Kittev attempted to alleviate the need of the starving mass of Jews. They established a public kitchen which gave a free meal once a day. The meal consisted of boiled water with a small potato and a sprinkling of flour. The public kitchen was located in the High Bet Midrash because of the fifteen prayer-houses, people davened secretly only in two. The others were deserted because the Germans did not allow Jews to assemble in public places. The Judenrat of Kolomei was the first to send in a few bags of potatoes to Kittev and a few Kittever Jews who still possessed something, contributed to the public kitchen.

In February, 1942, the Germans proclaimed a campaign (akzion) for wool. Representatives of the Judenrat went from house-to-house and demanded a certain amount of wool from every Jew. From the gathered wool, the Jewish women and girls who were doing forced labour for the Germans, knitted gloves and socks for the German Wehrmacht. Besides this, the women had to do the hardest and dirtiest service for the Germans and haul boards from the Kittever saw mills to Kossev on wheelbarrows.

The Kossev Judenrat fixed up several large villas for the Gestapo and its headman, the 26-year-old Falkman, several large villas in which the executioner settled his mother and bride who had come from Germany for their summer vacation. Falkman showed them around the city, took them to the huge mass graves on the Pistin Mountain and bragged to them on how thoroughly he had solved the "Juden problem".

The material for the villas was provided by the Kittever saw mills. Since all horses and wagons had been taken away from the Jews by the Germans in August, 1941, and they did not want to hire a Christian wagon-driver for money, the Kittev Judenrat borrowed wheelbarrows from the Ukrainian militia and harnessed the Jewish women and girls to haul the loads of boards from Kittev to Kossev.

*[Page 156]*

The attitude of the Ukrainian population of Kittev toward the Kittever Jews was inhuman and treacherous. Not only did the young Ukrainian nationalists collaborate and help the Germans to rob and murder the Jews, but even the older Ukrainians who had lived as close neighbours with the Jews for many years and did business with them, betrayed the Jews in those fateful days to their deadly enemy.

At first, when the Germans separated the Jews and forbade them to come in contact with non-Jews, the Ukrainians secretly sold grain and other products to the Jews for exorbitant prices. But later, when the Germans began their plundering and Jews entrusted their possessions to the Ukrainians and Poles, they happily took it with the objective of inheriting it. When the bloody Juden-akzions began and the Jews ran to those same Ukrainians and Poles to hide, they would not let the Jews into the house and those whom they did admit, they later betrayed into the murderers' hands. In September, 1942, when the Germans had made the whole area Judenrein and a few Jews were hiding out or trying to slip into Romania, the Ukrainians themselves liquidated them.

It is important to relate how the three priests of Kittev acted toward the Jewish population at the time that the Ukrainians wanted to make certain that not one living Jewish witness should remain.

The Polish priest, Samuel, was a big anti-Semite all his life. The Jews knew that they could not expect anything good from him.

*[Page 157]*

He had not even one good word for Jews and never tried to influence his obedient Poles to show sympathy to their Jewish fellow citizens.

The Ukrainian priest, Mikitiuk was known before the war as a decent person. Until the invasion by the Nazis, he lived in amity with the Jews of Kittev. He even had good friends among Jews. In the spring of 1941, when the Soviets wanted to send him to Siberia as a Ukrainian nationalist leader, a Jewish neighbour of his, Zaide Mandel, saved him. Risking his own life, he hid and fed Mikitiuk for three months until the Soviets left.

In the dreadful winter months of 1941-1942, when Kittever Jews were dying of hunger and cold, this same Mikitiuk priest shamelessly sermonized in the Ukrainian church every Sunday and warned his listeners not to dare sell food to a Jew or hide Jews. "The Jews", he said "are a cursed people. God Himself doesn't want to help them. You see", he concluded "how the German murder them en masse and God doesn't take their part. On the contrary, the Germans win one victory after another".

The only priest in Kittev who not only acted with sympathy and feeling toward the Jews but also had the courage to solidarize himself with the Jews was the Armenian priest, S. Maniugevitch. He spoke at every opportunity in the Armenian church and called on the Christians to help the Jews in their struggle for their lives. He called on his Armenians (Timches) (this is a nickname for Armenians used in Galicia) to sell food to the Jews and give them all possible support. The priest himself risked his life and hid Jews and fed them. He also hid, in his own place, a large number of Torah scrolls and saved them from the fire. To this day, the Torah scrolls must be in the house of the Armenian priest in Kittev.

*[Page 158]*

The Timchech priest, S. Maniugevitch, was the only Christian leader in Kittev who truly and with his whole heart and soul, wished to help the Jews of Kittev. None other than the Amalekite of Kittev, truly and legitimately deserved to be named as one of the Righteous Among the Gentiles.

## Chapter XXXI

# The Last Bloody Final Day of Passover (Achron shel Pesach) in Kittev

In the history of the Jewish community of Kittev, the Achron Shel Pesach (last day of Passover) of the year 1942, will remain a day of remembrance engraved in blood; the city's day of mourning when all the houses of prayer were destroyed. The Torah scrolls were burned, and 950 Jews were murdered by the German and Ukrainian murderers.

Prior to that Pesach when the fearsome famine raged and people died of hunger and cold, the Kittever Rabbi permitted us to eat flat rolls of maize on Pesach and permitted the grinding and baking of the rolls even during Chol Hamoed (the intermediate days of Passover). Any Jew who still possessed a garment or other valuable which he could, at risk of his life, barter with a peasant for a couple of kilos of wheat, the Rabbi permitted him (declared it permissible under Jewish law) to grind the wheat even in a coffee mill and bake a few matzos. But many Jews conducted the Seder with just a few potatoes and a beet. One's heart was torn from grief and pity seeing how elderly Jews, former businessmen, artisans, wagon drivers, emaciated and pale little Jewish children, knocked on doors and pleaded for a piece of matzo, a potato or even some potato peel.

Still, despite all the tragic conditions, large numbers of Kittev Jews exhibited a remarkable religious devotion. Such was the religious zeal that it was reminiscent of our ancestors of the dark Middle Ages, in the shadow of the Inquisition and the Pyres, when they jumped into the flames with Shema Yisrael on their lips.

*[Page 159]*

These pious Kittever Jews, whose lives hung by a hair, who were more enslaved than their ancestors in ancient Egypt – these same Jews in the Seder night of 1942, sat behind chained doors and like prices: "over goblets of borsht and matzos of bran", recited the old-new Haggadah and sang the ancient Jewish Marsellaise: "Avodim hayinu" - - once we were slaves and we were liberated from slavery - -

When the Nazi fiends entered the Vizshnitzer Klaus on the morning of Achron shel Pesach, they found Jews who looked more of the spirit than of the flesh, reciting Hallel with great ardour and much pathos. With heads held high, the Kittever Jews went to their death. A congregation of Sabbath-Yom Tov Jews, their eyes sparkling with fire and their souls beaming rays of light, and on their lips hovered the "Shema Yisrael"!

I want to record here the disputation that I had with the last Kittever Rabbi, Reb Yehuda Leib Yentshes, may God avenge his blood. He was yet a young man, a great scholar and he sympathized with Zionism. I brought him a few potatoes for his family, and I expressed the opinion that we, the Jews of Kittev, should be more sinful than the Jews of Kossev and Kolomei who were now at rest in mass graves while we, whom the same fate awaited us, would still have to suffer the seven fires of Hell through slave labour and starvation. "Is not death better than to witness the women, children and old people walk about like shadows?" I asked the Rabbi. If this was called life, then how bad would death be?

*[Page 160]*

It is a great sin to speak thus – so the last Rabbi answered me: "One must not even think about it. We must thank and praise the One above for every hour of life. This is not the first time in Jewish history that various Hamans want to destroy the Jewish people. But it always ended with the defeat of the evil ones. We too must believe and hope that we will merit to live to see Hitler's downfall. Even if not all Jews will survive until the day of victory, some of us will surely survive". "We Jews", the young Rabbi said as a prophecy, "will come out of the Hitler fire and the ghettos and the death camps, purified and strengthened and will be worthy to witness the "return of the children to their domain". "Jews will return to Zion and will again live as free people in their own homeland".

The prophecy of the last Kittever Rabbi was fulfilled only partially. Israel was established after the victory over Hitler, but he himself, the Rabbi, did not live to see it. The Rabbi accepted all sufferings with love. After the Juden akzion in Kittev in which he was miraculously saved, he cut off his beard and went to break rocks in the streets so that he could stay in Kittev and live to see the day of victory. In September, 1942, the Rabbi was murdered together with his congregation.

During the first days of Pesach, reports reached us about renewed Juden akzions that the German murderers carried out intensively in the neighbouring larger cities. In Stanislav, the murderers surrounded the public kitchen in broad daylight and set it on fire burning to death hundreds, maybe thousands of Jews. Those who ran from the flames were shot. In Kolomei, they set fire to part of the ghetto and burned to death a few thousand Jews.

The first day of Chol Hamoed Pesach, the Kossev Judenrat invited the chairman of the Kittev Judenrat, Mr. Tillinger, to an urgent conference. What happened at the conference remained a secret. The Kittever representatives returned from Kossev dejected and would not say anything. The president, Tillinger, took the register of all the Kittever Jews and studied the names carefully. This was a bad sign which called forth various conjectures.

[Page 161]

Each Jew warned the other to be alert and expect the worst.

The 4th day of Chol Hamoed, April 8th, the Germans carried out Juden akzions in Pistin and Yablonov. Kittev remained the only city in the entire region that was left alone by the mass murderers up until then. Until the horrible and bloody Achron shel Pesach arrived.

On Thursday, April 10th, on a sunny spring day, the darkness of Egypt descended on the Jews of Kittev. On the streets, it was dreadfully still, the quiet before the storm. The older Jews went to daven in the Beth-Midrash and the younger ones went to their forced labour, to the border defence, to bridge building, repairing streets or to the saw mills.

At eight o'clock in the morning, the great commotion began. Via the road from Kossev, there arrived from Kolomei, four trucks filled with Gestapo and SS men. They drove to the market square. On arriving, they shot from machine guns at the passing Jews on the streets. As soon as the Gestapo appeared, there suddenly popped up as though from under the ground, a lot of Ukrainian militia from Kittev and from the area who had secretly been mobilized for the akzion.

Through all the roads, highways and paths, Ukrainians and Hutzuls streamed in. Also, the German border guard from the surrounding villages were hurriedly mobilized for the akzion. Like the black crows that come in flocks when they smell blood, so did the rabble of sadistic murderers' rush together for the rob-feast and the slaughter of the defenseless Jews of Kittev.

The Gestapo knew well about the various bunkers and holes where the Jews were hiding. They understood that shouting "Jew come out!" would not bring one Jew into their bloody paws. So, they set fire with hand grenades to all the Jewish houses in the ghetto streets and to the Great Synagogue and the prayer houses.

[Page 162]

They only spared the Jewish houses that bordered on the center of town and those that were close to Christians.

In just a few minutes, a sea of fire and clouds of smoke covered the Jewish streets. From the burning houses and crashing walls, screams and cries for help were heard from the choking and burning victims. The reports of the gunfire mixed together with the bestial roaring and wild shouts of the sadistic murderers who, on seeing their victims hooked, grew even wilder and more feral and brayed like stallions, yelling with furious joyful murderousness. They hurled living children into the flames of the blazing synagogues and prayer houses. They tortured Jewish women before killing them. Mocked and derided the Jews and blasphemed the Jewish God. They defiled and violated the Torah scrolls and trod on the holy books with their filthy boots.

The fire and flame – this hell for the Jewish population of Kittev and the devilish dance of the Gestapo, the SS and the Ukrainians, lasted a whole day. Many Kittever Jews who had hidden in their dug-outs were burned and buried under the ruins. Those who tried to save themselves from the burning fires by jumping off roofs, were shot by the Nazi or else dragged to Kolomei and sent from there to the gas chambers.

Those directing the destruction akzion were the chief of the district, Gestapo Leitritz and the sturm-fuhrers, Huber and Shmeler.

Among the Ukrainian militia, those especially excelling in brutality were the commander of the Kittev militia – the sadist, Matveyov from Brod and the head of the Ukrainian militia in Kossev, the Kittever, Ukrainian, Derezshitski. They murdered many Jews with their own hands.

The total of the blood Achron shel Pesach in Kittev was about 950 victims.

*[Page 163]*

We buried, in two huge mass graves in the Kittev cemetery, 190 men, 148 women and 82 children who were shot or burned to death. The rest remained buried under the ruins. On that Achron shel Pesach, the Jewish Kittev was utterly destroyed. Generations of effort and creativity, the Germans and Ukrainians destroyed and burned together with the productive folk and builders of the city.

## Chapter XXXII

# The Death March

On Friday, the day after the Juden akzion, the remaining Kittever Jews came out into the streets and gathered the corpses of the holy martyrs in order to bring them to Jewish burial. It is impossible to describe the scenes that played out on to the streets, running with Jewish blood and among the sunken ruins. Parents were gathering up the burned and charred limbs and body parts of their children. Kittever Jews lamented aloud and clung to the dead bodies of their former friends and relatives. I am not able to describe even a small part of the tragic horror. Today, sixteen years later, my whole body falls into a tremble if I just recall the final day of the holiday in the spring of 1942. I am certain that the other Kittever landsleit who witnessed these horrors will also never in their lives forget them.

Wandering on the blood-spattered streets where lamentations and wailing came from all sides, I met my neighbour, Moshe Neiman, carrying his 22-year-old son, Hershele, to the cemetery on a wheel barrow. He had been shot. I met the girl, Ruth Olesker, who was bringing the bodies of her shot-to-death parents, the well-known Zionist activist, Doctor Marcus Olesker and his wife. Jewish young men were carrying in sacks and on stretchers, the half-burned bodies of their friends and neighbours. I saw in the middle of the street, Meshulam Landwehr, lying opposite his house, shot. He lay face up. His eyes bulging with fear. I was afraid to close his eyes. His Ukrainian neighbours, the Uraks, were watching and laughing loudly. I also came across Shlomo Breger of Yablonitse, carrying the crippled body of his brother-in-law, Israel Dermer, whom the Ukrainians had beaten murderously before shooting him. In a gutter there were 3 bodies lying there, children of Yankel the carrier. The pool of blood in which they lay stuck them together so that they appeared as one body! I helped wrap in sacks and carry out the bodies of Zaide Fisher and his wife and children. They had been burned in their hiding place. I met the wife of my good friend Arthur Locker. When I asked where Arthur was, she led me to their burnt-out dwelling and showed me the bodies of her husband and her mother. To write down all the names, to describe the appearance of the holy martyrs and to tell how each one perished, would take up an entire book. Such a book would horrify every reader just as I am shuddering now on recalling these sights. Because of this, alone, I must limit myself and mention only a few cases from memory.

*[Page 164]*

I am not capable of describing even a small part of my experiences and my feelings of that day when I wandered around the ruins, among the burnt-down homes and prayer houses. I walked through the unforgettable Jewish streets and lanes of Kittev where I once went to Cheder, to Synagogue and where I spent the best years of my life. Some of the houses were still smouldering and the walls were spattered with blood. I stopped near the Great Synagogue and the Hasidic Bet-Midrash where, as a child, I davened with my father, may he rest in peace. Strew about here were torn and burnt holy books and prayer books. Across the Bet-Midrash, in a gutter, lay the bodies of the Shamess' wife and her children. But as I have said, my vocabulary is limited and I can't describe my experiences of that day. To do that, one has to be a Lamenter such as the prophet Jeremiah or a Bialik.

*[Page 165]*

On Friday, April 11th, the Gestapo ordered that all remaining Jews in Kittev had to go to the Kolomei ghetto within 24 hours. But the Gestapo had to postpone for a few months its plan for the complete liquidation of the Jews in Kittev because there was still a lot of menial labour in the city which the Jews had to do. First of all, it was necessary to clear away the collapsed ruins and bring the dead to Jewish burial. All of these things the Jews had to complete before being liquidated.

Therefore, on Saturday, April 12th, the Gestapo commanded that there may remain in Kittev only those Jews whose work permit was confirmed by the German labour office in Kossev and by the Gestapo.

The business of the work permits (cards) is a sad chapter. I will not dwell too much on the politics that various groups played with regards to this matter. The Kittev Judenrat made up its lists of work permits. The community council had its own lists and the other places where Jews did forced labour did the same. A regular commerce developed with work permits. Naturally, the names of the Jews who paid off were placed on the list first. Only after this, names of the other Jews who were able to work were entered.

In connection with the work permits, there also arose fictitious weddings. A single man or a widower whose wife had perished during the Juden akzion was permitted to register a girl or another Jewish woman as his wife, and as his wife, she was allowed to remain in Kittev. Parents could not remain on the basis that their children were working, however, under-age children (minors) could remain with their parents.

*[Page 166]*

Until the second black day for the Jews of Kittev came, the day of April 24th, 1942. On that day, on all roads leading to Kolomei from Kittev and the surrounding towns, there moved long columns of the death-sentenced Jews. That was the death-march – the march of the living dead.

In these death-caravans, there mostly were old people, sick women and children and also young men who, for various reasons, could not get permission to remain at work.

Some of the sick were carried in wheel-barrows which the Judenrat supplied. The rest dragged along on their weak and ailing feet. They took nothing with them because they had nothing left and anyhow, this was their final trip. The death-sentenced Jews had given up all hope. They knew that there was no way back. A few older Jews committed suicide because they didn't want their old bones to be buried in a strange place. They preferred to lie in the cemetery in Kittev rather than undergo torture in the Kolomei ghetto and then be gassed or buried in some pit deep in the forest.

Among those who committed suicide before the death-march to Kolomei were Reb Nissen Krumholtz and Reb Wolf Steinbrecher who hanged themselves. Reb Leizer Weiss fulfilled the wish of his old sick mother and poisoned her.

*[Page 166]*

## Chapter XXXIII

# The Final Road

Even before the Juden akzion in Kittev took place, a small group of Kittever Jews, considering the hopeless situation and witnessing the systematic extermination campaigns of the Nazi, decided that there was no chance of rescue for Jews under the German occupation. This group began to seek other ways to save their own and other Jewish lives.

From the Ukrainian blackmarket operators, the Jews learned that in Chernovitz, Romania, about 80km from Kittev, nearly 40,000 Jews were living. The Jews of Chernovitz had to wear the yellow patch, had to go to the market in certain set hours to buy supplies but were living in their own homes and living 'normally'. Acting on this information, a small group of Kittever Jews, young men and two days after the Juden-akzion, set out on the dangerous path of escaping to Romania. These young men were followed by a number of other Kittever Jews and were saved.

The trip to Romania was, understandably, extremely difficult and risky. Romania was Germany's ally. Not all the Jews who set out on this dangerous path succeeded in reaching Chernovitz. Some were killed by those who were guiding them across the border after they had robbed them. Others were caught by the Romanians and sent to the camps in Transnistria

*[Page 168]*

But, despite the danger, a small number of Jews managed to get to Chernovitz, survive the War and be saved from the Nazi death. Regrettably, only a few Jews seized the opportunity to smuggle themselves in Romania. The greater part of the Kittever Jews, especially those who remained in the city after April 24th, on the basis of their work certificates, were lulled by the respite hoping that the murderers would now leave them alone. Some even received letters from those who were saved in Chernovitz, warning them to get over to Romania. But the Kittever Jews responded that for now they were not being bothered and if the situation were to change for the worse, they would flee at the last minute. However, not the Jews but the German murderers decided when the last hour would strike against the Jews. When the final hour came, it was too late and there no longer was any rescue for the Jews.

As previously mentioned, after April 24th, 1942, only Jews who had work certificates remained in Kittev. From time-to-time, the German labour supervisor would conduct new registrations. Then, the Jews had to assemble at the appointed time in the market square and have their certificates checked. This is how it went on until September 7th, 1942.

On Monday, September 7th, the history of the Jewish community in Kittev really ended. On that day, the remaining Jews were driven out and walked their final road. Kittev became Judenrein. The 18 Jewish artisans whom the Germans had left in the city were liquidated two months later. Only three of these managed to save themselves: the tinsmith, Aaron Goldshmidt; the tailor, Moshe Elenbogen and the apothecary, Pavel Remmer.

The Germans made Kittev Judenrein in the following manner: On the appointed Monday, the murderers ordered a new registration for the Jews of Kittev. The Judenrat requested the Jews to come to the registration and come decently dressed in order to find favour in the eyes of the overlord . . . But not all the Jews of Kittev trusted this: 250 Jews crossed the Romanian border that night toward Vizshnitz and turned themselves in to the Romanian border guard. A number of Jews hid themselves. By the way, the Germans carried out this kind of 'final' registration in every city on one same day so that the Jews would not be able to communicate with each other.

*[Page 169]*

When the Jews assembled on that Monday with their families in the Kittev market square, the Gestapo and SS with the Ukrainian militia surrounded the place and drove the Jews like cattle to the slaughter, to the courtyard of the Pole Tustanovski on the Kossev road and locked them into the attic. 564 Jews came to the registration. A few elderly Jews who attempted to run away were shot.

Monday afternoon, the Germans also drove into the same courtyard the 250 Jews who had fled to Romania and the Romanian border guard had turned them over into the murderers' hands. The head of the final extermination action was the well-known sadist and murderer, Frost.

After penning the Jews into the big house, the whole mob – Germans and Ukrainians – set out among the houses to look for hidden Jews. In the dwelling of my brother-in-law, Meshik Liebergall, they found his 4-week old baby lying in the crib. The mother who had run to hide, had left the infant in its cradle so that the child would not give away the hiding place by crying. The man-beasts forced the miserable Jewish father to take the child along on the final trip to the dark abyss. The Germans and the Ukrainians arranged the last Jews of Kittev in rows: the men in the middle and the women and children at the sides and kept watch that no one could escape. Upwards to 800 Jews were driven out of Kittev on that September 7th.

In that last transport of the Kittev Jewish community, there were the Baal Tefillah (prayer-leader) and sweet singer, Yakir Knall, the son-in-law of Rafael Shochet.

*[Page 170]*

His father-in-law and mother-in-law, his wife Batiah and her brother Shmulik had perished during the first Juden akzion on April 10th. The only thing which Yakir took along on the final trip was a Machzor (High Holiday prayer book). The SS executioner asked him what he was carrying under his arm and he answered "a prayer book". The executioner then commanded him to sing so as to make the death march interesting. Yakir turned to the prayers of the Yom Kippur Neilah and began singing with such cries that could make the heavens tremble. He sang and keened all the way. If it is true that stones can weep, they must have been moved by the heart-rending and heaven-splitting cries. Nevertheless, the whole community of Kittever Jews were not saved by the merit of the prayer. Only two were saved: Yakir Knall and Zelig Tillinger. The entire community was murdered.

On September 8th, the Germans and Ukrainians drove the remaining Jews of the Kossev district into Kossev and the following day, took them to Kolomei where they were locked up in the prison courtyard. On September 10th, the sadist and murderer, Wiessman, posted himself with a rubber whip and sorted all the Jews. The weaker ones he commanded to be shot and the younger and stronger ones to be sent to the forced labour camp in Lemberg. The remaining Jews were packed into railroad cars – 250 to 300 per car – and transported to Belz. In the cars, many were suffocated or expired from hunger such as Mordecai Preminger and my cousin, Joseph Meltzer. The rest of the Jews were forced into the slaughter houses where they were killed by an electric current.

The Kittever young men whom the Germans had sent to the Yanover labour camp near Lemberg, died one-by-one, some from hunger, some from beatings and some from hard labour. Every morning before work, the murderers commanded them to run and whoever was too weak to run, they drew them down onto the sand and fired a bullet into his head. In November, 1943, the Nazis liquidated the Yanover camp and thus, the last Jews of Kittev perished along with the remaining Jews of the neighbouring cities.

*[Page 171]*

September 7th was also the last day for the Jews of Sniatin. They were also loaded into freight cars and transferred to Belz. A month later, the Nazi liquidated the Jews of Kolomei. On October 11th, the Germans and Ukrainians surrounded the Kolomei ghetto, took the Jews out and locked them into railroad cars en route to Belz. After the Jews of Kolomei were on their way to Belz, the Sturm-fuhrer Weissmann and the head of the security police, Hertel, demanded from the Judenrat 100 more Jews to shoot. They explained they had not seen any blood! Their helpers caught a hundred Jews and turned them over to the sadists who led them out to the chicken farm, made them lie on the ground and shot bullets into their throats.

The remaining 250 Jewish artisans in Kolomei were liquidated by the Germans on November 6th, 1942. On that day they also torched the entire ghetto, shot the Jews and threw them into the flames. Some they also took into the woods.

Thus the entire Jewish settlement of the whole region was destroyed. Thus, the Germans destroyed the largest Jewish community in Poland.

## Chapter XXXIV

# The Dead City Kittev – Without Jews

In April, 1944, I was in Kittev for the last time after the Germans had left.

*[Page 172]*

Before setting out into the great world to look for a place of rest for me and my family, I wanted to see my birthplace and say farewell to the old home. I wanted, for the last time, to inscribe in my memory the ghastly destruction of Kittev. I looked at the burned Jewish homes and prayer-houses, trod on the dear Jewish streets and alleys where, as a boy I had played, and where my buddies and I spun the most beautiful dreams of youth. The last Jew of Kittev was taking leave of the holy martyrs.

I came into the city at three in the afternoon and did not meet a living soul. Kittev without Jews looked like a dead city. Even the center, which had always been lively and noisy, was now still, dead as a cemetery.

The burned-out Jewish houses lay in ruins as they did two years ago except that now, they were overgrown with grass and weeds. The Jewish streets were covered with green wild grasses which grew so tall that they completely covered and screened everything. It was obvious that in the last two years, the Ukrainian bandits who had participated in the murder and plundering of the Jews, had not set foot in a Jewish street. They had feared the dead Jews more than the living. I tried to recollect who had lived in the houses and it seemed to me that I heard the spirits moving and their wings hovering among the ruins. I recalled the scene in I.L. Peretz's: "A Night on the Old Marketplace" where the spirits come out and sing: "The paths where we went walking have long been overgrown". I myself, one Jew in the dead city, appeared like a ghost who came back from the other world and could find no rest. There were moments when I could not be sure if I were alive or if it were my ghost that wandered in search of purification.

On my way to the Kittever cemetery, I met Kittever Ukrainians with their murderous faces. They saw me and stood petrified. The Ukrainian, called Trishchuk, even came up to me and touched me as if to convince himself that it was I. He crossed himself and ran away.

*[Page 173]*

At the cemetery, I found out that the Ukrainian murderers did not content themselves with helping to murder the living Jews, but they did not even leave the dead alone. They tore out many of the monuments from the graves and used the stones to fortify the banks of the Mlunubke (a small stream which drove the Kittever mills and sawmills).

I came to two mass graves, took off my shoes not wanting to tread on the soft green grasses and fresh white spring flowers which looked like a beautiful carpet over the two huge graves of the holy martyrs. I held my breath, that the rapid rhythm of my heartbeat should not disturb the holy peace of the place. Thus, I took leave of the martyrs with bowed head and trembling knees. I revived in my memory the names of all my family members and comrades who were in these holy mass graves and bade farewell to each one. It was a quiet farewell. I did not hear my own voice, only felt the whisper of my lips which moved silently. A light breeze bent the thin young trees to the earth and it seemed to me as if the holy souls were hovering in their branches and saying to me: "farewell!"

With a pained and heavy heart, I took leave of the holy ones. I wished to leave a sign that I, Yitzchak Eisig ben Chaim, the last Kittever Jew, had been there. But I soon noticed that the temporary tombstone that we had erected over the mass graves in April 1942 had also vanished. My heart sank within me with pain, and my hands curled into fists at this murderous infamy, but I was helpless to act. In a nearby garden, I tore out a white-painted board from a fence and dug it into the earth like a tombstone. On this board I wrote with black charcoal:

*[Page 174]*

**Here Rest the Kittever Holy Martyrs**
**Men, Women and Children**
**Who on April Tenth, 1942**
**Were by the German and Ukrainian Murderers**
**Cruelly Done to Death.**

**May Their Souls Be Bound in the Bond of Life**[1]

With this ended the history of the Jews in Kittev. Jewish Kittev lies in ruins. The Jews were murderously destroyed. The voices of Torah of the famous Rabbis and Rebbes of Kittev, of the Yeshivos and Cheders, of teachers and pupils, Cantors and Baalei Tefillah (non-cantorial prayer leaders), were silenced for eternity.

There remains only the dear memory of the holy martyrs and the mass graves and the remaining violated tombstones which were torn out and used to pave the roads of Kittev.

We swear that we will never forget them and ever keep their remembrance holy.

Upon the remaining murderers, Ukrainians and others who remained in Kittev, one wishes to invoke the words of the great prophet and 80aughter80, Jeremiah:

"Repay them according to the deeds of their hands. Give them sorrow of heart; thy curse unto them. Pursue them in wrath and destroy them from under the heavens of the Lord." (Quoted from "Lamentations" 3:64-66).

*Translator's footnote:*

1.    In the original, only the 5 Hebrew initials appear: Tav, Nun, Tsadi, Bet, Hai

[Page 175]

**Third Part:**

# The Names of the Holy Martyrs

[Page 175]

*[Page 176 Blank [Pages 177-203]*

# The Names of the Martyrs

## Transliterated by Judy Petersen

| Family name | First name | Maiden name | Gender | Martal status | Father's name | Mother's name | Name of spouse | Remarks | Page |
|---|---|---|---|---|---|---|---|---|---|
| **א** Alef | | | | | | | | | |
| ABASH | Shimshon | | M | | | | | | 177 |
| ABASH | | | M | | Shimshon | | | | 177 |
| ABASH | | | M | | Shimshon | | | | 177 |
| ABASH | | | M | | Shimshon | | | | 177 |
| ABASH | Yosel | | M | | | | | children | 177 |
| ABASH | | | F | married | | | Yosel | children | 177 |
| ABASH | Meir | | M | married | | | Chaya | 1 child | 177 |
| ABASH | Chaya | SHECHTER | F | married | | | Meir | 1 child | 177 |
| ABASH | Meshulam | | M | married | | | | children | 177 |
| ABASH | | | F | married | | | Meshulam | children | 177 |
| ABASH | | | F | | Meshulam | | | | 177 |
| ABASH | | | F | | Meshulam | | | | 177 |
| SHAPIRA | Hodye | ABASH | F | married | | | Avraham | 3 children | 177 |
| SHAPIRA | Avraham | | M | married | | | Hodye | 3 children | 177 |
| ABASH | Yente | | F | | | | | | 177 |
| ABASH | Moshe | | M | married | | | | 1 child | 177 |
| ABASH | | | F | married | | | Moshe | 1 child | 177 |
| | | ABISH | F | | Alter | | | and family; eldest daughter of Alter ABISH | 177 |
| | | ABISH | F | | Alter | | | and family; middle daughter of Alter ABISH | 177 |
| | | ABISH | F | | Alter | | | and family; youngest daughter of Alter ABISH | 177 |
| ABISH | Sheidl | | F | | | | | | 177 |

| | | | | | | | | | |
|---|---|---|---|---|---|---|---|---|---|
| ABISH | Perl | | F | | | | | | 177 |
| ABISH | Moshe | | M | married | | | Ipika | children | 177 |
| ABISH | Ipika | SCHER | F | married | | | Moshe | children | 177 |
| AUFSEHER | Moritz | | M | | | | | children | 177 |
| AUFSEHER | Channah | | F | | | | | children | 177 |
| AUFSEHER | Berl | | M | | | | | and his family | 177 |
| ALPERN | Moshe | | M | married | | | Meite | children | 177 |
| ALPERN | Meite | | F | married | | | Moshe | children | 177 |
| ALPERN | Berl | | M | | | | | | 177 |
| ALPERIN | Pesach | | M | | | | | | 177 |
| ALPERIN | Chaya Sarah | | F | | | | | | 177 |
| FRIEDMAN ANTLER | | | M | | | | | | 177 |
| ARAN | Kalman Leizer | | M | | | | | | 177 |
| ARAN | Yisrael Mendel | | M | married | | | | | 177 |
| ARAN | | | F | married | | | Yisrael Mendel | | 177 |
| ARAN | | | M | | Yisrael Mendel | | | eldest daughter of Yisrael Mendel ARAN | 177 |
| ARAN | | | M | | Yisrael Mendel | | | youngest daughter of Yisrael Mendel ARAN | 177 |
| ARAN | Leibtsche | | M | married | | | | children | 177 |
| ARAN | | | F | married | | | Leibtsche | children | 177 |
| ARAN | Menashe | | M | married | | | | children | 177 |
| ARAN | | | F | married | | | Menashe | children | 177 |
| ALTMAN | Moshe | | M | married | | | | | 177 |
| ALTMAN | | | F | married | | | Moshe | | 177 |
| GRAU | | ALTMAN | F | married | Moshe | | Wolf | eldest daughter of Moshe ALTMAN | 177 |
| GRAU | Wolf | | M | married | | | | | 177 |
| ALTMAN | | | M | | Moshe | | | eldest of the youngest sons of Moshe ALTMAN | 177 |

| | | | | | | | | | |
|---|---|---|---|---|---|---|---|---|---|
| ALTMAN | | | M | | Moshe | | | second of the youngest sons of Moshe ALTMAN | 177 |
| ALTMAN | Chaim | | M | | | | | | 177 |
| ALTMAN | Efraim | | M | | | | | | 177 |
| ALTMAN | Sarah | | F | | | | | | 178 |
| ALTMAN | | | F | | | Sarah | | | 178 |
| ALTMAN | | | F | | | Sarah | | | 178 |
| ALTBACH | Mordechai | | M | married | | | | 1 child | 178 |
| ALTBACH | | | F | married | | | Mordechai | 1 child | 178 |
| UNGAR | Mechele | | M | | | | | and his family; on the list is written "Mechele the tailor" | 178 |
| URHEBER | Shmuel | | M | married | | | | | 178 |
| URHEBER | | | F | married | | | Shmuel | | 178 |
| | | URHEBER | F | | Shmuel | | | and family; eldest daughter of Shmuel URHEBER | 178 |
| | | URHEBER | F | | Shmuel | | | and family; youngest daughter of Shmuel URHEBER | 178 |
| URHEBER | | | M | | Shmuel | | | eldest son of Shmuel URHEBER | 178 |
| URHEBER | | | M | | Shmuel | | | youngest son of Shmuel URHEBER | 178 |
| URHEBER | Yosef | | M | | | | | and his family | 178 |
| URHEBER | Yehuda Leib | | M | | | | | and his family | 178 |
| URHEBER | Soshe | | F | | | | | mother of Shmuel | 178 |
| ALESKER | | | M | married | | | | | 178 |
| ALESKER | | | F | married | | | | Doctor's wife | 178 |
| ALESKER | | | F | | | | | Doctor's daughter | 178 |
| ALESKER | Rut | | F | | | | | | 178 |
| ARENSTEIN | Hersch | | M | | | | | and his family | 178 |
| ARENSTEIN | Alter | | M | married | | | | | 178 |
| ARENSTEIN | | | F | married | | | Alter | | 178 |

| | | | | | | | |
|---|---|---|---|---|---|---|---|
| ARENSTEIN | | | M | | Alter | | | 178 |
| ARENSTEIN | Yosel | | M | | | | | 178 |
| ARENSTEIN | Litman | | M | married | | | | 178 |
| ARENSTEIN | | | F | married | | | Litman | 178 |
| ARENSTEIN | | | F | | Litman | | | eldest daughter of Litman EHRENSTEIN | 178 |
| ARENSTEIN | | | F | | Litman | | | youngest daughter of Litman EHRENSTEIN | 178 |
| ARENSTEIN | Elke | | F | | | | | 178 |
| ARENSTEIN | Pepi | | F | | | | | 178 |
| ARENSTEIN | Miriam | | F | | | | | 178 |
| ARENSTEIN | | | M | | | Miriam | | elder son of Miriam EHRENSTEIN | 178 |
| ARENSTEIN | | | M | | | Miriam | | younger son of Miriam EHRENSTEIN | 178 |
| ARENSTEIN | Zalman | | M | married | | | | children | 178 |
| ARENSTEIN | | | F | married | | | Zalman | children | 178 |
| ARENSTEIN | Menashe | | M | married | | | | children | 178 |
| ARENSTEIN | | | F | married | | | Menashe | children | 178 |
| ARENSTEIN | Munye | | M | married | | | | children | 178 |
| ARENSTEIN | | | F | married | | | Munye | children | 178 |
| ARINGER | Meir | | M | married | | | | 3 children | 178 |
| ARINGER | | | F | married | | | Meir | 3 children | 178 |
| ARINGER | Lifshe | | M | | | | | 178 |

ב Bet

| | | | | | | | |
|---|---|---|---|---|---|---|---|
| BALTUCH | Yosel | | M | | | | | 178 |
| BALTUCH | | | F | married | | | Yosel | 178 |
| BARTFELD | Chaim | | M | married | | | Edel | 178 |
| BARTFELD | Edel | | F | married | | | Chaim | 178 |
| BARTFELD | Leon | | M | | | | | 178 |
| BARTFELD | Esther | | F | | | | | 178 |
| BARTFELD | Shlomo | | M | married | | | Beile | children | 178 |

| BARTFELD | Beile | | F | married | | Shlomo | children | 178 |
|---|---|---|---|---|---|---|---|---|
| BARTFELD | Idel | | M | | | | | 178 |
| BARTFELD | Shmuel | | M | | | | | 178 |
| BARTFELD | Motye | | M | married | | | children | 178 |
| BARTFELD | | | F | married | | Motye | children | 178 |
| BARTFELD | Peretz | | M | married | | Devorah | children | 179 |
| BARTFELD | Devorah | | F | married | | Peretz | children | 179 |
| BARTFELD | Shmuel | | M | | | | | 179 |
| BARTFELD | Tzipe | | F | | | | | 179 |
| BARTFELD | Nisan | | M | married | | | children | 179 |
| BARTFELD | | | F | married | | Nisan | children | 179 |
| BRODER | Aba | | M | married | | Tzipora | children | 179 |
| BRODER | Tzipora | KOIFMAN | F | married | | Aba | children | 179 |
| BRODER | Penina | | F | | | | | 179 |
| BRODER | Yitzchak | | M | | | | | 179 |
| BARTEL | Leon | | M | married | | Sarah | children | 179 |
| BARTEL | Sarah | TILINGER | F | married | | Leon | children | 179 |
| BARTEL | Max | | M | | | | | 179 |
| BARTEL | Giza | | F | | | | | 179 |
| BERGMAN | Yeshayahu | | M | married | | | | 179 |
| BERGMAN | | | F | married | | Yeshayahu | | 179 |
| BERGMAN | | | M | | Yeshayahu | | | eldest son of Yeshayahu BERGMAN | 179 |
| BERGMAN | | | M | | Yeshayahu | | | middle son of Yeshayahu BERGMAN | 179 |
| BERGMAN | | | M | | Yeshayahu | | | youngest son of Yeshayahu BERGMAN | 179 |
| BERGMAN | Avraham | | M | | | | and his family | 179 |
| BERGMAN | Berl | | M | | | | and his family | 179 |
| BERGMAN | Leibele | | M | | | | | 179 |
| BERGMAN | | | F | | Leibele | | | 179 |
| BERGMAN | | | F | | Leibele | | | 179 |
| BERGMAN | | | F | | Leibele | | | 179 |

| | | | | | | | | | |
|---|---|---|---|---|---|---|---|---|---|
| BERGMAN | Sarah | | F | | | | | and family | 179 |
| BERGMAN | Batya | | F | | | | | and family | 179 |
| BERGMAN | Malka | | F | | | | | and family | 179 |
| BERGMAN | Berke | | M | married | | | Eidel | | 179 |
| BERGMAN | Eidel | | F | married | | | Berke | | 179 |
| BERGMAN | | | F | | Berke | Eidel | | | 179 |
| MESINGER | Etel | BERGMAN | F | married | | | Beno | children | 179 |
| MESINGER | Beno | | M | married | | | Etel | children | 179 |
| MESINGER | | | M | | Beno | Etel | | eldest son of Beno and Etel MESINGER | 179 |
| MESINGER | | | M | | Beno | Etel | | middle son of Beno and Etel MESINGER | 179 |
| MESINGER | | | M | | Beno | Etel | | youngest son of Beno and Etel MESINGER | 179 |
| BERGMAN | Bobie | | M | | | | | | 179 |
| BERGMAN | Juli | | F | | | | | | 179 |
| BERGMAN | Loni | | F | | | | | | 179 |
| BERGMAN | Moshe | | M | married | | | | 2 children | 179 |
| BERGMAN | | | F | married | | | Moshe | 2 children | 179 |
| BERGMAN | Chaim Zev | | M | | | | | and his family | 179 |
| BERGMAN | Leibtsche | | M | | | | | children | 179 |
| BERGMAN | Herschel | | M | married | | | | children | 179 |
| BERGMAN | | | F | married | | | Herschel | children | 179 |
| BOCHNER | Mordechai | | M | married | | | | | 179 |
| BOCHNER | | | F | married | | | Mordechai | | 179 |
| | | BOCHNER | F | | Mordechai | | | and her family; eldest daughter of Mordechai BOCHNER | 179 |
| | | BOCHNER | F | | Mordechai | | | and her family, second oldest daughter of Mordechai BOCHNER | 179 |
| | | BOCHNER | F | | Mordechai | | | and her family, third oldest daughter of | 179 |

| | | | | | | | | |
|---|---|---|---|---|---|---|---|---|
| | | BOCHNER | F | | Mordechai | | | Mordechai BOCHNER and her family, youngest daughter of Mordechai BOCHNER | 179 |
| BUKSENBAUM | Berta | | F | | | | | | 179 |
| BUKSENBAUM | | | F | | | Berta | | | 179 |
| BUKSENBAUM | | | F | | | Berta | | | 179 |
| BERGRIN | Yosel | | M | married | | | Rabtshe | 1 child | 179 |
| BERGRIN | Rabtshe | LAKER | F | married | | | Yosel | 1 child | 179 |
| BERGRIN | Itzikel | | M | married | | | Sheina Etel | children | 180 |
| BERGRIN | Sheina Etel | | F | married | | | Itzikel | children | 180 |
| BERGRIN | Mendel | | M | | | | | | 180 |
| BERGRIN | Avraham | | M | | | | | | 180 |
| BERGRIN | Chaya | | F | | | | | | 180 |
| BERNSTEIN | Reuven | | M | married | | | | 2 children | 180 |
| BERNSTEIN | | | F | married | | | Reuven | 2 children | 180 |
| BOYER? / BAUER? | Henrik | | M | married | | | | children | 180 |
| BOYER? / BAUER? | | | F | married | | | Henrik | children | 180 |
| BOR | Rivka | | F | | | | | and family | 180 |
| BOR | | | M | | | | | and his family; brother of Rivka BOR | 180 |
| BULLER | David Yosef | | M | married | | | | | 180 |
| BULLER | | | F | married | | | David Yosef | | 180 |
| BULLER | | | M | | David Yosef | | | | 180 |
| BULLER | Avraham | | M | married | | | | and his only child (daughter) | 180 |
| BULLER | | | F | married | | | Avraham | and her only child (daughter) | 180 |
| BULLER | Devorah | | F | married | | | | children, husband. It is likely that her surname is different. | 180 |
| BULLER | Roza | | F | | | | | and family | 180 |
| BULLER | Mina | | F | | | | | | 180 |

| | | | | | | | | | |
|---|---|---|---|---|---|---|---|---|---|
| BARAN | Leon | | M | married | | | Roize | 1 child | 180 |
| BARAN | Roize | MANDEL | F | married | | | Leon | 1 child | 180 |
| BULLER | Molye | | F | | | | | | 180 |
| BULLER | | | M | | | Molye | | | 180 |
| BULLER | Alter | | M | married | | | | | 180 |
| BULLER | | | F | married | | | Alter | and her daughters | 180 |
| SHITZ | Shprintze | BULLER | F | married | | | Monek | | 180 |
| SHITZ | Monek | | M | married | | | Shprintze | | 180 |
| SHITZ | | | F | | Monek | | | | 180 |
| KREIZLER | Devorah | BULLER | F | married | | | David | children | 180 |
| KREIZLER | David | | M | married | | | Devorah | children | 180 |
| BULLER | Itzik | | M | married | | | | children | 180 |
| BULLER | | | F | married | | | Itzik | children | 180 |
| BULLER | | | M | married | | | | father of Itzik BULLER | 180 |
| BULLER | | | F | married | | | | mother of Itzik BULLER | 180 |
| | | BULLER | F | | | | | and her family; 1st sister of Itzik BULLER | 180 |
| | | BULLER | F | | | | | and her family; 2nd sister of Itzik BULLER | 180 |
| BULLER | Anschel | | M | married | | | | | 180 |
| BULLER | | | F | married | | | Anschel | | 180 |
| BULLER | | | M | | Anschel | | | and his family | 180 |
| | | BULLER | F | | Anschel | | | and her family; elder daughter of Anschel BULLER | 180 |
| | | BULLER | F | | Anschel | | | and her family; younger daughter of Anschel BULLER | 180 |
| BIRNBOIM | Sheina Etel | | F | married | | | | 2 children, husband. It is likely that the surname is different. | 180 |
| BIRNBOIM | Yosel | | M | married | | | | | 180 |
| BIRNBOIM | | | F | married | | | Yosel | | 180 |

| BIRNBOIM | | | M | | Yosel | | | | 180 |
|---|---|---|---|---|---|---|---|---|---|
| BIRNBOIM | Avraham | | M | | | | | | 180 |
| | | BIRNBAUM | F | married | Avraham | | | children | 180 |
| | | | M | married | | | | Children. Son in law of Avraham BIRENBOIM. Wife's maiden name BIRENBAUM. | 180 |
| BIRNBERG | Moshe Meir | | M | | | | | and his family | 180 |
| BINEWERT | Yudel | | M | married | | | | | 180 |
| BINEWERT | | | F | married | | Yudel | | | 180 |
| | | BINEWERT | F | | Yudel | | | and her family; elder daughter of Yudel BINEWERT | 180 |
| | | BINEWERT | F | | Yudel | | | and her family; younger daughter of Yudel BINEWERT | 180 |
| BLAUKOPF | Sender | | M | married | | | | children | 180 |
| BLAUKOPF | | | F | married | | Sender | | children | 180 |
| BLAUKOPF | Fishel | | M | married | | | | children | 180 |
| BLAUKOPF | | | F | married | | Fishel | | children | 180 |
| BLAUKOPF | | | F | | | | | the mother of Fishel BLAUKOPF. | 180 |
| BLAUKOPF | Gitel | | F | | | | | | 180 |
| BUCHER | Munye | | M | | | | | | 180 |
| BUCHER | | | F | | | | | the mother of Munye BUCHER | 180 |
| BUCHER | | | F | | | | | the sister of Munye BUCHER | 180 |
| BLUMENSTEIN | Etel | | F | | | | | | 180 |
| BLUMENSTEIN | | | F | | Etel | | | | 180 |
| BLUMENSTEIN | | | M | | Etel | | | | 180 |
| BLUMENSTEIN | Feige | | F | | | | | | 181 |
| BLUMENSTEIN | Binyamin | | M | | | | | | 181 |

ג **Gimmel**

| GOTLIEB | Moshe | | M | married | Chaim | | Bobeleh | | 181 |
|---------|-------|--|---|---------|-------|--|---------|--|-----|
| GOTLIEB | Bobeleh | | F | married | | | Moshe | | 181 |
| GOTLIEB | | | F | | Moshe | Bobeleh | | | 181 |
| GOTLIEB | Hantzel | | F | | | | | | 181 |
| GOTLIEB | Leizer | | M | married | | | Regina | | 181 |
| GOTLIEB | Regina | | F | married | | | Leizer | | 181 |
| GOTLIEB | Moshe | | M | | Zalman | | | and his family | 181 |
| GOTLIEB | Moshke | | M | married | | | | 2 children | 181 |
| GOTLIEB | | | F | married | | | Moshke | 2 children | 181 |
| GOTLIEB | | | M | | | | | brother of Moshke GOTLIEB | 181 |
| GOTLIEB | Motye | | M | | | | | | 181 |
| GOTLIEB | | | F | | | | | mother of Motye GOTLIEB | 181 |
| GOTLIEB | | | F | | Motye | | | elder daughter of Motye GOTLIEB | 181 |
| GOTLIEB | | | F | | Motye | | | younger daughter of Motye GOTLIEB | 181 |
| GOTLIEB | | | F | | | | Naftali | and family | 181 |
| GOTLIEB | | | F | | Naftali | | | | 181 |
| GOTLIEB | | | M | | Naftali | | | | 181 |
| GOTLIEB | Binyamin | | M | married | | | | 1 child | 181 |
| GOTLIEB | | | F | married | | | Binyamin | 1 child | 181 |
| GOTLIEB | Koppel | | M | | | | | | 181 |
| GOTLIEB | Pinye | | M | married | | | | | 181 |
| GOTLIEB | | | F | married | | | Pinye | | 181 |
| GRINBERG | Yosel | | M | married | | | | | 181 |
| GRINBERG | | | F | married | | | Yosel | | 181 |
| GRINBERG | | | M | | Yosel | | | | 181 |
| GRINBERG | Velvel | | M | | | | | and his family | 181 |
| GRINBERG | Moshe | | M | | | | | and his family | 181 |
| GRINBERG | Alter | | M | married | | | | the name on the list—GRINBER– is apparently in error | 181 |
| GRINBERG | | | F | married | | | Alter | the name on the list—GRINBER– | 181 |

| | | | | | | | is apparently in error | |
|---|---|---|---|---|---|---|---|---|
| GRINBERG | | | F | | Alter | | the name on the list—GRINBER– is apparently in error | 181 |
| GRINBERG | Sima | | F | married | | | 1 child; mother and husband; it's not clear who she is; possibly the surname is different | 181 |
| GRINBERG | Chatzkel | | M | | | | and his family | 181 |
| GEIER | Mendel | | M | | | | and his family | 181 |
| GEIER | | | M | | Mendel | | elder son of Mendel GEIER | 181 |
| GEIER | | | M | | Mendel | | younger son of Mendel GEIER | 181 |
| GEIER | Shlomo | | M | | | | and his family | 181 |
| GEIER | Moshe | | M | | | | and his family | 181 |
| | Tzipe | GEIER | F | married | Alter | | 1 child | 181 |
| | | | M | married | | Tzipe | 1 child | 181 |
| GEIER | Elek | | M | married | | | | 181 |
| GEIER | | | F | married | | Elek | | 181 |
| GEIER | Gavriel | | M | married | | | | 181 |
| GEIER | | | F | married | | Gavriel | | 181 |
| GEIER | | | F | | Gavriel | | | 181 |
| | Klara | GEIER | F | married | | | children | 181 |
| | | | M | married | | Klara | children | 181 |
| GEIER | Munye | | M | | | | and his family | 181 |
| GEIER | Montzye | | F | | | | and family | 181 |
| GEIER | | | F | | | Eizik | | 181 |
| | | GEIER | F | | Eizik | | and her family. Eldest daughter of the wife of Eizik GEIER | 181 |
| | | GEIER | F | | Eizik | | and her family. Middle daughter of the wife of Eizik GEIER | 181 |

| | | | | | | | | |
|---|---|---|---|---|---|---|---|---|
| | | GEIER | F | | Eizik | | | and her family. Youngest daughter of the wife of Eizik GEIER | 181 |
| GEIER | Leibenyo | | M | | | | | and his family | 181 |
| GEIER | Dugye | | F | | | | | and family | 181 |
| GASTER | | | F | | | | Leizer | | 181 |
| | | GASTER | F | | Leizer | | | and her family; eldest daughter of Leizer GASTER | 181 |
| | | GASTER | F | | Leizer | | | and her family; 2nd daughter of Leizer GASTER | 181 |
| | | GASTER | F | | Leizer | | | and her family; 3rd daughter of Leizer GASTER | 181 |
| | | GASTER | F | | Leizer | | | and her 93aught; youngest daughter of Leizer GASTER | 181 |
| GASTER | | | M | | Leizer | | | eldest son of Leizer GASTER | 181 |
| GASTER | | | M | | Leizer | | | middle son of Leizer GASTER | 181 |
| GASTER | | | M . | | Leizer | | | youngest son of Leizer GASTER | 181 |
| GASTER | Yosef | | M | married | | | Losye | 1 child | 182 |
| GASTER | Losye | LANDMAN | F | married | | | Yosef | 1 child | 182 |
| GASTER | Hillel | | M | | | | | | 182 |
| GASTER | Aharon | | M | | | | | | 182 |
| GELLES | | | F | | | | Leibtsche | | 182 |
| | | GELLES | F | | Leibtsche | | | and her family; eldest daughter of Leibtsche GELLES | 182 |
| | | GELLES | F | | Leibtsche | | | and her family; 2nd daughter of Leibtsche GELLES | 182 |
| | | GELLES | F | | Leibtsche | | | and her family, 3rd daughter of Leibtsche GELLES | 182 |

| Surname | Given name | | Sex | Status | Father | | Spouse | Notes | Page |
|---|---|---|---|---|---|---|---|---|---|
| | | GELLES | F | | Leibtsche | | | and her family; youngest daughter of Leibtsche GELLES | 182 |
| GREBLER | Hersch | | M | married | | | | 2 children; on the list the surname is GREBELER; corrected from a Page of Testimony | 182 |
| GREBLER | | | F | married | | | Hersch | 2 children; on the list the surname is GREBELER; corrected from a Page of Testimony | 182 |
| GREBLER | Eizik | | M | married | | | | | 182 |
| GREBLER | | | F | married | | | Eizik | | 182 |
| GREBLER | Mendel | | M | | | | | | 182 |
| GREBLER | | | M | | Yudel | | | and his family; elder son of Yudel GREBLER | 182 |
| GREBLER | | | M | | Yudel | | | and his family; younger son of Yudel GREBLER | 182 |
| GERTNER | Mechel | | M | | | | | and his family | 182 |
| GERTNER | Yoel | | M | married | | | | children | 182 |
| GERTNER | | | F | married | | | Yoel | children | 182 |
| GERTNER | Moshe | | M | married | | | | children | 182 |
| GERTNER | | | F | married | | | Moshe | children | 182 |
| GOLDSCHMID | Itzik Shmuel | | M | married | | | | children | 182 |
| GOLDSCHMID | | | F | married | | | Itzik Shmuel | children | 182 |
| GOLDSCHMID | Chantzel | | F | | | | | | 182 |
| GOLDSCHMID | | | M | | | Chantzel | | | 182 |
| GOLDSCHMID | Solomon Feivish | | M | married | | | | | 182 |
| GOLDSCHMID | | | F | married | | | Solomon Feivish | | 182 |
| GOLDSCHMID | Sima | | F | | Solomon Feivish | | | | 182 |
| GOLDSCHMID | | | M | | Solomon Feivish | | | elder son of Solomon GOLDSCHMID | 182 |

| | | | | | | | | | |
|---|---|---|---|---|---|---|---|---|---|
| GOLDSCHMID | | | M | | Solomon Feivish | | | younger son of Solomon GOLDSCHMID | 182 |
| GOLDSCHMID | Avraham | | M | | | | | and his family | 182 |
| GENZLER | Devorah | | F | | | | | Lived on Todyev Street | 182 |
| GENZLER | | | F | | | | | Lived on Todyev Street. First sister of Devorah GENZLER | 182 |
| GENZLER | | | F | | | | | Lived on Todyev Street. Second sister of Devorah GENZLER | 182 |
| GENZLER | Feigele | | F | married | | | | 1 child, husband. Probably the surname is different. | 182 |
| GENZLER | Soshe | | F | | | | | and family | 182 |
| GENZLER | Alter | | M | | | | | and his family | 182 |
| GENZLER | | | F | | | | | sister of Alter GENZLER | 182 |
| GLATTER | David | | M | married | | | | | 182 |
| GLATTER | | | F | married | | | David | | 182 |
| | | GLATTER | F | | David | | | and her family, elder daughter of David GLATTER | 182 |
| | | GLATTER | F | | David | | | and her family, younger daughter of David GLATTER | 182 |
| GOLDAPPER | Herschel | | M | | | | | and his family | 182 |
| GOLDAPPER | Alter | | M | | | | | and his family | 182 |
| GOLDAPPER | Anschel | | M | | | | | and his family | 182 |
| GOLDSCHMID | Moshe | | M | | | | | and his family | 182 |
| GOLDAPPER | Anschel | | M | | | | | and his family | 182 |
| GOLDAPPER | Alter | | M | | | | | and his family | 182 |
| GOLOPER | Herschel | | M | | | | | and his family | 182 |
| GLAZBERG | Tatke | | M | married | | | | | 182 |
| GLAZBERG | | | F | married | | | Tatke | | 182 |
| | | GLAZBERG | F | | Tatke | | | and family; eldest daughter of Tatke GLAZBERG | 182 |

| Surname | Given | Surname2 | Sex | Status | | Spouse | Notes | Page |
|---|---|---|---|---|---|---|---|---|
| | | GLAZBERG | F | | Tatke | | and family; youngest daughter of Tatke GLAZBERG | 182 |
| GLAZBERG | | | M | | Tatke | | elder son of Tatke GLAZBERG | 182 |
| GLAZBERG | | | M | | Tatke | | younger son of Tatke GLAZBERG | 182 |
| GLAZBERG | Berl | | M | | | | | 182 |
| GLAZBERG | Tonye | | M | married | | Rakhel | 1 child | 182 |
| GLAZBERG | Rakhel | HUTTERER | F | married | | Tonye | 1 child | 182 |
| GLAZBERG | Pitzye | | M | married | | Rakhel | | 182 |
| GLAZBERG | | | F | married | | Pitzye | | 182 |
| GLAZBERG | Dugye | | M | | | | and his family | 183 |
| GLAZBERG | Hersch | | M | married | | | | 183 |
| GLAZBERG | | | F | married | | Hersch | | 183 |
| GRAU | Wolf | | M | married | | | | 183 |
| GRAU | | | F | married | | Wolf | | 183 |
| GRAU | | | M | | Wolf | | | 183 |
| GRAU | Leibtsche | | M | | | | | 183 |
| GRAU | Wolf | | M | married | | | Lived on Todyev Street | 183 |
| GRAU | | | F | married | | Wolf | Lived on Todyev Street | 183 |
| GRAU | | | M | | | | father of Wolf GRAU | 183 |
| | | GRAU | F | married | | | and her family, sister of Wolf GRAU | 183 |
| GRAU | Ezra | | M | married | | | | 183 |
| GRAU | | | F | married | | Ezra | | 183 |
| GRAU | | | M | | Ezra | | | 183 |
| | | GRAU | F | | Ezra | | and family | 183 |
| GRAU | Shimshon | | M | | | | and his family | 183 |
| GRAU | Yosel | | M | | | | and his family | 183 |
| GRAU | Zeide | | M | | | | and his family | 183 |
| GLICKSTERN | Fishel | | M | married | | | | 183 |

| GLICKSTERN | | | F | married | | | Fishel | | 183 |
|---|---|---|---|---|---|---|---|---|---|
| GLICKSTERN | | | M | | Fishel | | | | 183 |
| GLICKSTERN | Shmuel | | M | | | | | and his family | 183 |
| GLICKSTERN | | | F | | Shmuel | | | | 183 |
| SHPINER | Danya | GLICKSTERN | F | married | | | Avraham | children | 183 |
| SHPINER | Avraham | | M | married | | | Danya | children | 183 |
| GOTHERTZ | Yente | | F | | | | | | 183 |
| GOTHERTZ | | | F | | | Yente | | elder daughter of Yente GOTHERTZ | 183 |
| GOTHERTZ | | | F | | | Yente | | younger daughter of Yente GOTHERTZ | 183 |
| GOTLIEB | Shimon | | M | | | | | and his family | 183 |
| GOLDSCHMID | Leizer | | M | | | | | and his family | 183 |
| GRINBLAT | Channah | | F | | | | | | 183 |
| | Hodye | GRINBLAT | F | | | Channah | | and family | 183 |

ד **Dalet**

| DOLOR | Aharon | | M | married | | | | | 183 |
|---|---|---|---|---|---|---|---|---|---|
| DOLOR | | | F | married | | | Aharon | | 183 |
| DOLOR | | | M | | Aharon | | | eldest daughter of Yisrael Mendel ARAN | 183 |
| DOLOR | | | M | | Aharon | | | youngest daughter of Yisrael Mendel ARAN | 183 |
| | | DOLOR | F | | Aharon | | | and family | 183 |
| DRUCK | Moshe Yehuda | | M | | | | | and his family. from Slobodka | 183 |
| DRUCK | Yosel | | M | | | | | and his family. from Kabaky | 183 |
| DRUCK | Pesach | | M | married | | | Rivka | | 183 |
| DRUCK | Rivka | | F | married | | | Pesach | | 183 |
| DRUCK | | | F | | Pesach | Rivka | | | 183 |
| DRUCK | Esther | | F | | | | | | 183 |
| DRUCK | Litman | | M | married | | | Reina | | 183 |
| DRUCK | Reina | | F | married | | | Litman | | 183 |

| | Blume | DRUCK | F | married | Litman | Reina | Noach | 2 children | 183 |
|---|---|---|---|---|---|---|---|---|---|
| | Noach | | M | married | | | Blume | 2 children | 183 |
| DRUCK | | | M | | Litman | Reina | | eldest son of Litman and Reina DRUCK | 183 |
| DRUCK | | | M | | Litman | Reina | | 2nd son of Litman and Reina DRUCK | 183 |
| DRUCK | | | M | | Litman | Reina | | 3rd son of Litman and Reina DRUCK | 183 |
| DRUCK | | | M | | Litman | Reina | | youngest son of Litman and Reina DRUCK | 183 |
| DRUCK | Zintsche | | M | married | | | | children | 183 |
| DRUCK | | | F | married | | | Zintsche | children | 183 |
| DRUCK | Shlomo | | M | married | | | | children | 183 |
| DRUCK | | | F | married | | | Shlomo | children | 183 |
| DRUCK | Alter | | M | | | | | | 183 |
| DRUCK | Moshe | | M | | | | | | 183 |
| DRUCK | Moshe | | M | married | Mendel Leib | | | 1 child | 183 |
| DRUCK | | | F | married | | | Moshe | 1 child | 183 |
| DRUCK | Rivka | | F | | | | | | 183 |
| DRUCK | | | M | | | Rivka | | eldest son of Rivka DRUCK | 183 |
| DRUCK | | | M | | | Rivka | | middle son of Rivka DRUCK | 183 |
| DRUCK | | | M | | | Rivka | | youngest son of Rivka DRUCK | 183 |
| DRUCK | Mendel | | M | married | | | | children | 184 |
| DRUCK | | | F | married | | | Mendel | children | 184 |
| DRUCK | Shlomo | | M | married | | | | children | 184 |
| DRUCK | | | F | married | | | Shlomo | children | 184 |
| DRUCK | Efraim | | M | married | | | | children | 184 |
| DRUCK | Unknown | | F | married | | | Efraim | 3 daughters and their families | 184 |
| DRUCKMAN | Reina | | F | | | | | | 184 |
| DRUCKMAN | | | F | | | Reina | | elder daughter of Reina DRUCKMAN | 184 |

| Surname | Given | Surname2 | Sex | Status | Father | Mother | Spouse | Notes | Page |
|---|---|---|---|---|---|---|---|---|---|
| DRUCKMAN | | | F | | | Reina | | younger daughter of Reina DRUCKMAN | 184 |
| SCHERF | Beile | DRUCKMAN | F | married | | | Shlomo | | 184 |
| SCHERF | Shlomo | | M | married | | | Beile | | 184 |
| LUSTIK | Yocheved | DRUCKMAN | F | married | | | Menye | | 184 |
| LUSTIK | Menye | | M | married | | | Yocheved | | 184 |
| LUSTIK | Toibele | | F | | Menye | Yocheved | | | 184 |
| LUSTIK | Mendel | | M | | Menye | Yocheved | | | 184 |
| DRUCKMAN | Yehoshua | | M | | | | | | 184 |
| DRUCKMAN | | | M | | Yehoshua | | | elder son of Yehoshua DRUCKMAN | 184 |
| DRUCKMAN | | | M | | Yehoshua | | | younger son of Yehoshua DRUCKMAN | 184 |
| DRUCKMAN | Berl | | M | married | | | | 1 child | 184 |
| DRUCKMAN | | | F | married | | | Berl | 1 child | 184 |
| DRUCKMAN | Gavriel | | M | | | | | | 184 |
| DRUCKMAN | Sarah | | F | | | | | | 184 |
| DRUCKMAN | | | F | | | Sarah | | | 184 |
| DRUCKMAN | | | M | | | Sarah | | eldest son of Sarah DRUCKMAN | 184 |
| DRUCKMAN | | | M | | | Sarah | | 2nd son of Sarah DRUCKMAN | 184 |
| DRUCKMAN | | | M | | | Sarah | | 3rd son of Sarah DRUCKMAN | 184 |
| DRUCKMAN | | | M | | | Sarah | | 4th son of Sarah DRUCKMAN | 184 |
| DRUCKMAN | | | M | | | Sarah | | youngest son of Sarah DRUCKMAN | 184 |
| DRUCKMAN | Motl | | M | married | | | | children | 184 |
| DRUCKMAN | | | F | married | | | Motl | children | 184 |
| DRUCKMAN | Chaim | | M | married | | | | children | 184 |
| DRUCKMAN | | | F | married | | | Chaim | children | 184 |
| DRUCKMAN | Yosel | | M | married | | | | children | 184 |
| DRUCKMAN | | | F | married | | | Yosel | children | 184 |

| DRUCKMAN | Itsche | | M | married | | | | children | 184 |
|---|---|---|---|---|---|---|---|---|---|
| DRUCKMAN | | | F | married | | | Itsche | children | 184 |
| DRUCKMAN | Baruch Hersch | | M | | | | | | 184 |
| DRACH | Yosel | | M | | | | | and his family | 184 |
| DRACH | Chaim | | M | married | | | | 2 children | 184 |
| DRACH | | | F | married | | | Chaim | 2 children | 184 |
| | | DRACH | F | | | | | and her family, 1st sister of Chaim DRACH | 184 |
| | | DRACH | F | | | | | and her family, 2nd sister of Chaim DRACH | 184 |
| DEMNER | Neta | | M | married | | | | | 184 |
| DEMNER | | | F | married | | | Neta | | 184 |
| DEMNER | | | M | | Neta | | | elder son of Neta DEMNER | 184 |
| DEMNER | | | M | | Neta | | | middle son of Neta DEMNER | 184 |
| DEMNER | | | M | | Neta | | | younger son of Neta DEMNER | 184 |
| DEMNER | Hersch | | M | married | | | | children | 184 |
| DEMNER | | | F | married | | | Hersch | children | 184 |
| DEMNER | Yisrael | | M | married | | | | children | 184 |
| DEMNER | | | F | married | | | Yisrael | children | 184 |
| DEMNER | Chaim | | M | | | | | | 184 |
| DEMNER | Feivel | | M | married | | | | | 184 |
| DEMNER | | | F | married | | | Feivel | | 184 |
| DRECHSLER | Zelig | | M | married | | | Etel | | 184 |
| DRECHSLER | Etel | | F | married | | | Zelig | | 184 |
| DRECHSLER | Avetzye | | M | married | | | | | 184 |
| DRECHSLER | | | F | married | | | Avetzye | | 184 |
| DRECHSLER | | | F | | Avetzye | | | elder daughter of Avetzieh DRECHSLER | 184 |
| DRECHSLER | | | F | | Avetzye | | | younger daughter of Avetzieh DRECHSLER | 184 |

**ה** Hey

| HABER | Moshe | | M | married | | Chava | 2 children | 184 |
|-------|-------|--|---|---------|--|-------|------------|-----|
| HABER | Chava | | F | married | | Moshe | 2 children | 184 |
| HABER | Henye | | F | | | | | 184 |
| HABER | Roize | | F | | | | | 184 |
| HABER | Leibke | | M | married | | Leah | 2 children | 184 |
| HABER | Leah | | F | married | | Leibke | 2 children | 184 |
| HABER | Hesye | | F | | | | | 185 |
| HABER | Batya | | F | | | | | 185 |
| HABER | Efraim | | M | married | | | children. From Slobodka | 185 |
| HABER | | | F | married | | Efraim | children. From Slobodka | 185 |
| HABER | David | | M | married | | | children | 185 |
| HABER | | | F | married | | David | children | 185 |
| HABER | Yosel | | M | married | | | | 185 |
| HABER | | | F | married | | Yosel | | 185 |
| HABER | | | M | | Yosel | | | 185 |
| HABER | Wolf | | M | married | | | 2 children | 185 |
| HABER | | | F | married | | Wolf | 2 children | 185 |
| HABER | | | F | | Wolf | | | eldest daughter of Wolf HABER | 185 |
| HABER | | | F | | Wolf | | | middle daughter of Wolf HABER | 185 |
| HABER | | | F | | Wolf | | | youngest daughter of Wolf HABER | 185 |
| HABER | Leah | | F | married | | | and her husband. Her surname is probably different. Children. | 185 |
| HABER | Sonye | | F | married | | | and her husband. Her surname is probably different. Children. | 185 |
| HABER | Roza | | F | married | | | and her husband. Her surname is probably different. Children. | 185 |

| | | | | | | | | | |
|---|---|---|---|---|---|---|---|---|---|
| HABER | Leibele | | M | | Motyeche | | | on the list is written "of Motyeche" | 185 |
| HABER | | | F | | | | | sister of Leibele HABER | 185 |
| HABER | Sarah | | F | | | | | | 185 |
| HABER | | | F | | | Sarah | | | 185 |
| HAZENFRATZ | Moshe | | M | married | | | Sheina Reize | | 185 |
| HAZENFRATZ | Sheina Reize | | F | married | | | Moshe | | 185 |
| HAZENFRATZ | | | F | | Moshe | Sheina Reize | | | 185 |
| KANTOR | Gitel | HAZENFRATZ | F | married | | | Leib | | 185 |
| KANTOR | Leib | | M | married | | | Gitel | | 185 |
| KANTOR | Ella | | F | | Leib | Gitel | | | 185 |
| KANTOR | | | M | | Leib | Gitel | | eldest daughter of Leib and Gitel KANTOR | 185 |
| KANTOR | | | M | | Leib | Gitel | | middle daughter of Leib and Gitel KANTOR | 185 |
| KANTOR | | | M | | Leib | Gitel | | youngest daughter of Leib and Gitel KANTOR | 185 |
| HAZENFRATZ | Mendel | | M | | | | | | 185 |
| HAZENFRATZ | Eliezer | | M | | | | | | 185 |
| HAZENFRATZ | Zev Wili | | M | | | | | | 185 |
| HAZENFRATZ | Yudel | | M | | | | | | 185 |
| HAZENFRATZ | | | F | | Yudel | | | elder daughter of Yudel HAZENFRATZ | 185 |
| HAZENFRATZ | | | F | | Yudel | | | younger daughter of Yudel HAZENFRATZ | 185 |
| HAZENFRATZ | Sarah | | F | | | | | | 185 |
| HAZENFRATZ | Manye | | | | | | | | 185 |
| HAGER | | | F | | | | Shlomo | | 185 |
| | | HAGER | F | | Shlomo | | | and her family. Elder daughter of the wife of Shlomo HAGER | 185 |

| | | HAGER | F | | Shlomo | | | and her family. Younger daughter of the wife of Shlomo HAGER | 185 |
|---|---|---|---|---|---|---|---|---|---|
| HAGER | | | M | | Shlomo | | | | 185 |
| HAGER | Montz | | M | married | | | | children | 185 |
| HAGER | | | F | married | | | Montz | children | 185 |
| HAGER | Shalom | | M | | | | | | 185 |
| HAGER | Binyamin | | M | | | | | | 185 |
| HAMMER | Shimon | | M | married | | | | 4 children | 185 |
| HAMMER | | | F | married | | | Shimon | 4 children | 185 |
| HAMMER | Berl Leib | | M | married | | | | children | 185 |
| HAMMER | | | F | married | | | Berl Leib | children | 185 |
| HAMMER | Velvel | | M | married | | | | children | 185 |
| HAMMER | | | F | married | | | Velvel | children | 185 |
| HAMMER | Avraham | | M | married | Itsche | | | children | 185 |
| HAMMER | | | F | married | | | Avraham | children | 185 |
| HAMMER | Yosel | | M | | | | | and his family | 185 |
| HAMMER | Yakov | | M | | | | | and his family | 185 |
| HAMMER | Zalman | | M | | | | | and his family | 185 |
| HAMMER | Moshe Yakov | | M | | | | | and his family | 186 |
| HAMMER | Yisrael | | M | | | | | and his family | 186 |
| HALEM | Velvel | | M | married | | | | Baker. 2 children. | 186 |
| HALEM | | | F | married | | | Velvel | 2 children | 186 |
| HALEM | Moshe | | M | married | | | | Tailor. Children | 186 |
| HALEM | | | F | married | | | Moshe | children | 186 |
| HALEM | Chaikele | | F | | | | | | 186 |
| HALEM | | | F | | Chaikele | | | | 186 |
| HARNER | Mechele | | M | married | | | | children | 186 |
| HARNER | | | F | married | | | Mechele | children | 186 |
| HARNER | Chaim Mendel | | M | | | | | | 186 |
| HARNER | | | F | | Chaim Mendel | | | | 186 |
| HARNER | Bobeleh | | F | married | | | | children, husband. It is likely that her | 186 |

| | | | | | | | | | |
|---|---|---|---|---|---|---|---|---|---|
| | | | | | | | | surname is different. | |
| HARTENSTEIN | Sovorin | | M | married | | | | daughters and her family. Has title of Dr. | 186 |
| HARTENSTEIN | | | F | married | | | Sovorin | daughters and her family. Has title of Dr. | 186 |
| HALPERN | Mendel | | M | married | | | | | 186 |
| HALPERN | | | F | married | | | Mendel | | 186 |
| HALPERN | | | F | | Mendel | | | elder daughter of Mendel HALPERN | 186 |
| HALPERN | | | F | | Mendel | | | younger daughter of HALPERN | 186 |
| HALPERN | Feige | | F | | | | | | 186 |
| HALPERN | | | M | | | Feige | | | 186 |
| HIBSCHMAN | Reizl | HALPERIN | F | married | | | Moshe | 1 child | 186 |
| HIBSCHMAN | Moshe | | M | married | | | Reizl | 1 child | 186 |
| HALPERIN | Yebye | | M | | | | | | 186 |
| HALPERIN | | | F | | Yebye | | | | 186 |
| HALPERIN | Rivka | | F | married | | | | husband and son. Probably the surname is different. | 186 |
| HALPERIN | Yoel | | M | | | | | and his family | 186 |
| HALER | Dugye | | M | married | | | | | 186 |
| HALER | | | F | married | | | Dugye | | 186 |
| HALER | | | M | | Dugye | | | elder son of Dugye HALER | 186 |
| HALER | | | M | | Dugye | | | younger son of Dugye HALER | 186 |
| | | HALER | F | married | Dugye | | Zeide | 1 child | 186 |
| | Zeide | | M | married | | | | 1 child | 186 |
| HARNIK | Yakov Berush | | M | married | | | | 1 child | 186 |
| HARNIK | | | F | married | | | Yakov Berush | 1 child | 186 |
| HARNIK | | | F | | | | | sister of Yakov Berush HARNIK | 186 |
| HARNIK | Sheindel | | F | married | | | | husband and 1 child. Probably | 186 |

| | | | | | | | | |
|---|---|---|---|---|---|---|---|---|
| | | | | | | | the surname is different. | |
| HUTTERER | Fishel | | M | | | | and his family | 186 |
| HUTTERER | Tzipe | | F | | | | | 186 |
| HUTTERER | Zeide | | M | married | | | | 186 |
| HUTTERER | | | F | married | | Zeide | | 186 |
| HUTTERER | | | F | | Zeide | | | 186 |
| HUTTERER | Channah | | F | | | | | 186 |
| HUTTERER | | | M | | Channah | | | 186 |
| HUTTERER | | | M | | | | Probably he is the son of Channah's son | 186 |
| HUTTERER | Avraham | | M | married | | | children | 186 |
| HUTTERER | | | F | married | | Avraham | children | 186 |
| HUTTERER | Avraham | | M | married | Moshe | | children | 186 |
| HUTTERER | | | F | married | | Avraham | children | 186 |
| HUTTERER | Mendel | | M | married | | Gitsche | | 186 |
| HUTTERER | Gitsche | | F | married | | Mendel | | 186 |
| HUTTERER | | | M | | Mendel | Gitsche | elder son of Mendel and Gitsche HUTTERER | 186 |
| HUTTERER | | | M | | Mendel | Gitsche | younger son of Mendel and Gitsche HUTTERER | 186 |
| HUTTERER | Shlomo | | M | married | | | children | 186 |
| HUTTERER | | | F | married | | Shlomo | children | 186 |
| HUTTERER | Leib | | M | married | | | children | 186 |
| HUTTERER | | | F | married | | Leib | children | 186 |
| HUTTERER | | | F | | Leib | | eldest daughter of Leib HUTTERER | 186 |
| HUTTERER | | | F | | Leib | | middle daughter of Leib HUTTERER | 186 |
| HUTTERER | | | F | | Leib | | youngest daughter of Leib HUTTERER | 186 |
| HUTTERER | Etel | | F | married | | | children, husband. It is likely that her | 186 |

| | | | | | | | | |
|---|---|---|---|---|---|---|---|---|
| | | | | | | | surname is different. | |
| HUTTERER | Leah | | F | | | | | 186 |
| HUTTERER | Sarah | | F | | | | | 186 |
| HUTTERER | Yisrael | | M | married | | | children | 187 |
| HUTTERER | | | F | married | | Yisrael | children | 187 |
| HUTTERER | Kamil | | M | married | | | 1 child | 187 |
| HUTTERER | | | F | married | | Kamil | 1 child | 187 |
| HUTTERER | Baruch | | M | | | | | 187 |
| HUTTERER | | | F | | Alter | | eldest daughter of Alter HUTTERER | 187 |
| HUTTERER | | | F | | Alter | | middle daughter of Alter HUTTERER | 187 |
| HUTTERER | | | F | | Alter | | youngest daughter of Alter HUTTERER | 187 |
| HUTTERER | Chaya | | F | married | | | children, husband. It is likely that her surname is different. | 187 |
| HUTTERER | Rakhel | | F | married | | | husband and 1 child. Probably the surname is different. | 187 |
| HUTTERER | Lotti | | F | married | | | husband and 1 child. Probably the surname is different. | 187 |
| HUTTERER | Itsche | | M | | | | | 187 |
| HIRSCH | Moshe | | M | | Zeidke | | | 187 |
| HIRSCH | Yosel | | M | married | | | children | 187 |
| HIRSCH | | | F | married | | Yosel | children | 187 |
| HENISH | Berl | | M | | | | | 187 |
| HENISH | Etel | | F | | | | | 187 |
| HELFER | David | | M | married | | | children | 187 |
| HELFER | | | F | married | | David | children | 187 |
| HELFER | Shmuel | | M | married | | Hoge | children | 187 |
| HELFER | Hoge | HEIT | F | married | | Shmuel | children | 187 |
| HECHLER | Tzirl Leah | | F | | | | | 187 |

| HECHLER | | | F | | | Tzirl Leah | | | 187 |
|---|---|---|---|---|---|---|---|---|---|
| FEIGER | Tzipora | HECHLER | F | married | | | Mendel | | 187 |
| FEIGER | Mendel | | M | married | | | Tzipora | | 187 |
| HECHLER | Shepsel | | M | | | | | | 187 |
| HECHLER | | | F | | | | | sister of Shepsel HECHLER | 187 |
| HEIT | Toibe | | F | | Yosel | | | | 187 |
| HOZEN | Simcha | | M | married | | | | | 187 |
| HOZEN | | | F | married | | | Simcha | | 187 |
| HOZEN | | | F | | Simcha | | | sister of Simcha HOZEN | 187 |
| HEBEL | Meir | | M | married | | | Babtsche | | 187 |
| HEBEL | Babtsche | | F | married | | | Meir | | 187 |
| HEBEL | | | M | | Meir | Babtsche | | | 187 |
| HEBEL | Yosef Hersch | | M | married | | | | 1 child | 187 |
| HEBEL | | | F | married | | | Yosef Hersch | 1 child | 187 |
| HITZIK | Roize | | F | | | | | children | 187 |
| HITZIK | Esther | | F | | | | | | 187 |
| HITZIK | Leizer | | M | | | | | | 187 |
| HITZIK | | | F | | | | Yakov | | 187 |
| HITZIK | | | F | | Yakov | | | elder daughter of the wife of Yakov HITZIK | 187 |
| HITZIK | | | F | | Yakov | | | younger 107aughter of the wife of Yakov HITZIK | 187 |
| HITZIK | Sarahke Sarah | | F | | | | | | 187 |
| HITZIK | Channah | | F | | | | | | 187 |
| HITZIK | | | M | | | | | brother of Channah HITZIK | 187 |
| HITZIK | Chaim | | M | | | | | | 187 |
| HELFER | | | F | | | | Zishe | | 187 |
| HELFER | | | M | | Zishe | | | and his family. Elder son of the wife of Zishe HELFER | 187 |

| | | | | | | | |
|---|---|---|---|---|---|---|---|
| HELFER | | M | Zishe | | | and his family. Younger son of the wife of Zishe HELFER | 187 |
| HABER | Fishel | M | | | | | 187 |
| HABER | | M | | | | first brother of Fishel HABER | 187 |
| HABER | | M | | | | second brother of Fishel HABER | 187 |
| HABER | Itsche | M | | | | and his family | 187 |
| HABER | Mendel | M | | | | and his family | 188 |
| HABER | | F | | | | Mother of Mendel HABER | 188 |

ר    Vav

| | | | | | | | |
|---|---|---|---|---|---|---|---|
| WAGSCHAL | Saike | F | | | | | 188 |
| WAGSCHAL | | F | | Saike | | eldest daughter of Saike WAGSCHAL | 188 |
| WAGSCHAL | | F | | Saike | | middle daughter of Saike WAGSCHAL | 188 |
| WAGSCHAL | | F | | Saike | | youngest daughter of Saike WAGSCHAL | 188 |
| WAGSCHAL | Perl | F | | | | | 188 |
| WAGSCHAL | Miriam | F | | | | | 188 |
| WAGSCHAL | Lotti | F | | | | | 188 |
| WAGSCHAL | | M | | | | brother of Lotti WAGSCHAL | 188 |
| WAGSCHAL | Sala | F | | | | | 188 |
| WOSHKOVITZER | Avraham | M | married | | | | 188 |
| WOSHKOVITZER | | F | married | | Avraham | | 188 |
| WOSHKOVITZER | | M | Avraham | | | | 188 |
| WOSHKOVITZER | Herschel | M | | | | | 188 |
| WOSHKOVITZER | Itsche | M | | | | and his family | 188 |
| WOLF | Meshulam | M | | | | and his family | 188 |
| WAURMAN | Shalom | M | married | | | | 188 |
| WAURMAN | | F | married | | Shalom | | 188 |
| WEISZ | Leizer | M | married | | | 2 children | 188 |

| WEISZ | | | F | married | | | Leizer | 2 children | 188 |
|---|---|---|---|---|---|---|---|---|---|
| WEISZ | Mendel | | M | | | | | | 188 |
| WEISZ | Baruch | | M | | | | | | 188 |
| WEICH | Yosel | | M | married | | | | | 188 |
| WEICH | | | F | married | | | Yosel | | 188 |
| WEICH | | | M | | Yosel | | | elder son of Yosel WEICH | 188 |
| WEICH | | | M | | Yosel | | | younger son of Yosel WEICH | 188 |
| WEICH | Yisrael | | M | | | | | and his family | 188 |
| WEICH | Moshe | | M | | | | | | 188 |
| WEINER | Zeide | | M | married | | | | on the list "cockroach" is written | 188 |
| WEINER | | | F | married | | | Zeide | | 188 |
| WINDRICH | Chaim | | M | married | | | | | 188 |
| WINDRICH | | | F | married | | | Chaim | | 188 |
| WINTER | Chaim | | M | | | | | and his family | 188 |

ז Zayin

| ZEIDMAN | Leibele | | M | married | | | | | 188 |
|---|---|---|---|---|---|---|---|---|---|
| ZEIDMAN | | | F | married | | | Leibele | | 188 |
| ZEIDMAN | Yosel | | M | married | | | | children | 188 |
| ZEIDMAN | | | F | married | | | Yosel | children | 188 |
| ZARGER | Avraham Itsche | | M | married | | | Babatsche | | 188 |
| ZARGER | Babatsche | | F | married | | | Avraham Itsche | | 188 |
| | | ZARGER | F | | Avraham Itsche | Babatsche | | and her family. Eldest daughter of Avraham Itsche and Babatsche ZARGER | 188 |
| | | ZARGER | F | | Avraham Itsche | Babatsche | | and her family. Middle daughter of Avraham Itsche and Babatsche ZARGER | 188 |
| | | ZARGER | F | | Avraham Itsche | Babatsche | | and her family. Youngest daughter of Avraham Itsche | 188 |

| Surname | Given name | | Sex | | | | | Notes | Page |
|---|---|---|---|---|---|---|---|---|---|
| | | | | | | | | and Babatsche ZARGER | |
| ZARGER | | | M | | Avraham Itsche | Babatsche | | | 188 |
| ZARGER | Shmuel | | M | married | | | | | 188 |
| ZARGER | | | F | married | | | Shmuel | | 188 |
| ZALTZMAN | Bobeleh | | F | married | | | | and her husband. Seamstress. It's likely the surname is different. | 188 |
| ZICHT | Efraim | | M | | | | | on the list "Chaya Sarah the Grete's man" is written | 188 |
| ZICHT | | | M | | Efraim | | | Elder son of Efraim ZICHT | 188 |
| ZICHT | | | M | | Efraim | | | younger son of Efraim ZICHT | 188 |
| ZICHT | Yisrael | | M | | | | | and his family | 188 |
| ZICHT | Moshe | | M | | | | | and his family | 188 |
| ZEKLER | Chaim | | M | married | | | Esther Eidel | | 188 |
| ZEKLER | Esther Eidel | | F | married | | | Chaim | | 188 |
| ZABLOTOWER | Meir Hersch | | M | married | | | | | 189 |
| ZABLOTOWER | | | F | married | | | Meir Hersch | | 189 |
| ZABLOTOWER | | | F | | Meir Hersch | | | | 189 |
| ZABLOTOWER | Alter | | M | married | | | | children | 189 |
| ZABLOTOWER | | | F | married | | | Alter | children | 189 |
| ZABLOTOWER | Yechiel | | M | married | | | | children | 189 |
| ZABLOTOWER | | | F | married | | | Yechiel | children | 189 |
| ZLATSHEWER | Motl | | M | | | | | and his family | 189 |
| ZLATSHOWER | Moshe | | M | | | | | and his family | 189 |
| ZLATSHOWER | Velvel | | M | | | | | and his family | 189 |

## ח Chet

| Surname | Given name | | Sex | | | | | Notes | Page |
|---|---|---|---|---|---|---|---|---|---|
| CHASID | Hersch Leib | | M | | | | | | 189 |
| CHASID | | | F | | Hersch Leib | | | eldest daughter of Hersch Leib CHASID | 189 |

| Surname | Given | Maiden | Sex | Marital | Father | Mother | Spouse | Notes | Page |
|---|---|---|---|---|---|---|---|---|---|
| CHASID | | | F | | Hersch Leib | | | middle daughter of Hersch Leib CHASID | 189 |
| CHASID | | | F | | Hersch Leib | | | youngest daughter of Hersch Leib CHASID | 189 |
| SHNEID | Perl | CHASID | F | married | | | Yitzchak | 2 children | 189 |
| SHNEID | Yitzchak | | M | married | | | Perl | 2 children | 189 |
| HARTMAN | Feige | CHASID | F | married | | | Moshe | children | 189 |
| HARTMAN | Moshe | | M | married | | | Feige | children | 189 |
| ERLICH | Freide | CHASID | F | married | | | Yehoshua | 1 child | 189 |
| ERLICH | Yehoshua | | M | married | | | Freide | 1 child | 189 |

ט Tet

| Surname | Given | Maiden | Sex | Marital | Father | Mother | Spouse | Notes | Page |
|---|---|---|---|---|---|---|---|---|---|
| TANNENTZAPF | Tzipora | | F | | | | | | 189 |
| TANNENTZAPF | | | F | | | Tzipora | | | 189 |
| | Rivka | TANNENTZAPF | F | married | | | Shlomo David | 1 child | 189 |
| | Shlomo David | | M | married | | | Rivka | 1 child | 189 |
| | | | M | | | Rivka | | elder son of Rivka TANNENTZAPF; mother's maiden name TANNENTZAPF | 189 |
| | | | M | | | Rivka | | younger son of Rivka TANNENTZAPF; mother's maiden name TANNENTZAPF | 189 |
| TANNENTZAPF | Yudel | | M | married | | | | children | 189 |
| TANNENTZAPF | | | F | married | | | Yudel | children | 189 |
| TANNENTZAPF | Tatke | | M | married | | | | children | 189 |
| TANNENTZAPF | | | F | married | | | Tatke | children | 189 |
| TAU | Hersch | | M | married | | | | | 189 |
| TAU | | | F | married | | | Hersch | | 189 |
| TAU | | | M | married | Hersch | | | 1 child | 189 |
| TAU | | | F | married | | | | 1 child; wife of the son Hersch TAU | 189 |

| | | | | | | | | |
|---|---|---|---|---|---|---|---|---|
| TAU | Avraham | | M | married | | | son in law of Zishe HELFER | 189 |
| TAU | | | F | married | | Avraham | | 189 |
| TAU | | | M | | Avraham | | | 189 |
| TILINGER | Butzye Chaim | | M | married | | Losya | | 189 |
| TILINGER | Losya | | F | married | | Butzye Chaim | | 189 |
| TILINGER | | | M | | Butzye Chaim | Losya | | 189 |
| TILINGER | Herschel | | M | | | | | 189 |
| TILLINGER | Meir | | M | | | | and his family | 189 |
| TILLINGER | Leizer | | M | married | Yose | | Yose's | 189 |
| TILLINGER | | | F | married | | Leizer | | 189 |
| TILLINGER | | | F | | Leizer | | Youngest daughter of Lezier TILLINGER | 189 |
| TILLINGER | | | F | | Leizer | | Second youngest daughter of Leizer TILLINGER | 189 |
| TILLINGER | | | F | | Leizer | | Third youngest daughter of Leizer TILLINGER | 189 |
| TILLINGER | Rakhel | | F | | | | | 189 |
| TILLINGER | | | M | | | Rakhel | elder son of Rakhel TILLINGER | 189 |
| TILLINGER | | | M | | | Rakhel | younger son of Rakhel TILLINGER | 189 |
| TILLINGER | Yakov Leib | | M | | | | and his family | 189 |
| TILLINGER | Zanye Yakov | | M | married | | Lortzye | | 189 |
| TILLINGER | Lortzye | KLAR | F | married | | Zanye Yakov | | 189 |
| TILLINGER | | | M | | Zanye Yakov | Lortzye | | 189 |
| TILLINGER | Gizella | | F | married | | Zelig | | 189 |
| TILLINGER | | | M | | Zelig | Gizella | | 189 |
| TILLINGER | Meir | | M | | | | | 189 |
| TILLINGER | Neche | | F | | | | | 189 |
| TILLINGER | | | F | | | Neche | | 189 |
| TREGER | Sima | | F | | | | | 189 |

ל **Lamed**

| | | | | | | | | | |
|---|---|---|---|---|---|---|---|---|---|
| LAKER | Meir | | M | married | | | Rivka | | 189 |
| LAKER | Rivka | | F | married | | | Meir | | 189 |
| LAKER | Artur | | M | married | | | Frimtshe | | 189 |
| LAKER | Frimtshe | | F | married | | | Artur | | 189 |
| LAKER | Nachum | | M | married | | | Malka | and his daughters | 189 |
| LAKER | Malka | | F | married | | | Nachum | and her daughters | 189 |
| LAKER | Sarah | | F | | | | | and family | 189 |
| LAKER | Channah | | F | | | | | | 190 |
| LANDVER | Irtzye | | M | | | | | | 190 |
| LANDVER | | | M | | Irtzye | | | | 190 |
| LANDVER | Matias | | M | | | | | | 190 |
| LANDVER | Rivka | | F | | | | | | 190 |
| LANDVER | Meshulam | | M | married | | | | | 190 |
| LANDVER | | | F | married | | | Meshulam | | 190 |
| LANDVER | | | M | | Meshulam | | | | 190 |
| LANDMAN | Yosel | | M | married | | | Golde | | 190 |
| LANDMAN | Golde | | F | married | | | Yosel | | 190 |
| LORBER | Markus | | M | married | | | Danya | | 190 |
| LORBER | Danya | PFAU | F | married | | | Markus | | 190 |
| LORISH | Itsche | | M | | | | | | 190 |
| LORISH | Perl | | F | | | | | | 190 |
| LORISH | Mendel | | M | | | | | | 190 |
| LEBEL | Herschel | | M | | | | | and his family | 190 |
| LEBEL | Efraim | | M | | | | | and his family | 190 |
| LEBEL | Moshe | | M | | | | | | 190 |
| LIBERGALL | Feige | | F | | | | Shmuel | | 190 |
| LIBERGALL | | | F | | Shmuel | Feige | | | 190 |
| LIBERGALL | | | F | | Shmuel | Feige | | | 190 |
| BLECHER | Reizel | LIBERGALL | F | married | | | Zeidel | | 190 |
| BLECHER | Zeidel | | M | married | | | Reizel | | 190 |
| BLECHER | Banyo Berl | | M | | Zeidel | Reizel | | | 190 |
| BLECHER | Efraim | | M | | Zeidel | Reizel | | | 190 |

| BLECHER | Shulamit | | F | | Zeidel | Reizel | | | 190 |
|---|---|---|---|---|---|---|---|---|---|
| FEIGER | Hodye | LIBERGALL | F | married | | | Mendel | | 190 |
| FEIGER | Mendel | | M | married | | | Hodye | | 190 |
| FEIGER | Solko | | M | | Mendel | Hodye | | | 190 |
| | | | M | | | Hodye | | elder son of Hodye LIBERGALL; mother's maiden name LIBERGALL | 190 |
| | | | M | | | Hodye | | younger son of Hodye LIBERGALL; mother's maiden name LIBERGALL | 190 |
| LIBERGALL | Mechel | | M | married | | | Batya | | 190 |
| LIBERGALL | Batya | SOCHER | F | married | | | Mechel | | 190 |
| LIBERGALL | Shmuel | | M | | Mechel | Batya | | | 190 |
| LIBERGALL | Moshe | | M | married | | | Tzipora | | 190 |
| LIBERGALL | Tzipora | BLECHER | F | married | | | Moshe | | 190 |
| LIBERGALL | Shmuel | | M | | Moshe | Tzipora | | | 190 |
| LEIWAND | Mordechai | | M | | | | | | 190 |
| LEIWAND | | | F | | Mordechai | | | | 190 |
| LEIWAND | Mutsha | | M | | | | | | 190 |
| LEIWAND | | | M | | Mutsha | | | elder son of Motshe LEIWAND | 190 |
| LEIWAND | | | M | | Mutsha | | | younger son of Motshe LEIWAND | 190 |
| LEIWAND | Zeinvel | | M | | | | | | 190 |
| LEIWAND | Munye | | M | | | | | | 190 |
| LINDER | Nachum | | M | | | | | and his family | 190 |
| LINDER | Metzye | | F | | | | | | 190 |
| LAUFER | Yosel | | M | | | | | and his family. From Kabaky | 190 |
| LUSTIK | Leizer | | M | | | | | and his family. From Kabaky | 190 |
| LAUB | Shmuel | | M | married | | | Berta | children | 190 |
| LAUB | Berta | | F | married | | | Shmuel | children | 190 |

| | | | | | | | | | |
|---|---|---|---|---|---|---|---|---|---|
| LAUB | Stefa | | F | married | | | | children, husband. It is likely that her surname is different. | 190 |
| LAUB | Inka | | F | | | | | | 190 |
| LAUB | Zigfried | | M | | | | | | 191 |
| LAUB | Richard | | M | | | | | | 191 |
| LAUB | Chaim | | M | married | | | | carpenter | 191 |
| LAUB | | | F | married | | | Chaim | | 191 |
| | | LAUB | F | | Chaim | | | and her family; elder daughter of Chaim LAUB | 191 |
| | | LAUB | F | | Chaim | | | and her family; younger daughter of Chaim LAUB | 191 |
| LAUB | Chaim Hersch | | M | married | | | | his children and mother in law; shoemaker | 191 |
| LAUB | | | F | married | | | Chaim Hersch | children | 191 |
| LUSTIK | Sarah | | F | | | | | the beadle of the Chassidic Beit Hamidrash | 191 |
| | | LUSTIK | F | | | Sarah | | and her family; elder daughter of Sarah LUSTIK | 191 |
| | | LUSTIK | F | | | Sarah | | and her family; younger daughter of Sarah LUSTIK | 191 |
| LINDER | Yosef | | M | | Moshe | | | and his family | 191 |

מ **Mem**

| | | | | | | | | | |
|---|---|---|---|---|---|---|---|---|---|
| MANDEL | Menashe | | M | | | | | | 191 |
| MANDEL | Zeide | | M | married | | | Frida | | 191 |
| MANDEL | Frida | | F | married | | | Zeide | | 191 |
| MANDEL | Anita | | F | | Zeide | Frida | | | 191 |
| MANDEL | Shimon | | M | married | | | | children | 191 |
| MANDEL | | | F | married | | | Shimon | children | 191 |
| MANDEL | Mutzye | | M | | | | | | 191 |
| MANDEL | Meir | | M | | | | | | 191 |
| MANDEL | Toibele | | F | | | | | | 191 |
| MANDEL | Liebe | | F | | | | | | 191 |

| Surname | Given | Surname2 | Sex | | | | | Notes | Year |
|---|---|---|---|---|---|---|---|---|---|
| MANDEL | | | M | | | Liebe | | elder daughter of Liebe MANDEL | 191 |
| MANDEL | | | M | | | Liebe | | younger daughter of Liebe MANDEL | 191 |
| MANDEL | Shemayahu | | M | | | | | and his family | 191 |
| MANDEL | Anschel | | M | | | | | | 191 |
| MANDEL | Rivka | | F | | | | | | 191 |
| MANDEL | | | M | | | Rivka | | | 191 |
| MANDEL | Avraham | | M | | | | | | 191 |
| MANDEL | Etel | | F | | | | | | 191 |
| MOCH | Wilhelm | | M | married | | | Pepi | | 191 |
| MOCH | Pepi | | F | married | | | Wilhelm | | 191 |
| MOSKOWITZ | | | F | | | | Shulke | | 191 |
| | Esther | MOSKOWITZ | F | | Shulke | | | and family | 191 |
| | | | M | | | Esther | | eldest son of Esther nee MOSKOWITZ | 191 |
| | | | M | | | Esther | | middle son of Esther nee MOSKOWITZ | 191 |
| | | | M | | | Esther | | youngest son of Esther nee MOSKOWITZ | 191 |
| MOSKOWITZ | Neta | | M | married | | | Gitel | | 191 |
| MOSKOWITZ | Gitel | | F | married | | | Neta | | 191 |
| MOSKOWITZ | Fridel | | M | married | | | | children | 191 |
| MOSKOWITZ | | | F | married | | | Fridel | children | 191 |
| MOSKOWITZ | Yechezkel | | M | married | | | | children | 191 |
| MOSKOWITZ | | | F | married | | | Yechezkel | children | 191 |
| MOSKOWITZ | Leah | | F | | | | | | 191 |
| HEIMAN | Andzye | MOSKOWITZ | F | married | | Leah | | 1 child | 191 |
| HEIMAN | | | M | married | | | Andzye | 1 child | 191 |
| PELPEL | Mina | MOSKOWITZ | F | | | | Aharon | children | 191 |
| MOSKOWITZ | Esther | | F | | | | | | 191 |
| MOSKOWITZ | Shimon | | M | married | | | Pepi | children | 191 |
| MOSKOWITZ | Pepi | | F | married | | | Shimon | children | 191 |

| | | | | | | | | | |
|---|---|---|---|---|---|---|---|---|---|
| MOSKOWITZ | Munzieh | | M | | | | | gender was determined from a Page of Testimony | 191 |
| MOSKOWITZ | Moshe | | M | | | | | | 192 |
| MOSKOWITZ | Shlomo | | M | married | | | Berta | children | 192 |
| MOSKOWITZ | Berta | | F | married | | | Shlomo | children | 192 |
| MOSKOWITZ | Avraham | | M | | | | | | 192 |
| MOSKOWITZ | Alter | | M | married | | | | | 192 |
| MOSKOWITZ | | | F | married | | | Alter | | 192 |
| MOSKOWITZ | Avraham David | | M | married | | | | children | 192 |
| MOSKOWITZ | | | F | married | | | Avraham David | children | 192 |
| MOSKOWITZ | Shimon | | M | | | | | "the mute" | 192 |
| MEIER | Yosel | | M | married | | | | | 192 |
| MEIER | | | F | married | | | Yosel | | 192 |
| MEIER | | | M | | Yosel | | | and his family; eldest son of Yosel MEIER | 192 |
| MEIER | | | M | | Yosel | | | and his family; middle son of Yosel MEIER | 192 |
| MEIER | | | M | | Yosel | | | and his family; youngest son of Yosel MEIER | 192 |
| | | MEIER | F | | Yosel | | | and her family; eldest daughter of Yosel MEIER | 192 |
| | | MEIER | F | | Yosel | | | and her family; middle daughter of Yosel MEIER | 192 |
| | | MEIER | F | | Yosel | | | and her family; youngest daughter of Yosel MEIER | 192 |
| MELTZER | Etel | | F | | | | | | 192 |
| MELTZER | | | F | | | Etel | | elder daughter of Etel MELTZER | 192 |
| MELTZER | | | F | | | Etel | | younger daughter of Etel MELTZER | 192 |
| GOLDREICH | Shprintze | MELTZER | F | married | | | Baruch | 2 children | 192 |
| GOLDREICH | Baruch | | M | married | | | Shprintze | 2 children | 192 |

| LETICH | Esther | MELTZER | F | married | | | Moshe | children | 192 |
|---|---|---|---|---|---|---|---|---|---|
| LETICH | Moshe | | M | married | | | Esther | children | 192 |
| LETICH | | | M | | Moshe | Esther | | elder son of Moshe and Esther LETICH | 192 |
| LETICH | | | M | | Moshe | Esther | | younger son of Moshe and Esther LETICH | 192 |
| MELTZER | Menye | | M | married | | | | | 192 |
| MELTZER | | | F | married | | | Menye | | 192 |
| MELTZER | Yosef | | M | married | | | | 1 child | 192 |
| MELTZER | | | F | married | | | Yosef | 1 child | 192 |
| MEHER | Gedalya | | M | | | | | and his family | 192 |
| MEHER | Frimtshe | | F | | | | | | 192 |
| MEHER | | | F | | | Frimtshe | | | 192 |
| MEHER | Yisrael | | M | | | | | | 192 |
| MEHER | Malka Esther | | F | | | | | | 192 |
| MEHER | Devorah | | F | | | | | | 192 |
| MEHER | Wolf | | M | married | | | | | 192 |
| MEHER | | | F | married | | | Wolf | | 192 |
| MAURER | | | F | | | | Avraham | and her family; wife of Avraham the teacher (melamed) | 192 |
| MAURER | | | F | | Avraham | | | elder daughter of the wife of Avraham MAURER the teacher (melamed) | 192 |
| MAURER | | | F | | Avraham | | | younger daughter of the wife of Avraham MAURER the teacher (melamed) | 192 |
| MAURER | Yosel | | M | | | | | and his family | 192 |
| MONTSCHIK | Yisrael | | M | | | | | and his family | 192 |
| MONTSCHIK | | | F | | | | | mother of Yisrael MONTSCHIK | 192 |

# ﬞ Nun

| | | | | | | | | |
|---|---|---|---|---|---|---|---|---|
| NEIMAN | Moshe | | M | married | | | 4 children | 192 |
| NEIMAN | | | F | married | | Moshe | 4 children | 192 |
| NEIMAN | Moshe | | M | | | | From Dolyna (Region: Stanislawow) | 192 |
| NEIMAN | | | F | | | | mother of Moshe NEIMAN. From Dolyna (Region: Stanislawow) | 192 |
| NEIMAN | | | F | | | | sister of Moshe NEIMAN. From Dolyna (Region: Stanislawow) | 192 |
| NEIBERGER | Izidor | | M | married | | | 1 child | 192 |
| NEIBERGER | | | F | married | | Izidor | 1 child | 192 |
| NADLER | Feivel | | M | | | | | 192 |
| NADLER | | | M | | Feivel | | and his family; elder son of Feivel NADLER | 192 |
| NADLER | | | M | | Feivel | | and his family; younger son of Feivel NADLER | 192 |
| | | NADLER | F | | Feivel | | and her family; eldest daughter of Feivel NADLER | 192 |
| | | NADLER | F | | Feivel | | and her family; middle daughter of Feivel NADLER | 192 |
| | | NADLER | F | | Feivel | | and her family; youngest daughter of Feivel NADLER | 192 |
| NACHMAN | Moshe | | M | | | | | 192 |

# ס Samech

| | | | | | | | | |
|---|---|---|---|---|---|---|---|---|
| SENDER | Chaim | | M | married | | | nicknamed Ketzeleh "the little cat" | 192 |
| SENDER | | | F | married | | Chaim | | 192 |
| SENDER | Binyamin | | M | married | | | | 192 |
| SENDER | | | F | married | | Binyamin | | 192 |

| Surname | First name | 2nd surname | Sex | Status | Name | Spouse | Notes | Page |
|---|---|---|---|---|---|---|---|---|
| SENDER | | | M | | Binyamin | | elder son of Binyamin SENDER | 192 |
| SENDER | | | M | | Binyamin | | younger son of Binyamin SENDER | 192 |
| SENDER | Manele | | M | married | | | | 192 |
| SENDER | | | F | married | | Manele | | 192 |
| | | SENDER | F | | Manele | | and her family; daughter of Manale SENDER | 192 |
| | | SENDER | F | | Manele | | and her family; daughter of Manale SENDER | 192 |
| SENDER | Mechele | | M | | | | and his family | 192 |
| SENDER | Moshe | | M | married | | | children | 193 |
| SENDER | | | F | married | | Moshe | children | 193 |
| SENDER | Otzye | | M | married | | | children | 193 |
| SENDER | | | F | married | | Otzye | children | 193 |
| BACHMAN | Etel | SENDER | F | married | | Eliahu | children | 193 |
| BACHMAN | Eliahu | | M | married | | Etel | children | 193 |
| FELDHAMER | Saike | SENDER | F | married | | David | children | 193 |
| FELDHAMER | David | | M | married | | Saike | children | 193 |
| SENDER | Chaim | | M | married | | | | 193 |
| SENDER | | | F | married | | Chaim | family and daughter | 193 |
| SENDER | | | M | | Chaim | | | 193 |
| SENDER | Yona | | M | married | | | children | 193 |
| SENDER | | | F | married | | Yona | children | 193 |
| SENDER | Motye | | M | married | | | 2 children | 193 |
| SENDER | | | F | married | | Motye | 2 children | 193 |
| SENDER | Motye | | M | married | | | children. "The Bulgarian" | 193 |
| SENDER | | | F | married | | Motye | "the Bulgarian" written next to her husband's name. | 193 |
| SENDER | Leizer | | M | married | | | children | 193 |
| SENDER | | | F | married | | Leizer | children | 193 |
| SENDER | David | | M | married | | Sarah | | 193 |

| | | | | | | | | |
|---|---|---|---|---|---|---|---|---|
| SENDER | Sarah | | F | married | | | David | 193 |
| SENDER | Hodye | | F | | David | Sarah | | 193 |
| SENDER | Reizel | | F | | David | Sarah | | 193 |
| SENDER | Neche | | F | | David | Sarah | | 193 |
| SENDER | | | F | | | | Avrahamtsche | 193 |
| SENDER | | | F | | Avrahamtsche | | | 193 |
| SENDER | | | F | | Avrahamtsche | | | 193 |
| SENDER | Beile | | F | | | | and family | 193 |
| SENDER | Liebe | | F | | | | | 193 |
| SENDER | Reuven | | M | | | Liebe | | 193 |
| SOCHER | | | M | | | | and his family; first of 2 brothers of the SOCHER family. On the list "at the Rosotke" is written. | 193 |
| SOCHER | | | M | | | | and his family; second of 2 brothers of the SOCHER family. On the list "at the Rosotke" is written. | 193 |
| SOCHER | Meir | | M | married | | | Yente | 193 |
| SOCHER | Yente | | F | married | | | Meir | 193 |
| SOCHER | | | F | | Meir | Yente | eldest daughter of Meir and Yente SOCHER | 193 |
| SOCHER | | | F | | Meir | Yente | middle daughter of Meir and Yente SOCHER | 193 |
| SOCHER | | | F | | Meir | Yente | youngest daughter of Meir and Yente SOCHER | 193 |
| SOCHER | Chaitsche | | F | | | | | 193 |
| SOCHER | Channah | | F | | | | | 193 |
| SOCHER | Sarah | | F | | | | | 193 |
| SOCHER | Moshe | | M | | | | | 193 |
| SOCHER | Moshe | | M | | Moshe | | it's possible his given name is different | 193 |
| SOCHER | Shlomo | | M | | Moshe | | | 193 |

| SOCHER | Moshe | | M | married | | | Polye | | 193 |
|--------|-------|--|---|---------|--|--|-------|--|-----|
| SOCHER | Polye | | F | married | | | Moshe | | 193 |
| | Batya | SOCHER | F | married | Moshe | Polye | | 1 child | 193 |
| | | | M | married | | | Batya | 1 child | 193 |
| SOBEL | Chaim | | M | married | | | Tzipe | | 193 |
| SOBEL | Tzipe | | F | married | | | Chaim | | 193 |
| | Klara | SOBEL | F | married | Chaim | Tzipe | | children; on the list her maiden name is written "SOBELEL" probably in error | 193 |
| | | | M | married | | | Klara | children, wife's maiden name SOBEL | 193 |
| SOBEL | Teador | | M | | | | | | 193 |
| SOFER | Mordechai | | M | | | | | and his family. From Slobodka | 193 |
| SOFER | Mendel | | M | | | | | and his family. From Yablunytsya | 193 |
| SOFER | | | M | | | | | and his family; brother of Mendel SOFER. From Yablunytsya | 193 |
| SOCHER | Eliahu | | M | married | | | | | 193 |
| SOCHER | | | F | married | | | Eliahu | | 193 |
| SOCHER | | | M | | Eliahu | | | | 193 |
| SOCHER | | | M | | Eliahu | | | | 193 |
| SOCHER | | | M | | Eliahu | | | | 193 |
| SOCHER | Herman | | M | married | | | | children; he is probably the son of Eliahu SOCHER | 193 |
| SOCHER | | | F | married | | | Herman | children | 193 |
| SOCHER | Max | | M | married | | | | children | 193 |
| SOCHER | | | F | married | | | Max | children | 193 |
| SOCHER | Brona | | F | | | | | | 193 |

**ע** Ayin

| ENGLER | Yute Leah | | F | | | | | | 193 |
|--------|-----------|--|---|--|--|--|--|--|-----|
| ENGLER | Hersch | | M | married | | Yute Leah | | children | 193 |

| | | | | | | | | | |
|---|---|---|---|---|---|---|---|---|---|
| ENGLER | | | F | married | | | Hersch | children | 193 |
| ENGLER | | | F | | | Yute Leah | | | 193 |
| GLICKSTERN | Gitel | ENGLER | F | married | | | Chaim | children | 193 |
| GLICKSTERN | Chaim | | M | married | | | Gitel | children | 193 |
| ENGLER | Yudel | | M | married | | | | children | 193 |
| ENGLER | | | F | married | | | Yudel | children | 193 |
| ENGLER | Zeide | | M | married | | | | children | 194 |
| ENGLER | | | F | married | | | Zeide | children | 194 |
| ENGLER | Miriam | | F | | | | | | 194 |
| ENGLER | | | F | | | | | mother of Miriam ENGLER | 194 |
| ENGEL | Moshe | | M | married | | | Rivka | | 194 |
| ENGEL | Rivka | | F | married | | | Moshe | | 194 |
| ENGEL | | | M | | Moshe | Rivka | | | 194 |
| ENGEL | Zeide | | M | married | | | | children | 194 |
| ENGEL | | | F | married | | | Zeide | children | 194 |
| ENGEL | | | F | | Zeide | | | | 194 |
| ENGEL | Pepi | | F | | | | | | 194 |
| EHRLICH | Yosel | | M | | | | | | 194 |
| ETTINGER | Meir | | M | married | | | Sheva | 2 children | 194 |
| ETTINGER | Sheva | | F | married | | | Meir | 2 children | 194 |
| ELSTER | Yudel | | M | married | | | | children | 194 |
| ELSTER | | | F | married | | | Yudel | children | 194 |
| ELSTER | Moshe | | M | married | | | | children | 194 |
| ELSTER | | | F | married | | | Moshe | children | 194 |
| ELENBOIGEN | | | F | | | | Moshe | children | 194 |

פ Peh

| | | | | | | | | | |
|---|---|---|---|---|---|---|---|---|---|
| PANKER | Hersch | | M | married | | | | 1 child | 194 |
| PANKER | | | F | married | | | Hersch | 1 child | 194 |
| PASTERNAK | Herschel | | M | married | | | | children | 194 |
| PASTERNAK | | | F | married | | | Herschel | children | 194 |
| POPPER | Yankel | | M | married | | | Jetti | | 194 |
| POPPER | Jetti | | F | married | | | Yankel | | 194 |

| | | | | | | | | | | |
|---|---|---|---|---|---|---|---|---|---|---|
| | Danya | POPPER | F | married | Yankel | Jetti | | | children | 194 |
| | | | M | married | | | | Danya | children | 194 |
| POPPER | Andzia | | F | | Yankel | Jetti | | | | 194 |
| PAUKER | Yente | | F | | | | | | | 194 |
| | | PAUKER | F | | | Yente | | | and her family; elder daughter of Yente PAUKER | 194 |
| | | PAUKER | F | | | Yente | | | and her family; younger daughter of Yente PAUKER | 194 |
| PFAU | Hinde | | F | | | | | | | 194 |
| | Toibe | PFAU | F | | | Hinde | | | children | 194 |
| | Sheindel | PFAU | F | | | Hinde | | | and family | 194 |
| | Danya | PFAU | F | married | | Hinde | | | | 194 |
| | | | M | married | | | | Danya | | 194 |
| | Roza | PFAU | F | married | | Hinde | | | 1 child | 194 |
| | | | M | married | | | | Roza | 1 child | 194 |
| PFAU | Avraham | | M | married | | | | | 2 children | 194 |
| PFAU | | | F | married | | | | Avraham | 2 children | 194 |
| PFAU | Shalom | | M | married | | | | | | 194 |
| PFAU | | | F | married | | | | Shalom | | 194 |
| | | PFAU | F | | Shalom | | | | and her family; elder daughter of Shalom PFAU | 194 |
| | | PFAU | F | | Shalom | | | | and her family; middle daughter of Shalom PFAU | 194 |
| | | PFAU | F | | Shalom | | | | and her family; younger daughter of Shalom PFAU | 194 |
| PFAU | Leib | | M | | | | | | and his family | 194 |
| PFAU | Herschel | | M | | | | | | and his family | 194 |
| PFAU | Moshe | | M | | | | | | | 194 |
| PFAU | Itsche | | M | married | | | | | | 194 |
| PFAU | | | F | married | | | | Itsche | | 194 |
| | | PFAU | F | | Itsche | | | | eldest daughter of Itsche PFAU | 194 |

| Surname | First Name | | Sex | | | | | Notes | Page |
|---|---|---|---|---|---|---|---|---|---|
| | | PFAU | F | | Itsche | | | middle daughter of Itsche PFAU | 194 |
| | | PFAU | F | | Itsche | | | youngest daughter of Itsche PFAU | 194 |
| | Etel | PFAU | F | married | | | | 2 children; sister of Moshe, Mendel and Herschel | 194 |
| | | | M | married | | | Etel | 2 children | 194 |
| PFAU | Moshe | | M | | | | | brother of Etel, Mendel and Herschel | 194 |
| PFAU | Mendel | | M | married | | | | brother of Etel, Moshe and Herschel | 194 |
| PFAU | | | F | married | | | Mendel | | 194 |
| PFAU | Herschel | | M | married | | | | brother of Etel, Moshe and Mendel | 194 |
| PFAU | | | F | married | | | Herschel | | 194 |
| PFAU | Leibenyo | | M | married | | | | 2 children; building contractor | 194 |
| PFAU | | | F | married | | | Leibenyo | 2 children | 194 |
| PFAU | Meir | | M | married | Leibenyo | | | children | 194 |
| PFAU | | | F | married | | | Meir | children | 194 |
| PFAU | Moshe | | M | married | Leibenyo | | | children | 194 |
| PFAU | | | F | married | | | Moshe | children | 194 |
| PREMINGER | Markus | | M | married | | | Gitel | 2 children | 194 |
| PREMINGER | Gitel | | F | married | | | Markus | 2 children | 194 |
| PREMINGER | Gedalyahu | | M | | | | | | 195 |
| FRIEZEL | Moshe | | M | married | | | Mintshe | children | 195 |
| FRIEZEL | Mintshe | | F | married | | | Moshe | children | 195 |
| PISTINER | Kalman | | M | married | | | | | 195 |
| PISTINER | | | F | married | | | Kalman | | 195 |
| PISTINER | Mechel | | M | married | | | | 1 child | 195 |
| PISTINER | | | F | married | | | Mechel | 1 child | 195 |
| FOIGEL | Zalman | | M | married | | | Hinde | | 195 |
| FOIGEL | Hinde | | F | married | | | Zalman | | 195 |
| FOIGEL | Moshe | | M | married | Zalman | Hinde | | children | 195 |

| FOIGEL | | | F | married | | | Moshe | children | 195 |
|--------|--|--|---|---------|--|--|-------|----------|-----|
| FOIGEL | Leibele | | M | married | Zalman | Hinde | | children | 195 |
| FOIGEL | | | F | married | | | Leibele | children | 195 |
| FOIGEL | Shaiye | | M | | Zalman | Hinde | | | 195 |
| FOIGEL | | | F | | Shaiye | | | eldest daughter of Shaiye FOIGEL | 195 |
| FOIGEL | | | F | | Shaiye | | | 2nd daughter of Shaiye FOIGEL | 195 |
| FOIGEL | | | F | | Shaiye | | | 3rd daughter of Shaiye FOIGEL | 195 |
| FOIGEL | | | F | | Shaiye | | | 4th daughter of Shaiye FOIGEL | 195 |
| FOIGEL | | | F | | Shaiye | | | 5th daughter of Shaiye FOIGEL | 195 |
| FOIGEL | Channah | | F | married | | | | children, husband. It is likely that her surname is different. | 195 |
| FOIGEL | Leah | | F | married | | | | children, husband. It is likely that her surname is different. | 195 |
| FOIGEL | Batya | | F | | | | | and her family. Her surname is probably different. | 195 |
| FOIGEL | Sima | | F | | | | | | 195 |
| FOIGEL | Elza | | F | | | | | | 195 |
| FOIGEL | Asher Eizik | | M | married | | | Bobe | | 195 |
| FOIGEL | Bobe | | F | married | | | Asher Eizik | | 195 |
| | Munye | FOIGEL | F | married | Asher Eizik | Bobe | | children | 195 |
| | | | M | married | | | Munye | children | 195 |
| | Chaya | FOIGEL | F | married | Asher Eizik | Bobe | | | 195 |
| | | | M | married | | | Chaya | | 195 |
| | Sheindele | FOIGEL | F | | Asher Eizik | Bobe | | | 195 |
| | Yosel | | M | | | Sheindele | | | 195 |
| FOIGEL | Shimon | | M | married | | | Yente | | 195 |
| FOIGEL | Yente | | F | married | | | Shimon | | 195 |
| | Roza | FOIGEL | F | married | Shimon | Yente | | | 195 |

| | | | | | | | | | |
|---|---|---|---|---|---|---|---|---|---|
| | | | M | married | | | Roza | | 195 |
| FOIGEL | Bella | | F | | Shimon | Yente | | | 195 |
| FOIGEL | Moshe | | M | married | | | | children; "the thief" | 195 |
| FOIGEL | | | F | married | | | Moshe | children | 195 |
| FOIGEL | Hersch | | M | married | | | | children | 195 |
| FOIGEL | | | F | married | | | Hersch | children | 195 |
| FOIGEL | Yosel | | M | married | | | | children | 195 |
| FOIGEL | | | F | married | | | Yosel | children | 195 |
| FOIGEL | Babtziye | | F | | | | | | 195 |
| | | FOIGEL | F | | Babtziye | | | and her family. Eldest daughter of Babtzieh FOIGEL | 195 |
| | | FOIGEL | F | | Babtziye | | | and her family. Youngest daughter of Babtzieh FOIGEL | 195 |
| FOIGEL | Simcha | | M | | Yosef Yehoshua | | | | 195 |
| FOIGEL | | | F | | | | Yosef Yehoshua | the mother of Simcha FOIGEL | 195 |
| FOIGEL | | | F | | | | | the sister of Simcha FOIGEL | 195 |
| FREILECH | Zeide | | M | married | | | Reina | | 195 |
| FREILECH | Reina | | F | married | | | Zeide | | 195 |
| | | FREILECH | F | | Zeide | Reina | | and her family. Elder daughter of Zeide and Reina FREILECH | 195 |
| | | FREILECH | F | | Zeide | Reina | | and her family. Younger daughter of Zeide and Reina FREILECH | 195 |
| FREILECH | Yosel | | M | | Zeide | Reina | | | 195 |
| FREILECH | Asher | | M | married | Zeide | Reina | | children | 195 |
| FREILECH | | | F | married | | | Asher | children | 195 |
| FREILECH | Shimon | | M | | Zeide | Reina | | | 195 |
| FRIEDENHEIM | Yosef | | M | | | | | and his family | 195 |
| FRENKEL | Baruch | | M | married | | | Feige | | 195 |
| FRENKEL | Feige | | F | married | | | Baruch | | 195 |

| FRENKEL | Katriel | | M | | Baruch | Feige | | | 195 |
|---|---|---|---|---|---|---|---|---|---|
| FRENKEL | Yona | | M | | Baruch | Feige | | | 195 |
| FRENKEL | Pepi | | F | | Baruch | Feige | | | 195 |
| FRENKEL | Eizik | | M | | | | Danya | the husband of Danya LANDMAN | 195 |
| FRIEDMAN | Julius | | M | married | | | | | 195 |
| FRIEDMAN | | | F | married | | | Julius | | 195 |
| FRIEDMAN | Henrietta | | F | | Julius | | | | 195 |
| FRIEDMAN | Manya | | F | | Julius | | | | 195 |
| FRIEDMAN | Miriam | | F | | Julius | | | | 195 |
| FRIEDMAN | Monek | | M | | Julius | | | | 195 |
| FREILICH | Dobtsche | | M | | | | | city beadle | 195 |
| FEINER | Alter | | M | married | | | | | 195 |
| FEINER | | | F | married | | | Alter | | 195 |
| FEINER | Reuven | | M | married | Alter | | | | 195 |
| FEINER | | | F | married | | | Reuven | | 195 |
| FEINER | Motl | | M | married | Alter | | | children | 195 |
| FEINER | | | F | married | | | Motl | children | 195 |
| FEINER | Yehuda Leib | | M | married | Alter | | | children | 195 |
| FEINER | | | F | married | | | Yehuda Leib | children | 195 |
| FEINER | Leibke | | M | married | | | Tzipre | | 195 |
| FEINER | Tzipre | | F | married | | | Leibke | | 195 |
| FEINER | Yitzchak | | M | married | Leibke | Tzipre | Feige | | 195 |
| FEINER | Feige | KASWAN | F | married | | | Yitzchak | | 195 |
| FEINER | Munzieh | | M | | Yitzchak | Feige | | | 195 |
| FEINER | Izye | | M | | Yitzchak | Feige | | | 195 |
| FEINER | | | F | | Yitzchak | Feige | | elder daughter of Yitzchak and Feige FEINER | 195 |
| FEINER | | | F | | Yitzchak | Feige | | younger daughter of Yitzchak and Feige FEINER | 195 |
| FEINER | Hentsche | | F | | | | | probably the surname is different | 195 |

| | | | | | | | | | |
|---|---|---|---|---|---|---|---|---|---|
| FEINER | Hersch Mordechai | | M | | | Hentsche | | probably the surname is different | 195 |
| FEINER | Esther | | F | | | Hentsche | | probably the surname is different | 195 |
| KIMEL | Shlima | FEINER | F | married | | | Mechel | | 195 |
| KIMEL | Mechel | | M | married | | | Shlima | | 195 |
| KIMEL | Peli | | F | | Mechel | Shlima | | | 195 |
| FEINER | Shlomo | | M | | | | | ro | 196 |
| FEIGENBOIM | Motl | | M | married | | | Sarahke | 2 children | 196 |
| FEIGENBOIM | Sarahke | HEIT | F | married | | | Motl | 2 children | 196 |
| FEIGENBOIM | | | F | | | | Berish | 3 children | 196 |
| FEIGER | Avraham | | M | | | | | and his family | 196 |
| FEIGER | Shimshon | | M | | | | | and his family | 196 |
| FEIGER | Chaim | | M | married | | | | children | 196 |
| FEIGER | | | F | married | | | Chaim | children | 196 |
| FISCHER | Zeide | | M | married | | | | children | 196 |
| FISCHER | | | F | married | | | Zeide | children | 196 |
| FISCHER | Zindel | | M | married | | | | brush manufacturer | 196 |
| FISCHER | | | F | married | | | Zindel | | 196 |
| FISCHER | | | F | | Zindel | | | eldest daughter of Zindel FISCHER | 196 |
| FISCHER | | | F | | Zindel | | | middle daughter of Zindel FISCHER | 196 |
| FISCHER | | | F | | Zindel | | | youngest daughter of Zindel FISCHER | 196 |
| FISCHER | Leibke | | M | married | | | | on the list "katschek" is written; unsure what this refers to | 196 |
| FISCHER | | | F | married | | | Leibke | by the name of her husband "katschek" is written | 196 |
| FISCHER | | | M | | Leibke | | | eldest son of Leibke FISCHER | 196 |
| FISCHER | | | M | | Leibke | | | middle son of Leibke FISCHER | 196 |

| FISCHER |  |  | M |  | Leibke |  |  | youngest son of Leibke FISCHER | 196 |
|---|---|---|---|---|---|---|---|---|---|
| FISCHER |  |  | F |  | Leibke |  |  | elder daughter of Leibke FISCHER | 196 |
| FISCHER |  |  | F |  | Leibke |  |  | younger daughter of Leibke FISCHER | 196 |
| FELDHAMER | Zeide |  | M | married |  |  | Gitschke |  | 196 |
| FELDHAMER | Gitschke |  | F | married |  |  | Zeide |  | 196 |
| FELDHAMER | Motye |  | M | married |  |  |  | children | 196 |
| FELDHAMER |  |  | F | married |  |  | Motye | children | 196 |
| FELDHAMER | Hersch |  | M | married |  |  |  |  | 196 |
| FELDHAMER |  |  | F | married |  |  | Hersch |  | 196 |
| FELDHAMER | Leib |  | M | married | Hersch |  |  | children | 196 |
| FELDHAMER |  |  | F | married |  |  | Leib | children | 196 |
| FELDHAMER | Dotsche |  | M | married | Hersch |  | Zelde | children | 196 |
| FELDHAMER | Zelde | KORN | F | married |  |  | Dotsche | children | 196 |
| FELDHAMER | Perl |  | F |  | Hersch |  |  |  | 196 |
| FELDHAMER | Moshe |  | M | married |  |  |  | children | 196 |
| FELDHAMER |  |  | F | married |  |  | Moshe | children | 196 |
| FELDHAMER | Aba |  | M | married |  |  |  | children | 196 |
| FELDHAMER |  |  | F | married |  |  | Aba | children | 196 |
| FELDHAMER | Zeide |  | M |  |  |  |  | and his family | 196 |
| FELDHAMER | Itzik |  | M | married |  |  |  |  | 196 |
| FELDHAMER |  |  | F | married |  |  | Itzik |  | 196 |
| FELDHAMER |  |  | F |  | Itzik |  |  |  | 196 |
| FELDHAMER | Herschel |  | M |  | Itzik |  |  | and his family | 196 |
| FELDHAMER | Shmerl |  | M |  | Itzik |  |  | and his family | 196 |
| FELDHAMER | Mordechai |  | M |  | Itzik |  |  |  | 196 |
| FELDHAMER | Moshe |  | M |  |  |  |  | and his family | 196 |
| FUCHS | Moshe |  | M | married |  |  |  | the mute tailor, children | 196 |
| FUCHS |  |  | F | married |  |  | Moshe | wife of the mute tailor. Children | 196 |
| FUCHS | Esther |  | F |  |  |  |  |  | 196 |
| FUCHS | Bobie |  | M |  |  | Esther |  |  | 196 |

| | | | | | | | | |
|---|---|---|---|---|---|---|---|---|
| FISCHBACH | Moritz | | M | married | | | children | 196 |
| FISCHBACH | | | F | married | | Moritz | children | 196 |
| PLACHNER | Naftali | | M | married | | | children | 196 |
| PLACHNER | | | F | married | | Naftali | children | 196 |
| PLACHNER | Moshe | | M | married | | | children. Carpenter | 196 |
| PLACHNER | | | F | married | | Moshe | children | 196 |
| | | FRIED | F | | Hersch | | and her family. Eldest daughter of Hersch FRIED | 196 |
| | | FRIED | F | | Hersch | | and her family. Middle daughter of Hersch FRIED | 196 |
| | | FRIED | F | | Hersch | | and her family. Youngest daughter of Hersch FRIED | 196 |
| FINKELSTEIN | Miriam Devorah | | F | | | | | 196 |
| | | FINKELSTEIN | F | | | Miriam Devorah | and her family. Elder daughter of Miriam Devorah FINKELSTEIN | 196 |
| | | FINKELSTEIN | F | | | Miriam Devorah | and her family. Younger daughter of Miriam Devorah FINKELSTEIN | 196 |
| FINKELSTEIN | Itzye | | M | | | | and his family | 196 |
| FLEISCHER | Menye | | F | | | Fishel | | 196 |
| FLEISCHER | Pina | | F | | Fishel | Menye | | 196 |
| FLEISCHER | Mendel | | M | | Fishel | Menye | | 196 |
| FLEISCHER | Moshe | | M | | Fishel | Menye | | 196 |

### צ Tzadik

| | | | | | | | | |
|---|---|---|---|---|---|---|---|---|
| TZVEIBACH | Tatke Berl | | M | married | | Nesya | | 196 |
| TZVEIBACH | Nesya | | F | married | | Tatke Berl | | 196 |
| TZVEIBACH | Avraham Yitzchak | | M | | Tatke Berl | Nesya | | 196, 197 |
| TZVEIBACH | Yakov | | M | | Tatke Berl | Nesya | | 197 |
| TZVEIBACH | Pepi | | F | | Tatke Berl | Nesya | | 197 |
| TZVEIBACH | Shlima | | F | | Tatke Berl | Nesya | | 197 |

| | | | | | | | | | |
|---|---|---|---|---|---|---|---|---|---|
| TZVEIBACH | Chaim | | M | married | | | | | 197 |
| TZVEIBACH | | | F | married | | | Chaim | | 197 |
| TZVEIBACH | | | F | | Chaim | | | elder daughter of Chaim TZVEIBACH | 197 |
| TZVEIBACH | | | F | | Chaim | | | younger daughter of Chaim TZVEIBACH | 197 |
| TZVEIBACH | Meir | | M | | Chaim | | | | 197 |
| TZIRL | Shlomo | | M | | | | | and his family. From Rybno | 197 |
| TZIRL | Shimon | | M | | | | | | 197 |
| TZIRL | | | F | | | | | mother of Shimon TZIRL | 197 |
| TZIRL | Meir | | M | married | | | | children. On the list "fuftziker" (fifty?) is written | 197 |
| TZIRL | | | F | married | | | Meir | children | 197 |
| TZEIGER | Yosel | | M | married | | | Motel | | 197 |
| TZEIGER | Motel | | F | married | | | Yosel | | 197 |
| | Fantzye | TZEIGER | F | married | Yosel | Motel | | children | 197 |
| | | | M | married | | | Fantzye | children | 197 |
| | Yute | TZEIGER | F | married | Yosel | Motel | | children | 197 |
| | | | M | married | | | Yute | children | 197 |
| TZEIGER | Herschel | | M | | Yosel | Motel | | | 197 |
| TZEIGER | Leibele | | M | | Yosel | Motel | | | 197 |
| TZACH | Moshe Chaim | | M | | | | | and his family | 197 |
| TZUKERMAN | Avraham | | M | married | | | | | 197 |
| TZUKERMAN | | | F | married | | | Avraham | | 197 |
| TZUKERMAN | Mendel | | M | married | Avraham | | | | 197 |
| TZUKERMAN | | | F | married | | | Mendel | | 197 |
| TZUKERMAN | Moshe | | M | | Avraham | | | | 197 |
| TZUKERMAN | Yakov | | M | married | Avraham | | | children | 197 |
| TZUKERMAN | | | F | married | | | Yakov | children | 197 |
| | Danya | TZUKERMAN | F | married | Avraham | | | children | 197 |
| | | | M | married | | | Danya | children | 197 |
| | Esther | TZUKERMAN | F | married | Avraham | | | children | 197 |

| Surname | Given name | Surname | Sex | Married | Father | Mother | Spouse | Notes | Page |
|---|---|---|---|---|---|---|---|---|---|
| | | | M | married | | | Esther | children | 197 |

ק **Kof**

| Surname | Given name | Surname | Sex | Married | Father | Mother | Spouse | Notes | Page |
|---|---|---|---|---|---|---|---|---|---|
| KOHEN | Herschel | | M | married | | | Keile | 6 children | 197 |
| KOHEN | Keile | | F | married | | | Herschel | 6 children | 197 |
| KAHANE | Munye | | M | married | | | | 2 children | 197 |
| KAHANE | | | F | married | | | Munye | 2 children | 197 |
| KAHANE | Esther | | F | | | | | and family | 197 |
| KOHEN | Leibish | | M | | | | | and his family | 197 |
| KOHEN | Itzik | | M | | Leibish | | | and his family | 197 |
| KOHEN | Herschel | | M | | Leibish | | | and his family | 197 |
| KOHEN | Zeide | | M | | Leibish | | | and his family | 197 |
| KASWAN | Ribe | | F | | | | Moshe Meir | | 197 |
| KASWAN | Chaim Avraham | | M | married | | Ribe | | Children; he is probably the son of Moshe Meir KASWAN | 197 |
| KASWAN | | | F | married | | | Chaim Avraham | children | 197 |
| KASWAN | Itzik | | M | married | | Ribe | | Children; he is probably the son of Moshe MeirKASWAN | 197 |
| KASWAN | | | F | married | | | Itzik | children | 197 |
| | Beile Feige | KASWAN | F | married | | Ribe | | 2 children; she is probably the daughter of Moshe Meir KASWAN | 197 |
| | | | M | married | | | | 2 children | 197 |
| | Minye | KASWAN | F | married | | Ribe | | 1 child; she is probably the daughter of Moshe Meir KASWAN | 197 |
| | | | M | married | | | | 1 child | 197 |
| KASNER | Avraham | | M | | | | | and his family | 197 |
| KASNER | Leizer | | M | married | | | | | 197 |
| KASNER | | | F | married | | | Leizer | | 197 |
| KASNER | Sarah | | F | | | | | sister of Yankel; on the list "the black" is written | 197 |

| | | | | | | | | | |
|---|---|---|---|---|---|---|---|---|---|
| KASNER | Yankel | | M | | | | | brother of Sarah KASNER; probably his surname is different | 197 |
| KASNER | Itzye | | M | married | | | | bath attendant | 197 |
| KASNER | | | F | married | | | Itzye | | 197 |
| | Etel | KASNER | F | married | Itzye | | | 1 child | 197 |
| | | | M | married | | | Etel | 1 child | 197 |
| KASNER | Leizer | | M | married | Itzye | | | children | 197 |
| KASNER | | | F | married | | | Leizer | children | 197 |
| KASNER | Shimon | | M | married | Itzye | | | children | 197 |
| KASNER | | | F | married | | | Shimon | children | 197 |
| KOLER | Hersch | | M | | | | | and his family. From Kabaky | 197 |
| KOLER | Shalom | | M | | | | | and his family. From Kabaky | 197 |
| KATZ | Feige | | F | | | | | on the list "of Rafael" is written; it's unclear whether this refers to her husband or brother | 197 |
| KATZ | Rafael | | M | married | | | Elka | | 197 |
| KATZ | Elka | | F | married | | | Rafael | | 197 |
| KATZ | Avraham Itzye | | M | married | Rafael | Elka | | children | 197 |
| KATZ | | | F | married | | | Avraham Itzye | children | 197 |
| KATZ | Anschel | | M | married | Rafael | Elka | | children | 197 |
| KATZ | | | F | married | | | Anschel | children | 197 |
| KATZ | Baruch | | M | married | | | | | 198 |
| KATZ | | | F | married | | | Baruch | | 198 |
| KATZ | | | M | | Baruch | | | and his family; elder son of Baruch KATZ | 198 |
| KATZ | | | M | | Baruch | | | and his family; younger son of Baruch KATZ | 198 |
| | | KATZ | F | | Baruch | | | and her family; elder daughter of Baruch KATZ | 198 |

| Surname | Given name | | Sex | Status | Father | Mother | Spouse | Notes | Year |
|---|---|---|---|---|---|---|---|---|---|
|  |  | KATZ | F |  | Baruch |  |  | and her family; younger daughter of Baruch KATZ | 198 |
| KLINGER | Anschel |  | M | married |  |  | Channah |  | 198 |
| KLINGER | Channah |  | F | married |  |  | Anschel |  | 198 |
| KLINGER | Yosel |  | M |  | Anschel | Channah |  |  | 198 |
| KLINGER | Moshe |  | M |  | Anschel | Channah |  |  | 198 |
| KLINGER | Leib |  | M |  | Anschel | Channah |  |  | 198 |
| KLINGER | Gershon |  | M | married |  |  | Breintsche |  | 198 |
| KLINGER | Breintsche |  | F | married |  |  | Gershon |  | 198 |
| KLINGER | Channah |  | F |  | Gershon | Breintsche |  |  | 198 |
| KLINGER | Leib Bunye |  | M |  | Gershon | Breintsche |  |  | 198 |
| KLINGER | Karl |  | M |  | Gershon | Breintsche |  |  | 198 |
| KLINGER | Hersch Leib |  | M | married |  |  | Loira |  | 198 |
| KLINGER | Loira |  | F | married |  |  | Hersch Leib |  | 198 |
| KLINGER | Lianye |  | M |  | Hersch Leib | Loira |  |  | 198 |
| KLINGER | Niamye |  | M |  | Hersch Leib | Loira |  |  | 198 |
| KLINGER | Mendel |  | M |  | Meir Wolf |  |  |  | 198 |
| KLINGER | Shimon |  | M |  | Meir Wolf |  |  |  | 198 |
| KLETERER | Yisrael |  | M | married |  |  |  |  | 198 |
| KLETERER |  |  | F | married |  |  | Yisrael |  | 198 |
| KLETERER |  |  | F |  | Yisrael |  |  |  | 198 |
| KLETERER | Binyamin |  | M | married |  |  |  |  | 198 |
| KLETERER |  |  | F | married |  |  | Binyamin |  | 198 |
|  | Sheva | KLETERER | F |  | Yehoshua |  |  | and family | 198 |
|  | Witel | KLETERER | F |  | Yehoshua |  |  | and family | 198 |
|  | Eidel | KLETERER | F |  | Yehoshua |  |  | and family | 198 |
| KLIEGER | Shmuel |  | M | married |  |  |  | 2 children | 198 |
| KLIEGER |  |  | F | married |  |  | Shmuel | 2 children | 198 |
| KLAR | Shlomo |  | M |  |  |  |  | brother of Shprinye, Sarah and Lortzieh | 198 |
|  | Shprinye | KLAR | F | married |  |  |  | sister of Shlomo, Sarah and Lortzieh | 198 |

| Surname | Given | | Sex | Married | Father | Mother | Spouse | Notes | Year |
|---|---|---|---|---|---|---|---|---|---|
| | | | M | married | | | Shprinye | | 198 |
| | Sarah | KLAR | F | married | | | | children; sister of Shlomo, Shprinye and Lortzieh | 198 |
| | | | M | married | | | Sarah | children | 198 |
| | Lortzye | KLAR | F | married | | | | sister of Shlomo, Shrpinye and Sarah | 198 |
| | | | M | married | | | Lortzye | | 198 |
| | | | M | | | Lortzye | | | 198 |
| KORN | Kopl | | M | married | | | | | 198 |
| KORN | | | F | married | | | Kopl | | 198 |
| KORN | | | M | | Kopl | | | elder son of Koppel | 198 |
| KORN | | | M | | Kopl | | | younger son of Koppel | 198 |
| KORN | Moshe | | M | | | | | | 198 |
| KORN | Rivkele | | F | | Moshe | | | | 198 |
| KORN | Asher Eizik | | M | married | Moshe | | | children | 198 |
| KORN | | | F | married | | | Asher Eizik | children | 198 |
| KORN | Herschele | | M | | Moshe | | | | 198 |
| KORN | | | F | | | | Zalman | | 198 |
| KORN | Yisrael | | M | married | Zalman | | | children | 198 |
| KORN | | | F | married | | | Yisrael | children | 198 |
| KREMER | Avraham | | M | married | | | Sarahtze | | 198 |
| KREMER | Sarahtze | | F | married | | | Avraham | | 198 |
| KREMER | Hersch | | M | married | | | Toibe | children | 198 |
| KREMER | Toibe | SOFER | F | married | | | Hersch | children | 198 |
| KREMER | Moshe | | M | married | | | | children | 198 |
| KREMER | | | F | married | | | Moshe | children | 198 |
| KREMER | Chaim Leib | | M | | | | | | 198 |
| | | KREMER | F | | Chaim Leib | | | and her family; elder daughter of Chaim Leib KREMER | 198 |
| | | KREMER | F | | Chaim Leib | | | and her family; younger daughter | 198 |

| Surname | Given | Surname | Sex | Married | Father | | Spouse | Notes | Page |
|---|---|---|---|---|---|---|---|---|---|
| | | | | | | | | of Chaim Leib KREMER | |
| KRUMHOLTZ | Nisan | | M | | | | | | 198 |
| KRUMHOLTZ | Moshe | | M | married | | | | | 198 |
| KRUMHOLTZ | | | F | married | | | Moshe | | 198 |
| | | KRUMHOLTZ | F | | Moshe | | | and family; eldest daughter of Moshe KRUMHOLTZ | 198 |
| | | KRUMHOLTZ | F | | Moshe | | | and family; youngest daughter of Moshe KRUMHOLTZ | 198 |
| KRUMHOLTZ | Nachum Yosel | | M | married | | | | | 198 |
| KRUMHOLTZ | | | F | married | | | Nachum Yosel | | 198 |
| | | KRUMHOLTZ | F | | Nachum Yosel | | | eldest daughter of Nachum Yosl KRUMHOLTZ | 198 |
| | | | M | | | | | children; husband of the elder daughter of Nachum Yosel KRUMHOLTZ | 198 |
| | | KRUMHOLTZ | F | | Nachum Yosel | | | middle daughter of Nachum Yosl KRUMHOLTZ | 198 |
| | | | M | | | | | children; husband of the middle daughter of Nachum Yosel KRUMHOLTZ | 198 |
| | | KRUMHOLTZ | F | | Nachum Yosel | | | children; youngest daughter of Nachum Yosl KRUMHOLTZ | 198 |
| | | | M | | | | | children; husband of the younger daughter of Nachum Yosel KRUMHOLTZ | 198 |
| KRUMHOLTZ | Pinye | | M | married | Nachum Yosel | | | children | 198 |
| KRUMHOLTZ | | | F | married | | | Pinye | children | 198 |
| KRUMHOLTZ | Moshe | | M | | Nachum Yosel | | | | 198 |

| | | | | | | | | | | |
|---|---|---|---|---|---|---|---|---|---|---|
| KRUMHOLTZ | Wolf | | M | married | | | | | | 198 |
| KRUMHOLTZ | | | F | married | | | Wolf | | | 198 |
| KRUMHOLTZ | Bertzye | | M | married | | | | 2 children | | 198 |
| KRUMHOLTZ | | | F | married | | | Bertzye | 2 children | | 198 |
| KRUMHOLTZ | Zeide | | M | married | | | | | | 198 |
| KRUMHOLTZ | | | F | married | | | Zeide | | | 198 |
| KRUMHOLTZ | | | M | | Zeide | | | and his family | | 198 |
| | | KRUMHOLTZ | F | | Zeide | | | and family | | 198 |
| KOIFMAN | Anschel | | M | married | | | Blime | | | 198 |
| KOIFMAN | Blime | | F | married | | | Anschel | | | 198 |
| KOIFMAN | Chaim | | M | | Anschel | Blime | | | | 198 |
| KANALLER | Zigmunt | | M | married | | | Tina | | | 199 |
| KANALLER | Tina | | F | married | | | Zigmunt | | | 199 |
| KANALLER | Edmund | | M | | Zigmunt | Tina | | | | 199 |
| KANALLER | Risi Richard | | M | | Zigmunt | Tina | | | | 199 |
| KEZ | Zeide | | M | married | | | Neche | 4 children | | 199 |
| KEZ | Neche | | F | married | | | Zeide | 4 children | | 199 |
| KIMEL | Berl | | M | married | | | Channah | | | 199 |
| KIMEL | Channah | | F | married | | | Berl | | | 199 |
| KIMEL | Mechel | | M | married | Berl | Channah | | 1 child | | 199 |
| KIMEL | | | F | married | | | Mechel | 1 child | | 199 |
| KEZ | Yankel | | M | married | | | | | | 199 |
| KEZ | | | F | married | | | Yankel | | | 199 |
| KRUMHOLTZ | Chaike | STIER | F | married | | | Moris | granddaughter of Yankel KEZ | | 199 |
| KRUMHOLTZ | Moris | | M | married | | | Chaike | From Yablunytsya | | 199 |
| KRUMHOLTZ | | | M | | Moris | Chaike | | | | 199 |
| KLEIN | Wolf | | M | married | | | | | | 199 |
| KLEIN | | | F | married | | | Wolf | | | 199 |
| KERNER | Shmuel | | M | married | | | | | | 199 |
| KERNER | | | F | married | | | Shmuel | | | 199 |
| KERNER | Mechel | | M | married | Shmuel | | | children | | 199 |
| KERNER | | | F | married | | | Mechel | children | | 199 |

| | | | | | | | | | |
|---|---|---|---|---|---|---|---|---|---|
| KERNER | Moshe | | M | married | Shmuel | | | children | 199 |
| KERNER | | | F | married | | | Moshe | children | 199 |
| | | KERNER | F | married | Shmuel | | | on the list "their sister" is written. Apparently this means she was the sister of Mechel and Moshe and the daughter of Shmuel KERNER | 199 |
| | | | M | married | | | | Wife's maiden name KERNER. On the list next to his wife "their sister" is written. Apparently this means she was the sister of Mechel and Moshe and the daughter of Shmuel KERNER | 199 |

ר **Resh**

| | | | | | | | | | |
|---|---|---|---|---|---|---|---|---|---|
| RAPAPORT | Yosef | | M | married | | | Dina | | 199 |
| RAPAPORT | Dina | | F | married | | | Yosef | | 199 |
| RAPAPORT | Menachem | | M | | Yosef | Dina | | | 199 |
| RAPAPORT | Leib | | M | | Yosef | Dina | | | 199 |
| RAPAPORT | Moshele | | M | | Yosef | Dina | | | 199 |
| ROZNER | Moshe | | M | married | | | | | 199 |
| ROZNER | | | F | married | | | Moshe | | 199 |
| RIEBER | Yosel | | M | | | | | and his family | 199 |
| RIEBER | Anschel | | M | married | | | Golde | | 199 |
| RIEBER | Golde | | F | married | | | Anschel | | 199 |
| RIEBER | David Dugye | | M | | Anschel | Golde | | | 199 |
| | Sutze | | F | | | | | on the list "his cousin" is written and it's not clear if she is the cousin of Anschel RIEBER or his son David (Dugye) | 199 |
| ROZENHECK | | | F | married | | | Hersch | | 199 |
| | | ROZENHECK | F | | Hersch | | | and family; eldest daughter of the | 199 |

| Surname | Given Name | | Sex | | Father | Mother | Spouse | Comments | Year |
|---|---|---|---|---|---|---|---|---|---|
| | | | | | | | | wife of Hersch ROZENHECK | |
| | | ROZENHECK | F | | Hersch | | | and family; middle daughter of the wife of Hersch ROZENHECK | 199 |
| | | ROZENHECK | F | | Hersch | | | and family; youngest daughter of the wife of Hersch ROZENHECK | 199 |
| RINDNER | Leah | | F | | Moshe | | | 2 children; daughter of Moshe SHUSTER | 199 |
| REIZER | Chaim Meir | | M | married | | | Devorah Henye | | 199 |
| REIZER | Devorah Henye | | F | married | | | Chaim Meir | | 199 |
| REIZER | Avraham Leib | | M | | Chaim Meir | Devorah Henye | | | 199 |
| REIZER | Shlomo | | M | | Chaim Meir | Devorah Henye | | | 199 |
| REIZER | Yakov | | M | | Chaim Meir | Devorah Henye | | | 199 |
| REIZER | Yakov | | M | | | | | | 199 |
| REIZER | Chaim | | M | | | | | | 199 |
| REIZER | Rentze | | F | | | | | | 199 |
| REIZER | Rakhel | | F | | | | | | 199 |
| REMER | Toibe | | F | | | | Paul | 2 children | 199 |
| REGENSTREIF | Avraham | | M | married | | | | | 199 |
| REGENSTREIF | | | F | married | | | Avraham | | 199 |
| REGENSTREIF | | | F | | Avraham | | | | 199 |
| REGENSTREIF | Herschel | | M | married | | | | children | 199 |
| REGENSTREIF | | | F | married | | | Herschel | children | 199 |
| REGENBOIGEN | Zeide | | M | | | | | | 199 |
| REGENBOIGEN | | | F | | Zeide | | | | 199 |
| REGENBOIGEN | | | M | | Zeide | | | and his family; elder son of Zeide REGENBOIGEN | 199 |
| REGENBOIGEN | | | M | | Zeide | | | and his family; younger son of | 199 |

| Surname | First name | Maiden name | Sex | Status | Relation | Spouse | Notes | Page |
|---|---|---|---|---|---|---|---|---|
| | | | | | | | Zeide REGENBOIGEN | |
| RESCH | Itzik | | M | married | | | | 199 |
| RESCH | | | F | married | | Itzik | | 199 |
| | | RESCH | F | | Itzik | | and her family; elder daughter of Itzik RESCH | 199 |
| | | RESCH | F | | Itzik | | and her family; younger daughter of Itzik RESCH | 199 |
| RESCH | Zeide | | M | | Itzik | | | 199 |

**ש Shin**

| SHAM | Chaim | | M | married | | Pesi Roize | | 199 |
| SHAM | | | F | married | | Chaim | | 199 |
| | | SHAM | F | | Chaim | | and family | 199 |
| SHATNER | Zeide | | M | married | | | | 199 |
| SHATNER | | | F | married | | Zeide | | 199 |
| SHATNER | Moshe | | M | married | Zeide | | children | 199 |
| SHATNER | | | F | married | | Moshe | children | 199 |
| SHATNER | Yakov | | M | | Zeide | | | 199 |
| | Moltzye | SHATNER | F | | Zeide | | children | 199 |
| SHATNER | Gedalya | | M | married | | | 2 children | 200 |
| SHATNER | | | F | married | | Gedalya | 2 children | 200 |
| SHATNER | Eliahu | | M | married | | | | 200 |
| SHATNER | | | F | married | | Eliahu | | 200 |
| SHATNER | Chaim | | M | married | | | | 200 |
| SHATNER | | | F | married | | Chaim | | 200 |
| | Toibe | SHATNER | F | | Chaim | | and family | 200 |
| SHARFSTEIN | Chaim | | M | married | | | children | 200 |
| SHARFSTEIN | | | F | married | | Chaim | children | 200 |
| SCHERTZER | Itzye | | M | married | | | | 200 |
| SCHERTZER | | | F | married | | Itzye | | 200 |
| SCHERTZER | Ireh | | M | | Itzye | | | 200 |
| SCHERTZER | Leib | | M | married | Itzye | Roza | 1 child | 200 |
| SCHERTZER | Roza | PFAU | F | married | | Leib | 1 child | 200 |

| | | | | | | | | | |
|---|---|---|---|---|---|---|---|---|---|
| | Moltzye | SCHERTZER | F | married | Itzye | | | children | 200 |
| | | | M | married | | | Moltzye | children | 200 |
| | Etke | SCHERTZER | F | married | Itzye | | | | 200 |
| | | | M | married | | | Etke | | 200 |
| SCHERTZER | Sheindel | | F | | | | | on the list "their mother" is written; probably her surname is different as it's not clear who this refers to. | 200 |
| SHECHTER | Avraham | | M | married | | | | bookbinder | 200 |
| SHECHTER | | | F | married | | | Avraham | bookbinder's wife | 200 |
| SHECHTER | | | M | | Avraham | | | eldest son of Avraham SHECHTER | 200 |
| SHECHTER | | | M | | Avraham | | | middle son of Avraham SHECHTER | 200 |
| SHECHTER | | | M | | Avraham | | | youngest son of Avraham SHECHTER | 200 |
| SHECHTER | Hendel | | M | married | | | | 1 child | 200 |
| SHECHTER | | | F | married | | | Hendel | 1 child | 200 |
| SHECHTER | Avraham | | M | married | | | | leather merchant | 200 |
| SHECHTER | | | F | married | | | Avraham | leather merchant's wife | 200 |
| SHECHTER | Mordechai Itzik | | M | married | | | | | 200 |
| SHECHTER | | | F | married | | | Mordechai Itzik | | 200 |
| SHECHTER | David | | M | | Mordechai Itzik | | | and his family | 200 |
| SHECHTER | Neta | | M | married | Mordechai Itzik | | | children | 200 |
| SHECHTER | | | F | married | | | Neta | children | 200 |
| SHECHTER | Yisrael | | M | | Mordechai Itzik | | | | 200 |
| | Rivka | SHECHTER | F | | Mordechai Itzik | | | and family | 200 |
| | Henye | SHECHTER | F | | Mordechai Itzik | | | and family | 200 |

| | Chaya | SHECHTER | F | | Mordechai Itzik | | | and family | 200 |
|---|---|---|---|---|---|---|---|---|---|
| SHECHTER | Chaitze | | F | | | | Yakov | | 200 |
| SHECHTER | Mordechai | | M | | Yakov | Chaitze | | | 200 |
| SHECHTER | Yitzchak | | M | | Yakov | Chaitze | | | 200 |
| SHECHTER | Rafael | | M | married | | | Babtziye | | 200 |
| SHECHTER | Babtziye | | F | married | | | Rafael | | 200 |
| SHECHTER | Batya | | F | | Rafael | Babtziye | | | 200 |
| SHECHTER | Shmuel | | M | | Rafael | Babtziye | | | 200 |
| SHECHTER | Shmuel | | M | | | | | | 200 |
| SHECHTER | Hendel | | M | | | | | | 200 |
| SHECHTER | Mindel | | F | | Hendel | | | | 200 |
| SHECHTER | Esther | | F | | Hendel | | | | 200 |
| SHECHTER | Avraham | | M | | Hendel | | | | 200 |
| SHECHTER | Pesye | | F | | Hendel | | | | 200 |
| SHECHTER | Devorah | | F | | Hendel | | | | 200 |
| SHECHTER | Naftali | | M | | Hendel | | | | 200 |
| SHECHTER | Sheindel | | F | | | | Meir | | 200 |
| MENTSCHEL | Devorah | SHECHTER | F | married | Meir | Sheindel | Zelik | 2 children | 200 |
| MENTSCHEL | Zelik | | M | married | | | Devorah | 2 children | 200 |
| SHECHTER | Gitsche | | F | | Meir | Sheindel | | | 200 |
| SHECHTER | Sarah | | F | | Meir | Sheindel | | | 200 |
| SHECHTER | Shlomo | | M | married | | | | 1 child | 200 |
| SHECHTER | | | F | married | | | Shlomo | 1 child | 200 |
| SHMERTZ | Nisan | | M | married | | | | children | 200 |
| SHMERTZ | | | F | married | | | Nisan | children | 200 |
| SHMERTZ | Moshe | | M | married | | | Malka | | 200 |
| SHMERTZ | Malka | | F | married | | | Moshe | | 200 |
| SHMERTZ | Avraham | | M | married | Moshe | Malka | Feige | | 200 |
| SHMERTZ | Feige | | F | married | | | Avraham | | 200 |
| SHMERTZ | Beti | | F | | Avraham | Feige | | | 200 |
| SHMERTZ | Peretz | | M | | Avraham | Feige | | | 200 |
| SHMERTZ | Zalman | | M | | | | | | 200 |
| SHMERTZ | Shlomo | | M | | | | | and his family | 200 |

| | | | | | | | | | |
|---|---|---|---|---|---|---|---|---|---|
| SHMERTZ | Peretz | | M | | | | | and his family | 200 |
| | Reina | SHTRAUS | F | | Manele | | | and family | 200 |
| SHTRAUS | Moshe | | M | married | | | | | 200 |
| SHTRAUS | | | F | married | | | Moshe | | 200 |
| SHTRAUS | Zeide | | M | married | Moshe | | | children | 200 |
| SHTRAUS | | | F | married | | | Zeide | children | 200 |
| SHTRAUS | Noach | | M | married | Moshe | | | children | 200 |
| SHTRAUS | | | F | married | | | Noach | children | 200 |
| SHTRAUS | Binyamin | | M | married | Moshe | | | children | 200 |
| SHTRAUS | | | F | married | | | Binyamin | children | 200 |
| SHTRAUS | Reuven | | M | married | Moshe | | | children | 200 |
| SHTRAUS | | | F | married | | | Reuven | children | 200 |
| SHTRAUS | Chaim | | M | | Moshe | | | | 201 |
| | Sheindel | SHTRAUS | F | married | | | | children | 201 |
| | | | M | married | | | Sheindel | children | 201 |
| SHTRAUS | Yisrael | | M | | | | | | 201 |
| STEINBRECHER | Moshe | | M | | | Channah | | and his family; on the list "Hannah's" is written | 201 |
| STEINBRECHER | Chaim Leib | | M | married | | | | | 201 |
| STEINBRECHER | | | F | married | | | Chaim Leib | | 201 |
| STEINBRECHER | | | M | | Chaim Leib | | | and his family; elder son of Chaim Leib STEINBRECHER | 201 |
| STEINBRECHER | | | M | | Chaim Leib | | | and his family; younger son of Chaim Leib STEINBRECHER | 201 |
| | | STEINBRECHER | F | | Chaim Leib | | | and her family; elder daughter of Chaim Leib STEINBRECHER | 201 |
| | | STEINBRECHER | F | | Chaim Leib | | | and her family; younger daughter of Chaim Leib STEINBRECHER | 201 |
| STEINBRECHER | Breintziye | | F | | | | | children | 201 |
| STEINBRECHER | Meir | | M | married | | | | | 201 |

| STEINBRECHER | | | F | married | | | Meir | | 201 |
|---|---|---|---|---|---|---|---|---|---|
| | | STEINBRECHER | F | | Meir | | | and family | 201 |
| STEINBRECHER | Itschele | | M | married | | | | children | 201 |
| STEINBRECHER | | | F | married | | | Itschele | children | 201 |
| STEIGMAN | Avraham | | M | married | | | Reina | | 201 |
| STEIGMAN | Reina | ETINGER | F | married | | | Avraham | | 201 |
| STEIGMAN | Zigfried | | M | | Avraham | Reina | | | 201 |
| STEIGMAN | Yulek | | M | | Avraham | Reina | | | 201 |
| STEIGMAN | Berta | | F | | | | | | 201 |
| STEIGMAN | | | F | | | | | mother of Berta STEIGMAN; her surname is probably different | 201 |
| STEIGMAN | Peritz | | M | | | | | | 201 |
| STEIGMAN | Wolf | | M | | | | | and his family | 201 |
| STEIGMAN | Pinye | | M | | | | | and his family | 201 |
| STEIGMAN | | | F | | | | | on the list "their mother" is written. She is probably the mother of Pinye STEIGMAN | 201 |
| STEIGMAN | | | F | | | | | elder daughter of the mother of Pinye STEIGMAN | 201 |
| STEIGMAN | | | F | | | | | younger daughter of the mother of Pinye STEIGMAN | 201 |
| SHTETNER | Mendel | | M | married | | | | | 201 |
| SHTETNER | | | F | married | | | Mendel | | 201 |
| SHTENGEL | Shlomo | | M | | | | | and his family. From Rybno | 201 |
| STEIN | Leibish | | M | | | | | and his family | 201 |
| STEIN | Pesye | | F | | | | | | 201 |
| | Beile | STEIN | F | | | Pesye | | and family | 201 |
| STEIN | Sheva | | F | | | Pesye | | | 201 |
| STEINKAHEL | Eliahu | | M | married | | | Freide | | 201 |
| STEINKAHEL | Freide | MANDEL | F | married | | | Eliahu | | 201 |

| | | | | | | | | | |
|---|---|---|---|---|---|---|---|---|---|
| STEINKAHEL | Medzia | | M | | Eliahu | Freide | | gender determined by a Page of Testimony | 201 |
| STEINKAHEL | Hesya | | F | | Eliahu | Freide | | | 201 |
| SHTENGEL | Hendel | | M | | | Minge | | and his family | 201 |
| SHTENGEL | Minge | | F | | | | | | 201 |
| SHTENGEL | | | F | | | Minge | | elder daughter of Minge SHTENGEL | 201 |
| SHTENGEL | | | F | | | Minge | | younger daughter of Minge SHTENGEL | 201 |
| SHTENGEL | Dotsche | | M | | | | | | 201 |
| SHTENGEL | | | F | | | | | mother of Dotsche SHTENGEL | 201 |
| SHTENGEL | | | F | | ' | | | sister of Dotsche SHTENGEL | 201 |
| SCHVARTZ | Moshe | | M | | | | | and his family | 201 |
| SCHVARTZ | Yosel | | M | married | | | | | 201 |
| SCHVARTZ | | | F | married | | | Yosel | | 201 |
| SCHVARTZ | | | M | | Yosel | | | elder daughter of Yosel SCHVARTZ | 201 |
| SCHVARTZ | | | M | | Yosel | | | younger daughter of Yosel SCHVARTZ | 201 |
| SHOIMAN | Zeide | | M | married | | | | | 201 |
| SHOIMAN | | | F | married | | | Zeide | | 201 |
| SHOIMAN | Danya | | F | | Zeide | | | | 201 |
| SHOIMAN | Avraham | | M | | Zeide | | | | 201 |
| SHOIMAN | Chaim | | M | | Zeide | | | | 201 |
| SHOIMAN | Yudel | | M | married | | | Roza | | 201 |
| SHOIMAN | Roza | | F | married | | | Yudel | | 201 |
| | Gusta | SHOIMAN | F | married | Yudel | Roza | | | 201 |
| | | | M | married | | | Gusta | | 201 |
| SHOIMAN | Izye | | M | | Yudel | Roza | | | 201 |
| SHOIMAN | Fuge | | M | | Yudel | Roza | | | 201 |
| SHIEBER | Yente | | F | | | | | | 201 |

| Surname | First name | | Sex | Status | Father | Mother/Spouse | Notes | Page |
|---|---|---|---|---|---|---|---|---|
| | | SHIEBER | F | | | Yente | and her family; elder daughter of Yente SHIEBER | 201 |
| | | SHIEBER | F | | | Yente | and her family; younger daughter of Yente SHIEBER | 201 |
| SHIEBER | | | M | | | Yente | and his family; eldest son of Yente SHIEBER | 201 |
| SHIEBER | | | M | | | Yente | and his family; middle son of Yente SHIEBER | 201 |
| SHIEBER | | | M | | | Yente | and his family; youngest son of Yente SHIEBER | 201 |
| SHIZEL | Zeide | | M | married | | Meta | 3 children | 202 |
| SHIZEL | Meta | | F | married | | Zeide | 3 children | 202 |
| SHIREN | Wolf | | M | married | | Esther | children | 202 |
| SHIREN | Esther | SENDER | F | married | | Wolf | children | 202 |
| SHIREN | Gavriel | | M | married | | | children | 202 |
| SHIREN | | | F | married | | Gavriel | children | 202 |
| SHUSTER | Moshe | | M | | | | and his family | 202 |
| SHLAU | | | | | | | the entire family of Motye SHLAU | 202 |
| SHLAU | Sarah | | F | | | | | 202 |
| SHLAU | | | M | | Sarah | | and his family; eldest son of Sarah SHLAU | 202 |
| SHLAU | | | M | | Sarah | | and his family, middle son of Sarah SHLAU | 202 |
| SHLAU | | | M | | Sarah | | and his family; youngest son of Sarah SHLAU | 202 |
| SHMETERER | Yudel | | M | married | | | | 202 |
| SHMETERER | | | F | married | | Yudel | | 202 |
| SHMETERER | | | M | | Yudel | | and his family; eldest son of Yudel SHMETERER | 202 |
| SHMETERER | | | M | | Yudel | | and his family; middle son of | 202 |

| | | | | | | | | |
|---|---|---|---|---|---|---|---|---|
| SHMETERER | | | M | | Yudel | | | Yudel SHMETERER and his family; youngest son of Yudel SHMETERER | 202 |
| | | SHMETERER | F | | Yudel | | | and family | 202 |
| SHMETERER | Mindel | | F | | | | | | 202 |
| SHMETERER | Shmuel | | M | married | | | Sarah | | 202 |
| SHMETERER | Sarah | | F | married | | | Shmuel | | 202 |
| SHMETERER | Bobeleh | | F | | Shmuel | Sarah | | | 202 |
| SHMETERER | Hersch | | M | married | Shmuel | Sarah | | children | 202 |
| SHMETERER | | | F | married | | | Hersch | children | 202 |
| SHMETERER | Shalom | | M | married | Shmuel | Sarah | | children | 202 |
| SHMETERER | | | F | married | | | Shalom | children | 202 |
| SHMETERER | Zeide | | M | | Shmuel | Sarah | | | 202 |
| SHMETERER | Lozer | | M | | Shmuel | Sarah | | | 202 |
| SHMID | Mechel | | M | | | | | and his family | 202 |
| SHNAPF | David | | M | | | | | | 202 |
| SHNAPF | | | F | | | | | mother of David SHNAPF | 202 |
| SHNAPF | Yosel | | M | married | | | Leah | | 202 |
| SHNAPF | Leah | | F | married | | | Yosel | | 202 |
| SHNAPF | Chaim | | M | married | Yosel | Leah | Chaya | 3 children | 202 |
| SHNAPF | Chaya | | F | married | | | Chaim | 3 children | 202 |
| SHNAPF | Malka | | F | | | | | and family | 202 |
| SHNITZER | Chaim | | M | | | | | and his family | 202 |
| SHNITZER | Kalman | | M | married | | | | | 202 |
| SHNITZER | | | F | married | | | Kalman | | 202 |
| SHNITZER | Herschel | | M | married | Kalman | | Henye | | 202 |
| SHNITZER | Henye | MOSKOWITZ | F | married | | | Herschel | | 202 |
| SHNITZER | Chaya Sarah | | F | | Herschel | Henye | | | 202 |
| SHNITZER | Aba | | M | married | Kalman | | | children | 202 |
| SHNITZER | | | F | married | | | Aba | children | 202 |
| SHNITZER | Aba | | M | married | | | | Lived on Gericht's Street | 202 |

| | | | | | | | | | |
|---|---|---|---|---|---|---|---|---|---|
| SHNITZER | | | F | married | | | Aba | Lived on Gericht's Street | 202 |
| | | SHNITZER | F | | Aba | | | and family. Lived on Gericht's Street | 202 |
| SCHER | Butze | | F | | | | | | 202 |
| | Ipika | SCHER | F | married | | Butze | | children | 202 |
| | | | M | married | | | Ipika | children | 202 |
| SCHER | Moshe | | M | | | Butze | | | 202 |
| SCHER | Moshe | | M | | | | | flour merchant | 202 |
| | | SCHER | F | | Moshe | | | and her family; elder daughter of Moshe SCHER | 202 |
| | | SCHER | F | | Moshe | | | and her family; younger daughter of Moshe SCHER | 202 |
| SCHER | | | M | | Moshe | | | and his family; eldest son of Moshe SCHER | 202 |
| SCHER | | | M | | Moshe | | | and his family; 2nd son of Moshe SCHER | 202 |
| SCHER | | | M | | Moshe | | | and his family, 3rd son of Moshe SCHER | 202 |
| SCHER | | | M | | Moshe | | | and his family; youngest son of Moshe SCHER | 202 |
| SCHER | Eizik | | M | married | | | Beile | | 202 |
| SCHER | Beile | | F | married | | | Eizik | | 202 |
| SCHER | Hersch | | M | | Eizik | Beile | | | 202 |
| SCHER | Leizer | | M | | Eizik | Beile | | | 202 |
| SCHER | Feige | | F | | | | | | 202 |
| FLEISCHER | Etel | SCHER | F | married | | Feige | Mutzik | 2 children | 202 |
| FLEISCHER | Mutzik | | M | married | | | Etel | 2 children | 202 |
| SCHERF | Pinye | | M | married | | | | children | 202 |
| SCHERF | | | F | married | | | Pinye | children | 202 |
| SCHERF | Yehoshua | | M | married | | | | children | 202 |
| SCHERF | | | F | married | | | Yehoshua | children | 202 |
| SCHERF | Pesach | | M | married | | | | 1 child | 202 |

| | | | | | | | | | |
|---|---|---|---|---|---|---|---|---|---|
| SCHERF | | | F | married | | | Pesach | 1 child | 202 |
| SCHERF | Mendel | | M | married | | | | children | 203 |
| SCHERF | | | F | married | | | Mendel | children | 203 |
| SCHERF | Shmuel | | M | married | | | Gusta | 1 child | 203 |
| SCHERF | Gusta | STEIGMAN | F | married | | | Shmuel | 1 child | 203 |
| SCHERF | Shlomo | | M | married | | | | | 203 |
| SCHERF | | | F | married | | | Shlomo | | 203 |
| SCHERF | Alter | | M | | | | | | 203 |
| SCHERF | | | F | | | | | and her family; mother of Alter SCHERF | 203 |
| | | SCHERF | F | | | | | and her family; sister of Alter SCHERF | 203 |
| SCHERF | Gedalya | | M | | | | | and his family | 203 |
| SHMID | Zeide | | M | | | | | and his family | 203 |
| SHPERBER | Meshulam | | M | | | | | | 203 |
| SHPERBER | | | M | | Meshulam | | | | 203 |
| SHPERBER | Sheintshe | | F | | | | Hersch | | 203 |
| KORN | Dina | SHPERBER | F | married | | Sheintshe | Kopl | | 203 |
| KORN | Kopl | | M | married | | | Dina | | 203 |
| KORN | | | M | | Kopl | Dina | | elder son of Kopl and Dina KORN | 203 |
| KORN | | | M | | Kopl | Dina | | younger son of Kopl and Dina KORN | 203 |
| LAUB | Bobeleh | SHPERBER | F | married | | Sheintshe | Yosel | 1 child | 203 |
| LAUB | Yosel | | M | married | | | Bobeleh | 1 child | 203 |
| SHPIEGEL | Leibtsche | | M | | | | | and his family | 203 |
| SHPIEGEL | Itzik | | M | married | | | | children | 203 |
| SHPIEGEL | | | F | married | | | Itzik | children | 203 |
| SHIEBER | Itzik | | M | married | | | | children | 203 |
| SHIEBER | | | F | married | | | Itzik | children | 203 |
| SHIEBER | Bertzye | | M | married | | | | children | 203 |
| SHIEBER | | | F | married | | | Bertzye | children | 203 |
| SHIEBER | Batya | | F | married | | | | children, husband. It is likely that her | 203 |

| | | | | | | | |
|---|---|---|---|---|---|---|---|
| | | | | | | surname is different. | |
| SHIEBER | Rakhel | | F | married | | children, husband. It is likely that her surname is different. | 203 |
| SHENKEL | Wolf Ber | | M | married | | | 203 |
| SHENKEL | | | F | married | | Wolf Ber | 203 |
| SHENKEL | | | F | | Wolf Ber | | 203 |

[Page 204]

# Final Word

### Ezekiel 37, according to the translation of Yehoash

Throughout the Polish fields and forests, among the mountains and valleys of Galicia and Ukraine, there lie, spread far and wide as a remembrance of the once great Jewish settlement in Poland – a long chain of large and small mass-graves. In these graves rest the bones of the millions of Jewish martyrs who perished in a brutal manner at the hands of the German murderers and their Ukrainian helpers during the blood war years of 1942-1944.

In the overgrown pass graves, under young saplings and grasses, lie the dried bones of our dear and unforgettable sisters and brothers. They rest there and wait until the vision of the prophet Ezekiel, by the river Chebar, shall be fulfilled.

"And he set me down in the midst of the valley which was full of bones.
And caused me to pass by them round about: and behold there were very many in the
open valley; and lo, they were very dry.
And he said unto me, Son of man, can these bones live?
And I answered, O Lord God, thou knowest.
Again, he said unto me, Prophesy upon these bones, and say unto them,
O ye dry bones, hear the word of the Lord.

[Page 205]

Thus, saith the Lord God unto these bones; Behold, I will cause breath
To enter into you, and you shall live: And I will lay sinews upon you.
* * *

And say to the wind, Thus, saith the Lord God; Come from the four winds, O breath,
And breathe upon these slain, that they may live.
So, I prophesised as he commanded me, and the breath came into them, and they lived,
and stood upon their feet, an exceeding great army.
Then he said unto me, Son of man, these bones are the whole house of Israel:
Behold, they say. Our bones are dried, and our hope is lost; we are cut off.
Therefore, prophesy and say unto them, Thus, saith the Lord God;
Behold, I will open your graves, and cause you to come up out of your graves,
And bring you to the land of Israel.

*[Page 206]*

*Blank*

*[Page 207]*

# First Kittever Illness Support Association in New York
# On Its Sixty Year Jubilee

*[Page 208]*

*Blank*

*[Page 209]*

## First Kittever Support Association of N.Y.
### (On its Sixty Year Jubilee)

After the dreadful destruction of Kittev, after the Germans and the Ukrainians did in the years 1942 and 1943, destroy all the Jews in a gruesome manner and, thereby, destroyed every trace of Jews and remnant of Jewish life in the historic city, afterward, the Kittever Association of New York remained as the only organized group of Kittever Jews which carries on a many-branched social-philanthropic work under the name: *"Kittever Sick and Benevolent Society of New York"*. (This name is in English, written with Yiddish letters).

The history of the KIttever Association in New York began in the year 1897 when the Kittever pioneers who had immigrated to America organized and founded the first Kittever illness-support organization.

The first Jewish immigrants from Kittev to America in the last years of the 19th century, were children of poor parents who lived in Kittev in want and poverty. When they grew up and considered their situation, they came to the conclusion that in the small and backward Kittev, without the necessary schools and institutions of education, there was no future for them. They sought ways to break out of poverty and backwardness and to forge for themselves a better existence.

At that time, the first reports about life in the "Golden Medina" reached Kittev. In free America, the land which is the place of refuge for all the oppressed and persecuted, the land which greets with open arms every person without discrimination as to religion or race, the land of limitless possibilities where everyone according to his talents can work himself up and even get rich, and the main thing, where every can live and conduct himself according to his conscience and persuasion.

*[Page 210]*

During the first few years, the Kittever landsleit in New York did not lick honey. It was natural that people who came from a small town, where everyone knew everyone, should feel lonely in the big and noisy New York.

Lacking the language of the land, without relatives and friends but full of confidence in their pioneering mission, our first Kittever set to work. They worked under the most difficult conditions, in various shops, 12-14 hours a day. Mostly, they slept at their places of work fearing that if they left the spot, someone else would take their place. In the hardest of conditions of sweat-shops, the Jews of Kittev worked and dreamed of a better and easier tomorrow for themselves and their families. Thus, they worked day-in-day out, saved on food and piled together a dollar-to-a-dollar in order to help their relatives in the old home.

When the Kittever immigrants became somewhat acclimatized, they began to think and look for ways to bring over their relatives from the old home. They also planned on how to get together from time-to-time and mutually help each other and generally, on how to create a Kittever environment in great New York. Then, in the year 1897, the first few Kittever landsleit of New York came together and established the first Kittever illness-support organization.

The tasks and aims which the organization set for itself were: to help the sick and need members here, locally, and to establish a continuing programme of assistance for the poor classes of Jews in the old home. In the year 1897, the organization numbered ten members but thanks to informational activity and constructive aid for members, and also thanks to the growing immigration, the number of members grew from day-to-day and year-to-year. In the year 1937, the Kittever organization numbered 135 member families. Not all the Kittever Jews of New York belong to the Kittever organization and only a small proportion of Kittever landsleit outside of New York are members of the organization.

*[Page 211]*

During its 60 years of existence, the Kittever organization has fulfilled the aims for which the first immigrants from Kittev founded the organization and the responsibilities which they assumed on behalf of their members and landsleit – fulfilled them fully and even surpassed them.

The organization is a thoroughly democratic one. The organizational work, the various aid activities and all the work within and outside the organization are carried out in a completely democratic fashion. At the meetings which are held once a month, all current questions and problems affecting the organization are discussed and decided democratically and every member can express his opinion and vote for or against.

The organization conducts elections once a year in the months of November and December. Before the elections, first and second nominations are made and members can nominate candidate for each office. After this, the elections are held and the leaders of the organization for the coming year are elected by majority vote.

The regular income of the organization comes from the fee which each member pays every quarter. In order to cover the necessary special expenses, the members are assessed a special tax or they collect the necessary sum through voluntary contributions.

The main regular benefits which the organization gives to its members are financial aid, sick benefit, death benefit, cemetery lots, their own Synagogue and so on.

*[Page 212]*

Before the war, the organization used to send to Kittev each year money for Maos Chittim (money for what – the designation for Passover supplies) and yearly subsidies for the Kittever charity institutions and for the religious necessities of the Jews of Kittev.

Aside from aid to the home city, the organization also provided annual subsidies to local Jewish philanthropic institutions such as HIAS, Joint, United Jewish Appeal and others.

After World War I, when the Kittever Jews had left the city for fear of the Cossacks, returned and found their homes destroyed; when the misery and poverty among the widows and orphans; victims of the horrible war were great, the Kittever organization of New York extended its brotherly hand across the sea and sent generous help to alleviate the neediness and suffering of the impoverished Jews of Kittev.

Besides the financial aid which the organization sent at that time, it also helped to solve one of the painful post-war problems in Kittev which was that of the poor Jewish orphans. Thanks to the sizeable amount that the organization sent to Kittev for this purpose, and thanks to the energetic work of the martyrs, Dr. Marcus Alesker and my friend

Eisig Grebler, the Jewish orphans' home was founded in Kittev which was a warm home and education institution as well as a trade school for the Jewish orphans.

In the year 1925, the Association also sent money which was used to buy a house opposite the Chassidic Bet Midrash, wherein a factory for rugs was set up and where the orphans learned the trade and became skilled workmen.

After the great national catastrophe, the horrible war-years 1939-1944 when only a small number of our landsleit (countrymen) succeeded in saving themselves from certain death, began to wander from country-to-country, city-to-city, homeless and rootless, hungry and naked, without a roof over their head, in the hour of destiny for the surviving remnant of Kittev, the small Kittever Association of New York proved, through deeds that it was equal to the historic role which the Jewish national destiny had placed upon it. The association gave help at that time for which it truly deserves great recognition.

*[Page 213]*

In various ways and in rapid and effective fashion, the association sent aid for every landsman. Whatever was needed was sent: medication, clothing, cash. The association also helped to connect the remaining landsleit with the near ones.

Since the end of the last World War, our landsleit who settled in Israel, stay in communication with the Association in New York. They turn to us with their requests and problems and the Association attempts to comply with the requests as much as possible and in general, exhibits great interest in every landsman who was saved.

Here, we must mention with special recognition, the aid activity which the Kittev Ladies Auxiliary, under the leadership of its dynamic President, *Ray Hai*, has carried out during the past ten years for the Association and the Kittever landsleit.

Let us declare here that, without the cooperation and assistance of the Ladies Auxiliary, the Association would have been unable to carry through its aid programme in such a broad scope. The women of the Ladies Auxiliary understood how to utilize each suitable opportunity to raise funds, such as Yizkor appeals, a Maos Chitim campaign, "card parties", which they especially organized. Every enterprise of the women was highly successful and produced the desired results. For its wonderful work, therefore, the Ladies Auxiliary has earned the recognition and won the respect of all Kittever landsleit.

In the confines of one chapter, it is understandably impossible to describe all the leaders, presidents and secretaries of the Association such as: *Simcha Zwiebach, Max* Reiser, *Joseph Hebl, Isidor Eisenberg* and others and all the active members who, from the first day of the Association's existence until today, with perseverance and endurance, have helped to build and develop the Association and to form it into an aid institution that is the pride of every Kittever landsman. Therefore, I will mention just a few long-time active members who lead the Association today and are the chief pillars of the organizational work.

*[Page 214]*

Our long-time president, *Willie Soifer*, possesses all the good qualities which a responsible president of such an association should have. He is a friendly and good-natured person who always has a good word for every member. He exhibits a lot of patience at the sessions of the Association, even toward the temperamental members, and always strives to find a way to fulfil the requests of its members.

Besides his duties as president, Willie Soifer also faithfully carries out his duties as the long-time hospital visitor of the Association. When a member becomes ill, Willie is the first one who feels a responsibility to the patient. He visits him at home or in hospital and does what he can to help.

The vice-president of the Association, *Morris Haitt*, also takes an active part in every activity. He has exhibited particular understanding and interest in the campaigns which were carried out to perpetuate the memory of the Kittever martyrs. Morris Haitt supported and energetically carried out the plan to unveil a large gravestone, a monument to the Kittever holy martyrs, on the grounds of the new Kittev cemetery on Montefiore Cemetery.

*Kalman Shnapf* is the long-time recording secretary (protocol secretary) of the Association.

He is the best interpreter of the Association's constitution which serves as a sort of Oral Law which the old guard had worked out. Kalman has years of faithful work behind him for the Kittever Association.

The long-time chairman of relief in the Association is Nathan Gottlieb. This is a person with a warm Jewish heard and a sympathetic Jewish soul. Of him it can be said: Good is it for the landsmanshaft (association of countrymen) that has such a landsman and happy is the association that possesses such a member. The relief work gives meaning to his life and his life is one great and wonderful story of relief work.

*[Page 215]*

I recall on this occasion the dreadful post-war years when I and my family, together with hundreds more refugees, among the Kittever people, found ourselves in 1947 in Prague, Czechoslovakia. While there, I heard from a landsman about the Kittever Association in New York and the help it gave the refugees. I did not know Nathan and he also did not know me from Kittev. Nevertheless, I wrote to him a letter and how astonished I was to receive, by return airmail, a letter with a check. More important than the check was the warm tone of the letter which made us feel that we were not deserted in time of trouble. And that in the Kittever Association, we had faithful sisters and brothers, landsleit who were ready to help us.

During the post-war years, Nathan Gottlieb stood on guard and sent aid to every surviving Kittever landsman wherever he found himself – Israel, Poland, Czechoslovakia, Italy, Romania and other countries. Nathan's house was then transformed into a great warehouse where all the members brought various clothing and footwear. Gottlieb and his late wife, Dora, peace be upon her, and their children worked day and night packing packages and sending them off to the sufferers in Europe.

Nathan Gottlieb continues his aid-activity and when he receives a letter from a landsman urgently asking for help, he does not wait to find out from the Association if the needed funds are available, but immediately sends off what is requested. He says: "If the Association won't reimburse me, I'll survive. I must not keep the landsman who needs help waiting"!

*[Page 216]*

I am sure that every member of the Association is proud of such a devoted relief chairman and gives him recognition and send him the heartiest blessing and good wishes for his great work.

I attempt to fulfil the duties of secretary of the Association and do my work with love and devotion. I do it because I consider the Association which bears the name of our despoiled and destroyed city as the only living remembrance of the city which is so beloved and dear to me as it is to everyone.

The holy principle of brother love, understanding and readiness to help every landsman, is the main motive which moves me to make my contribution to the Association and is the chief reason for my attachment to my landsleit.

This is briefly the summation of the first 60 years of activity of the Kittever sickness support association in New York. Sixty years of great historical world-events, years of war and revolutions, years which had such dreadful consequences for the Jewish people.

During World War II, we experienced the most dreadful tragedy in our history of martyrdom. We lost six million of our Jewish sisters and brothers. We also lived to see the most beautiful and exalted miracle when the 2,000-years' dream of the Jews came true and Jews are again a free nation in their historic homeland – Israel.

During these historic years, the small Kittever Association fulfilled completely its historic mission. As an association of Kittever landsleit, it was a bright haven in the stormy sea of suffering of our sisters and brothers who suffered in the two dreadful World Wars. The Association also participated actively in helping Israel.

*[Page 217]*

This year, at the 60th anniversary of the Kittever Association, when we write the balance sheet and sum up the total of the years that have passed, when we analyse and appraise all the historic events and their meaning, we are convinced that we may be justly proud. We are happy that our 60th anniversary falls in the same year as the 10th anniversary of the State of Israel which received with open arms the scattered and wandering children of our people, among them, also the homeless children of Kittev.

We stand with a silent prayer in our hearts and thank God that have lived to see these two anniversary dates. We wish all our members: may we all together and for many more years, be able to continue the fraternal and philanthropic work which have done for 60 whole years; and may we live to celebrate many more joyous jubilees and Jewish national celebrations.

*[Page 218]*

# Tenth Anniversary
## of the Kittev Ladies Relief Auxiliary

The first Ladies Auxiliary of the Kittever Association was organized right after World War I, in the years 1918-1919. But after a few years' work, having accomplished its mission to help collect the needed funds for the war-impoverished and despoiled Jews in Kittev, it dissolved and liquidated itself.

The current Ladies Auxiliary organized itself in the final months of the year 1947. This was in the post-war years of 1945-1947 when every Jewish heart would tremble with pain and hope at every report which came from Europe and at every single letter that arrived from a surviving countryman. This was in the post-war years when every American Jew and Kittever landsleit among them besieged their Landsman-societies in the hope of obtaining some information about the fate of their nearest and dearest in Europe.

And when the first letters from individual surviving landsleit began arriving, heart-rending letters which confirmed the awful truth of our great disaster, letters in which the persecuted homeless ones begged for urgent help to barely sustain their tortured lives; then; in the seriousness of the time, our Kittever ladies showed their understanding and compassion for the painful problem of our surviving landsleit and volunteered to work with and assist the Kittever Association in the sacred task of aiding our landsleit. At that time, they organized for this purpose and established the Kittev Ladies Relief Auxiliary.

The founding meeting of the Ladies Auxiliary was held on November 2, 1947 at the home of Mrs. Rosa Goldhagen and the participants were the following members of the founding committee:

*[Page 219]*

Mrs. D. Haitt, Mrs. Dora Gottlieb, Mrs. L. Haitt, Mrs. E. Hechler, Mrs. B. Ball, Mrs. B. Goldapper, Mrs. W. Soifer, Mrs. Goldhagen and Mrs. Zwiebach.

Elections were held and the following were elected: As President, Mrs. Raie Haitt; as Vice-President, Mrs. B. Shechter, as Treasurer, Mrs. P. Hallem and as Secretary, Mrs. L. Klinger.

At the above founding meeting, a complete working programme was also set up and the necessary plans were made for recruiting more members and raising funds.

The first two public undertakings of the Ladies Auxiliary were the printing of the first "raffle" books and the scheduling of a public card-party in the Schiff centre in the Bronx.

Both activities were very successful. They popularized the work of the Ladies Auxiliary among the Kittever ladies and the number of members kept increasing unceasingly.

In this way, thanks to its excellent organizational work, the Kittev Ladies Relief Auxiliary succeeded in organizing nearly all Kittever women and making them active in the aid activity for the Association and the landsleit.

Since then and even today, the Ladies Auxiliary carries on an independent and well-organized philanthropic action. They hold their plenary meetings each month and once a year, they hold elections for their officers.

In the latest elections, the following officers were chosen: Mrs. Rae Haitt, President; Mrs. Bella Shechter, Vice-President; Mrs. Elsa Neiman, Secretary and Mrs. Frieda Hallem, Treasurer. The long-term Chairman of Relief is Mr. Nathan Gottlieb.

Prominent among the active members of the Kittev Ladies Auxiliary are:

*[Page 220]*

Mrs. B. Ball, Mrs. Birnberg, Mrs. Anchelovitch, Mrs. L. Bogish, Mrs. M. Cherner, Mrs. G. Eisenberg, Mrs. H. Freimoirer, Mrs. B. Goldopper, Mrs. Ethel Glossberg, Mrs. R. Goldschmid, Mrs. M. Gottlieb, Mrs. Grosbard, Mrs. A. Goldschmid, Mrs. D. Goldhagen, Mrs. P. Hallem, Mrs. R. Haitt, Mrs. Z. Haitt, Mrs. L. Haitt, Mrs. J. Hager, Mrs. Ethel Hutner, Mrs. A. Held, Mrs. Lillian Klinger, Mrs. Rae Mandel, Mrs. Rosa Mandel, Mrs. Elsa Neiman; Mrs. Anna Novack, Mrs. R. Peltz, Mrs. R. Rosenfeld, Mrs. P. Rechter, Mrs. M. Reiser, Mrs. M. Singer, Mrs. B. Shechter, Mrs. G. Seiderer, Mrs. B. Shnapf, Mrs. Sarah Soifer, Mrs. A. Weiss, Mrs. Weinstein, Mrs. A. Zablatover, Mrs. V. Zarref, Mrs. Zwiebel and others.

This year, at the 10th anniversary of the Kittev Ladies Relief Auxiliary, when we assess the sum-total of their service, we can all aver with pride that in the first decade of their existence, with their organizational publicity and their social philanthropic work, they have shown great achievement and thus have earned great recognition and thanks from all our members and landsleit.

Utilizing the present opportunity, that of their 10th anniversary, we wish here, in the name of the Kittever Association and all its members and landsleit, to express our great confidence and recognition to the officers and members of the Kittev Ladies Relief Organization for their wonderful service and wish them all success in their work and much happiness and joy in their family lives.

*[Page 221]*

November 20th, 1958

To our most honoured Secretary

Brother Eisig Husen!

At our last meeting on November 9th, 1958, it was decided to express our thanks and recognition for your devoted work as Secretary of our Society and in particular, to salute you for writing the Kittever Yizkor Book.

Through your work as Secretary and with your experience in the field of organizational activity, you have brought new life and interest into the work of our Association. With your warm and brotherly attitude toward every one of our members, you have earned the friendship and the respect of us all.

In the Yizkor Book, into which you have poured so much heart and soul, and which is written in a beautiful folksy-style, you have immortalized the greatest beauty which Jewish Kittev represented. You have, thereby, brought honour to and exalted the prestige of our Society and thus earned the eternal gratitude and recognition and the heartfelt blessings of all Kittever landsleit for whom the memory of the martyrs of Kittev is holy and dear.

We wish to assure you, dear brother Husen, that all the members value your contribution and are proud to have a secretary like you! On my behalf and on behalf of all our members, I want to wish you and your dear family, many healthy and happy years. May we altogether continue for many years our creative work for the welfare of all the members.

Willie Soifer
President

*[Page 222]*

*Blank*

*[Page 223]*

# Kittever Pictures Section

*[Page 224]*

*Blank*

*[Page 225]*

***This is Rabbi Chaim Gelernter, the former 10th Rav (Rabbi) upon the
Rabbinic Throne of Kittev***

*This is the former Kittever Rebbe Zvi Yehuda Grossman, known as a Tzaddik and wonder worker. He stems from the hereditary line of the Baal Shem Tov, from the Angel son of the Maggid (preacher) of Mezritch. He was the Kittever Rebbe from the year 1906-1918. His oldest son, R. Shimon Menachem was ordained as the Rebbe and filled his position.*

[Page 226]

First row, standing: Hershel Zeiger. Sitting: Max Mandel, Itzik Poiker, Benjamin Orenstein,
Abba Shnitzer, Abraham Hutterer and Moshe Geyer.
Second row, standing: Mendel Pfui. Sitting: Moshe Neiman, Eisig Husen, Mechel Liebergall,
Abraham Buller, Yossel Hirsh, the then president, Hillel Gaster, Alter Buller, Samuel Zorger,
Moshe Gaster, Joshua Nachman, Pinchas Shoiman. Standing: Moshe Klinger, Zanye Tillinger.
Third row, standing: Moshe Goldshmid, Mendel Grebler, Yossel Uhrheber, Isaac Shmerz,
Moshe Zuckerman, Mendel Druckman, Notte Shechter, Mordecai Kasvan, Tunye Glassberg,
Moshe Shatner, Berel Bergman, David Shnapf, Feivel Bergman.
Fourth row, standing: M. Reizer, Hershel Vashkavitzer, Anshel Mandel, Moshe Foigel, Jacob
Shatner, Leib Bergman, Zanye Kremer, Berke Eisenberg, Yossel Orenstein.
The survivors are: Husen, Hutterer, Moshe Gaster, Nachman, Shoiman, Klinger, Kremer,
Benjamin Orenstein, Mendel Druckman, Mordecai Kasvan and Berel Shmerz.

[Page 227]

**Kittever Women's Organization –" WIZO"**

*First row, standing: Mrs. Larish, the youngest daughter of Moshe Neiman; the youngest daughter of Jacob Popper. Sitting: Danya Shizell, Lartsia Klar, Feigel Uhrheber, Ch. Schechter, Peppi Orenstein, Hannah'le Abbash, Gottlieb, Lotti Hutterer, Shrenzel (the child is unknown).*
*Second row: Leiter, Danya Pfui, Shev Ettinger, Victoria Mandel, Rivkah Grebler, Rivkah Grebler's little sister, her mother, Mrs. Falkenflig, Breintshe Klinger, Hersh Grebler's youngest daughter, Freide Steinkahl, Frimtshe Locker.*
*Third row: Jacob Popper, Ethel Pfui, Moshe Neiman's wife, R. Sherman, R. Freid, Peppi Engle, Foigel, H. Shechter, Eidel Kletterer, Vitel Kletterer, Unknown, Mrs. Grebler, Krumholz.*
*Fourth row: Moshe Shatner's wife, Jacob Popper's wife, unidentified man, Narka Weiner, Esther Zuckerman, Freide Krumholz, Baumgarten, Elka Orenstein, Shliemeh Feiner, Feigele Sucher, Rivkah Vashkavitzer Grebler, Rosa Buller, Rivkah Glozberg, Rachel Hutterer, Fiena Fleisher.*
*The survivors: Hannah'le Abbash, Shrenzel, Mandel, Rivkah Grebler, Mrs. Falkenlieg, Narka Weiner, Feige'le Sucher, Rivkah Vashkavitzer Grebler.*

[Page 228]

**Histadrut Hashomer Hatzair of Kittev**

*First row from right to left: A. Birnberg, S. Aufzeher, M. Soicher, Reizer, S. Bergman, M. Landwehr and B. Kremer.*
*Second row: B. Landwehr, Sh. Leivand, Feldhammer, Kasner, Nadler, Bergrin, Sh. Haitt, Hutterer, M. Rieber, N. Shtetner and Joseph Leivand.*
*Third row: M. Aron, A. Greenblatt, A. Shatner, Z. Meltzer, N. Tillinger, Sh. Freilich, N. Hallem, A. Bergman and Bergrin.*
*Fourth row: Ch. Shoiman, B. Foigel, Buchner, Freid, M. Freid, J. Hitzig, Ch. Foigel, F. Korn, G. Hozenfratz, R. Hallem, J. Korn, N. Meltzer, P. Steigman, T. Fleiss and A. Geyer.*
*Fifth row: M. Derchsler, A. Feldhammer, J.H. Habbel, D. Orenstein, H. Drechler, M. Hozenfratz, Sh. Drechsler, M. Tannentsapf and J. Grebler.*
*The following survived: B. Landvehr, Sh. Leivand, Sh. Haitt, N. Shtetner, Joseph Leivand, M. Aron, M. Krumholz, A. Greenblatt, A. Shatner, Z. Meltzer, N. Tillinger, A. Bergman, M. Freid, F. Korn; J. Korn, N. Meltzer, M. Drechsler, A. Feldhammer, H. Drechsler, Sh. Drechsler and J. Grebler.*

[Page 229]

**The Family of Shmuel Liebergall**

*Seated: Shmuel Liebergall holding his oldest grandchild, Banyu Blecher, his wife Faige Liebergall holding her niece, Sarah'le Rappoport, Bertha Kimmel and B. Feiger.*
*Standing: Their oldest son Mechel, a Warsaw Beth Jacob teacher (female), their niece Sh. Liebergall from Kolomei, their son-in-law Eisig Husen, his wife Rivkah, their youngest daughter, their middle daughter Hudye, their youngest son Moshe'le, their oldest daughter Reizel and her husband Zaidel Blecher.*

*[Page 230]*

**Hersh Mandel's son and daughter with their wives and husbands:**

*From left to right, standing: Zaide Mandel, Dr. Menashe Mandel, Dr. Baron, Gershon Klinger, Eliahu Steinkahl.*
*Seated: the wife of Zaide Mandel and her child, Roize Mandel, the wife of Dr. Baron, Victoria Mandel, wife of Dr. Menashe Mandel (the name of the older daughter is not known), Breinze Mandel, wife of Gershon Klinger and Freide Mandel, wife of Eliahu Steinkahl. … their children.*
*The men perished as well as the women except for Victoria Mandel and her daughter Lucia who are in Israel.*

*[Page 231]*

**The wedding picture of Shprinze Meltzer, daughter of Ethel Meltzer**

*Front row: the two children Bubi Meltzer and Yente Abash.*
*First row, standing: Menie Meltzer and his wife seated: Batia Bergman, Baruch Goldreich, his bride Shprinze Meltzer, Sarah Bergman, Mrs. Kramer and Esther Meltzer.*
*Second row: Abraham Shapiro below his wife Hudye Abash, B. Kimmel, Hudye Liebergal, Sh. Milbauer, Nechama Meltzer, Yetti Gaster, Leah Kremer, Reizel Liebergal, B. Shechter and Rivkah Liebergal.*
*(not clear what the word "below" means here).*
*Third row: Milbauer, Sender, Moshe'le Liebergal, Menachem Rappoport, Meshulam Abash, Malkah Bergman, Hannah'le Abash, Joseph Meltzer, Mechel Liebergal and Zaidel Blecher.*
*Surviving: Nechama Meltzer, Rivkah Liebergal, Milbauer, Hannah'le Abash.*

*[Page 232]*

**The family of Joseph Rappoport**

*Seated: Joseph Rappoport, his wife Dinah.*
*Standing: Their oldest son Menachem, their second son Leibele and their*
*youngest son Moshe'le.*
*In front stands their little daughter Sarah'le. Sarah Rappoport is the only one*
*remaining of the whole Rappoport family.*

*This is Mendel Shtetner with his wife and their son Natus. (The little girl is Geltsia Shibber). Aside from Natus Shtetner who is in Israel, they all perished.*

[Page 233]

*Dr. Menashe ben Zvi Mandel, beloved leader of the last generation of Kittever Jews, who perished for the Sanctification of God's Name (Kiddush Hashem) and his wife Victoria Mandel who is in Israel.*

*From right to left:*
*Sitting: Berel Bergman and Mordecai Kasvan.*
*Standing: Joseph Meltzer, Mendel Pfui and Notte Shechter.*

**Aside from Mordecai Kasvan who is in Israel, they all perished.**

*[Page 234]*

*From right to left: Beile (pronounced Bay-le) Feige (Fay-ge) Kaswan, Koppel Korn, Shaike (pronounced Shy-ke) Shtetner and Dinah Sperber (wife of Koppel Korn).*
*Seated: Bobbele Shparber, Yitzchak Feiner, husband of Beile Feige Kaswan, a Kaswan from Kolomei, Minnie Kaswan.*
*The children are: Yitzchak and Beile Feige Feiner's and Koppel and Dinah Korn's. Shaike was the only one who was saved.*

*This is Itzik Shibber with his wife Salli and their daughter Neltzia. They all perished.*

[Page 235]

*This is a picture of Mottel Feigenbaum (a son of Berish the baker) with his wife Surke Haitt and their child. They all perished.*

*Sheindel Shechter (wife of Meir the shochet). Their three daughters, the oldest Dvora, the middle one Gittele and the youngest Sarah. The entire family perished.*

[Page 236]

**This is a picture of the author of this book, Eisig Husen and his family
(from the year 1937)**

*From left to right: Eisig Husen and wife Rivka (Rebecca), his mother Sheindel, may she rest in peace, his nephew
Chaim Druckman in Israel and sister Malka Druckman in Israel and his brother-in-law, Abraham Druckman, may
he rest in peace.*

**Kittever Association in New York**

*Mr & Mrs Morris Haitt greet in the name of the Association, Mr. & Mrs. Nathan Gottlieb and present, as a symbol of recognition and thanks for their relief work, an electric boiler as a gift. This picture was taken in the year 1953.*

[Page 237]

**Kittever Association in New York. Officers**

*First row: Mrs. Goldopper, Mr. Goldopper, Mrs. Husen, Mrs. Soifer, Mrs. Rae Haitt, President of the Ladies Auxiliary, Mrs. Elsa Neiman, secretary, Mrs. Shechter, Vice-President.*
*Second row: Mr. Eisig Husen, secretary, Mr. Nathan Gottlieb, Chairman of the Relief, Mr. Willie Soifer, President, Mr. A. Gottlieb, Mr. Morris Haitt, Vice-President, Mr. Joseph Snapf, recording secretary.*

*[Page 238]*

**Kittever Ladies Auxiliary**
**(This picture is from the year 1953)**

*From right to left: Mrs. Goldopper, Mrs. L. Haitt, Mrs. Peltz, Mrs. G. Haitt, the late Mrs. Hager, Mrs. F. Hallem, Mrs. R. Haitt, Mrs. Goldhagen, the late Mrs. Dora Gottlieb, Mrs. Siderer, Mrs. B. Shnapf and Mrs. Elsa Neiman.*

[Page 239]

**Kittever Association in New York**

*Seated from right to left: Mr. B. Birnberg, Mr. Fr. Birnberg, Mr. Leon Zwiebel, Mr. J. Zwiebel, Mr. A. Sander, Mr. A. Gottlieb and children.*
*Standing: Mr. Shatner, Mr. Grosbard, Mr. J. Shnapf, Mr. K. Shnapf, Mr. Antshelovitz, Mr. Reiser, Mr. Wallach, Mr. M. Shnapf, Mr. Dornstein, Mr. M. Haitt, Mr. Ch. Haitt, Mr. Grill, Mr. N. Gottlieb, Mr. A. Husen, Mr. Goldopper, Mr. Willie Soifer, Mr. A. Gottlieb, Mr. Hager and Mr. Weiss.*

*[Page 240]*

**Kittever Ladies Auxiliary**

*Standing from right to left: Mrs. Goldopper, Mrs. Reiser, Mrs. Husen, Mrs. Gottlieb, Mrs. Ball,*
*Mrs. Hager, Mrs. Zwiebel, Mrs. Sucher, Mrs. Neiman, Mrs. Richter, Mrs. Birnberg, Mrs. Weiss,*
*Mrs. Held, Mrs. Siderer, Mrs. Grosbard, Mrs. Shechter and Mrs. Gottlieb.*
*(the names of the ladies who are seated are missing from the caption)*

## NAME INDEX